RAF Fighter Airfields
OF WORLD WAR 2

JONATHAN FALCONER

IAN ALLAN Publishing

Acknowledgements

The author would like to thank the following organisations and individuals for their invaluable assistance in the preparation of this book:
Bristol Evening Post, Cambridgeshire Evening News, Camelford & Delabole Post, Derby Evening Telegraph, East Anglian Daily Times, Lincolnshire Echo, Liverpool Echo, Manchester Evening News, Newcastle Evening Chronicle, Northants Evening Telegraph, Portsmouth News, Yorkshire Evening Press.

J.Barrien; Ray Beeforth; Chaz Bowyer for his help in supplying many of the photographs; Seb Cox of the RAF Air Historical Branch, Great Scotland Yard, for help and guidance with primary research sources; Eric Davey; W.Huntley; Z.Hurt; Mrs I.M.Hockin; Sqn Ldr W.L.H. 'Johnny' Johnston, pilot with Nos 152, 92, 234 Squadrons 1940-44; Ken Merrick; Alan Thorpe, Company Historian and Archivist, John Laing Plc; N.D.Welch; Alan White; Clive Williams for help with secondary research sources; Public Record Office, Kew; Commonwealth War Graves Commission, Marlow; Imperial War Museum, London; Royal Air Force Museum, Hendon; Public Archives of Canada; and Military Aircraft Photographs.

The large airfield plans are reproduced with permission of the Controller of HMSO. Those reproduced in *RAF Bomber Airfields of World War 2* should also have been credited as such.

Jacket illustration:
Digby, October 1941 – a Canadian pilot is strapped into his No 411 Squadron Spitfire IIa. *from an original painting by Michael Stride*

Title illustration:
Spitfire pilots of No 453 (RAAF) Squadron at Hornchurch in the spring of 1943.
J. Barrien via K. Merrick

First published 1993
Second impression 1998

ISBN 0 7110 2175 9

Published by Ian Allan Publishing

an imprint of Ian Allan Publishing Ltd, Terminal House, Station Approach, Shepperton, Surrey TW17 8AS.
Printed by Ian Allan Printing Ltd at its works at 'Riverdene', Molesey Road, Hersham, Surrey KT12 4RG

Code: 9806/1

Contents

Introduction   3

Author's Note   5

Hangar Designs Commonly Seen at RAF Fighter Command Airfields 1939-45   6

The Airfields: An A to Z   7

Airfield Locations in Great Britain   95

War Over the West   99

Growing Up in No 10 Group   104

Daylight Bomber Escort   107

Flak Clipped My Wings   109

A Decaying Legacy   113

Appendices

  I: RAF Fighter Command Headquarters and Air Officer Commanders-in-Chief 1939-45   117

 II: RAF Fighter Command & Air Defence of Great Britain, Home-based Frontline Unit Strengths 1939-45   119

III: RAF Fighter Command Training Unit Strengths 1939-45   125

Bibliography   128

Introduction

In 1938, the author of a book entitled *Air Power in the Next War* predicted that a future encounter between fighters and bombers 'should be an epic one, stupendously staged...when a huge formation of powerfully armed fighters engages a huge formation of only slightly less powerfully armed bombers, against a background of the heaven's embroidered cloths...'. How right he was for he had accurately prophesied the epic aerial struggles of the Battle of Britain two years later and the massive Allied daylight raids into Germany later in World War 2.

The author of that book was a civil servant named J. M. Speight who had occupied several important posts at the Air Ministry before his retirement in 1937. He was also widely respected for his writings on the laws of warfare. In his book he also spoke of a 'long-range, high-speed, heavily-armed fighter equipped with guns as well as machine guns...' capable of firing 'explosive shells and ultra-velocity bullets...a fighter that can carry the war into the bomber's own country' — visions, perhaps, of the de Havilland Mosquito and North American P-51 Mustang long-range fighters that were soon to fly from English fighter airfields to targets as far afield as Berlin and back, escorting Allied bomber formations or flying intruder operations.

During the 1930s it was the predictions of men such as Speight and the dire warnings of a handful of politicians like Winston Churchill, which cajoled the twin sloths of the Air Ministry and the British government into expanding the Royal Air Force to meet the growing threat of the German Luftwaffe. Thus, the RAF was the only air force in the developed world prior to 1939 to have given much thought to the defensive capabilities of the fighter – thoughts well placed as events were ultimately to prove.

In 1935 the RAF was forced by the government into accepting the Re-orientation Plan under which a greater emphasis than before was placed on air defence. However, this emphasis on the production of defensive fighters and AA weapons was met with some scepticism by the RAF's advocates of the bomber strategy. In admitting there was a defence against the bomber, the concept of the invincible bomber that would always get through to its target had been undermined and with it the philosophy on which the independent Royal Air Force had been created in 1918.

Notwithstanding these arguments, a decision to adopt an expansion programme, known as 'Scheme C', was set in motion which provided for a home-based air force of 70 bomber and 35 fighter squadrons. The scheme presented certain difficulties of administration under the existing RAF organisation and, as a consequence, the Service was completely reorganised into four new commands: Fighter, Bomber, Coastal and Training. RAF Fighter Command came into existence on 14 July 1936 under the command of Air Vice-Marshal Sir Hugh C.T.Dowding at a new headquarters in Bentley Priory, Stanmore, Middlesex.

Scheme C was one of a number of pre-war expansion schemes for the RAF that not only provided for an increase in the number of aircraft, but also for a comprehensive programme of airfield construction to house the new squadrons and aircraft of the various Commands. Known as Expansion stations, details of their construction are given in this book's companion volume *RAF Bomber Airfields of World War 2* and so will not be related here. A number of fighter airfields were amongst the first Expansion stations begun in 1935 – Cranfield, Church Fenton, Tern Hill and Odiham. Several of the existing fighter stations were also brought up to Expansion standard – these were Catterick, Hornchurch, North Weald, Tangmere, Turnhouse and Wittering. The last permanent fighter stations to be constructed before the war were Middle Wallop, Ouston and West Malling.

Group Structure

Initially, the new Fighter Command comprised four principal internal formations: Nos 11 and 12 (Fighter) Groups – the former tasked with all defence south of a line east-west through Bedford, the latter to cover the UK north of this same dividing line – No 22 (Army Cooperation) Group, and the civilian Observer Corps. However, the gradual expansion of Fighter Command in the years leading up to the war necessitated the formation of more groups to further divide the original two into

The rugged Gloster Gamecock typified the single-engined biplane fighter aircraft that equipped the RAF's frontline fighter squadrons during the interwar period. Gamecocks equipped five RAF fighter squadrons during the 1920s, a Mk 1 of No 43 Squadron is illustrated. *via Author*

more manageable units of control. At the outbreak of war in September 1939, the following fighter groups were in existence: No 11 Group (Southern England), No 12 Group (Midlands) and No 13 Group (North). By the early summer of the following year, three more fighter groups had been formed to help tackle the grave threat of invasion posed by the Nazis and to spread the burden of the UK's fighter defence, hitherto the task of the existing three groups. These were No 9 Group (Northwest Midlands) in August, No 10 Group (West) in July, and No 14 Group (Scotland, Orkneys, Shetlands), also in July.

Airfield Infrastructure

Despite Dowding's pleas to the Air Ministry for runways at his fighter airfields to improve their operational status and to avoid serious drainage problems in the winter months, he had to wait until shortly before the outbreak of war for his wishes to be granted. Then priority was given only to Kenley, Biggin Hill, Church Fenton, Debden, Northolt, Tangmere, Turnhouse and Hendon. There were only three fighter stations known to have had one or more runways before World War 2 and these were Odiham, Aldergrove and North Weald.

Generally speaking, the early runways were graded tarmac coated with asphalt laid over a hardcore base and were not as

durable as many built later in the war. Fighter Command airfields equipped with surfaced runways and perimeter tracks generally fared better and suffered less damage than those in Bomber Command, for the simple reason that a fully loaded four-engined Short Stirling bomber weighed considerably less than a single-engined Spitfire. However, despite the benefits to be gained from surfaced runways, many fighter airfields retained their grass-surfaced runways throughout the war. By virtue of the fact that it operated smaller aircraft, Fighter Command's new or updated airfields generally needed fewer large hangars and technical buildings than those of Bomber Command.

In common with Bomber Command, fighter aircraft were dispersed in paved hard-standings off the perimeter tracks to minimise losses in the event of enemy air attacks. They only returned to the hangars for essential damage repairs and major servicing. The number of dispersals varied from 50 at sector stations to 25 at satellites.

In 1937 the first of the new breed of single-seat monoplane fighters began to replace the comparatively primitive biplanes. Pictured here at Northolt in early 1938 are Hawker Hurricane Is of No 111 Squadron, the first squadron to equip with the type. *via K. Merrick*

Restructuring Fighter Command

With the approach of the invasion of Europe by Allied forces, the home-based elements of the RAF underwent a major structural reorganisation in 1943. On 13 November the Allied Expeditionary Air Force came into being under the command of Air Chief Marshal Sir Trafford Leigh-Mallory and it had three elements. The first was the US 9th AF. The second and third were formed two days later on 15 November with the dissolution of RAF Fighter Command: the tactical elements became 2nd Tactical Air Force, while the remaining squadrons came under the command of a new organisation named Air Defence of Great Britain.

The 2nd Tactical Air Force (2 TAF) was made up of four groups: Nos 83 and 84 Groups were known as 'composite' groups which meant that they contained fighter, fighter-bomber and recce squadrons tasked with continental tactical strike operations; No 2 (Bomber) Group, hived off from Bomber Command on 1 June 1943, came temporarily under the control of Fighter Command until on 15 November that same year it became part of 2 TAF for tactical light bombing operations; and No 85 Group, which was tasked with the air defence of the Allied armies and air forces on the continent. The remaining fighter squadrons came under ADGB control. However, following D-Day,

any 2 TAF flying units which remained in the UK came under the nominal control of No 11 Group ADGB. On 15 October 1944, ADGB was disbanded and Fighter Command came into existence once again.

Advanced Landing Grounds

Most airfields constructed for the RAF during the prewar Expansion period were sited in East Anglia but, with the outbreak of war and the eventual plans for the invasion of the Continent in 1944, the handful of airfields in the south and east of England which were closest to the planned invasion area were insufficient in number. Therefore plans were drawn up and work started in late 1942 on the construction of temporary airfields in Hampshire, Sussex and Kent, known as Advanced Landing Grounds (ALGs). From these ALGs the RAF and USAAF fighter and fighter-bomber squadrons operated to help establish a vital foothold in Europe – aircraft like the Spitfire, Typhoon and Tempest.

Because at this time civilian labour in the UK was largely taken up in the construction of airfields for Bomber Command, much of the building of ALGs was undertaken by RAF and Army Airfield Construction Units. Once completed, ALGs had two metal track runways, one 1,600yd and the other 1,400yd in length, surrounded by a perimeter track running as close to the runways as possible in order to save valuable agricultural land. Initially, all of the RAF's ALGs were surfaced with Sommerfeld Track – basically a mesh of steel rods and bars held on the ground by angle iron pickets. Wear and tear resulted in their replacement by a similar design called Square Mesh Track (SMT). ALGs used by the USAAF were surfaced with Pierced Steel Plank (PSP) and Bar & Rod Track. These different types of tracking all possessed the same requisite qualities of ease of manufacture

Development of the high performance monoplane fighter continued throughout the war. The Spitfire Mk XIV which entered RAF service in January 1944 with No 610 Squadron, boasted a maximum speed of 448mph and a service ceiling of 44,500ft. Armament was two 20mm British Hispano cannon and four 0.303in or two 0.50in Browning Mk II machine guns — a far more lethal mix of firepower than the eight 0.303in Brownings that armed the RAF's Spitfire and Hurricanes early in the war.

Illustrated is a Mk XIV, RB159, flown by the OC No 610 Squadron, Sqn Ldr R. A. Newbury, operating anti-'Diver' (V1 flying bomb) patrols from Lympne in September 1944. *via Author*

using available raw materials, speed of laying and dismantling for use elsewhere and durability in use. They also had to be easy to repair and to be inconspicuous from the air.

A maximum of 50 aircraft and four Blister hangars were planned for each ALG, together with tented accommodation and locally requisitioned property for some 100 officers and 2,000 men. No night flying or landing aids were considered necessary but a central bomb store was provided for a cluster of ALGs. Ammunition and fuel was stored on site, with up to 18,000gal of storage capacity for the latter.

Once the beachhead had been consolidated in France and new ALGs established on the Continent, the ALGs in southern England had served their purpose and were abandoned. They were soon all ripped up and, in most cases, by early 1945 the land had been quickly returned to agriculture. Much of the usable PSP was transported to Normandy for re-use on ALGs there.

Author's Note

This book is the logical follow-on from *RAF Bomber Airfields of World War 2* by the same author, published by Ian Allan Ltd in 1992. It deals specifically with airfields, squadrons and units in the British Isles under the operational control of RAF Fighter Command, Air Defence of Great Britain (ADGB) and the 2nd Tactical Air Force (2 TAF) between 1939 and 1945.

On some airfields, squadrons and units took up residence before the outbreak of war; on others they remained after the war's end. With instances such as these, the dates pre-3 September 1939 and post-8 May 1945 have been included for the sake of clarity and accuracy, even though they fall outside the book's time frame.

A number of different documentary sources have been consulted in the preparation of this book. Details, particularly dates, often vary from source to source when referring to individual squadrons and units, or when an airfield opened 'officially'. For this reason, some dates may be open to dispute. All airfields appear within the county boundaries as they were at the outbreak of war in 1939.

The following fighter groups are covered in the book: Nos 9, 10, 11, 12, 13, 14, 38 (Airborne), 70 (OTU), 81 (OTU), 82 Groups – Fighter Command and Air Defence of Great Britain; Nos 83, 84, 85, Groups – 2nd Tactical Air Force. No 38 (Airborne) Group with its Stirlings, Halifaxes and Albemarles was tasked with Special Duties, paratroop and glider operations, which made it the odd man out, administered as it was by No 3 Group Bomber Command but controlled by Fighter Command which had a say in the operations undertaken by the Group.

The following do not fall within the scope of this book:
- Lodger squadrons and units from other Commands;
- Army co-operation squadrons at any stage of the war, although they fell under the temporary jurisdiction of Fighter Command between 1 June and 15 November 1943, following the disbandment of Army Co-operation Command on 1 June;
- No 2 Group Bomber Command squadrons under the control of Fighter Command between 1 June and 15 November 1943 and 2 TAF thereafter;
- Fighter squadrons attached to No 100 (SD) Group, Bomber Command;
- Anti-Aircraft Co-operation Units (AACU), (eg: Bodorgan, Anglesey);
- Calibration Units;
- Air-Sea Rescue squadrons;
- Any fighter squadron on detachment from its home base.

Aircraft operated by a squadron or unit are listed in the order in which they served: Spitfire I, Vb; Typhoon Ib. It does not necessarily mean that the squadron in question operated all of these types at the same time. In the Orders Of Battle, where a squadron or a unit's aircraft types are listed thus: Mosquito II/VI or Beaufighter VIf/Mosquito II this denotes that the squadron or unit was in the process of converting from one mark or type of aircraft to another at that particular time.

Any work of this nature makes it an 'open season' on the author. As already stated, some dates, unit allocations and their equipment are open to varying interpretations, and errors can creep in, but all information contained in this book is, to the best of the author's knowledge, correct and true. Constructive comments will be welcomed.

Jonathan Falconer
Bradford-on-Avon
February 1993

Hangar Designs Commonly Seen at RAF Fighter Command Airfields 1939-45

'A' Type (1924)
Open span: 120ft; length: 250ft; max door height clearance: 25ft.
With the expansion of the RAF during the 1930s, and the anticipation of larger aircraft entering service, the 'A' Type proved ultimately to be unsuitable and thus a larger hangar was required.

Belfast Truss or General Service Shed (GS) (1917)
One of the most successful of the early designs of hangar, the Belfast was a buttressed structure built of brick and so-called because of its Belfast roof trusses.

Bellman (8349/37) (1937)
Open span: 87ft 9in; length: 175ft; max door height: 26ft.
Of steel construction with steel doors at each end, the Bellman was the most common steel hangar on RAF airfields up until 1940 when it was superseded by the 'T' Types.

Bessoneau (1916)
Temporary structures with wooden frames covered with canvas. Many were produced and a large number were brought out of storage during World War 2 for emergency use.

Blister (1939)
Designed with the dispersal principle in mind, Blisters were small open-ended hangars, all to a standard length of 45ft but in the following three permutations: 'Standard' Blister, with wooden arched-rib construction clad with corrugated iron sheeting (span 45ft); 'Over' Blister, the same basic construction as the 'Standard' but with steel cladding (span 65ft);

'Extra Over' Blister, the same construction as 'Over' Blister but with a 69ft span. Blister hangars had canvas curtains at each end although in many cases these were discarded. Some were bricked up at one end.

Butler Combat Hangar and 'Merton' Type (1939-45)
The former was an American-built steel-framed hangar used only on a few RAF fighter airfields. The RAF equivalent was the smaller Merton with tubular steel framework covered with canvas.

Callender-Hamilton (1937, 1940)
Open span: 90ft; length: 185ft; max door height: 25ft.
Transportable steel hangar with steel doors at each end, similar in design and appearance to the Bellman.

'B1' and 'B2' Types (1942)
Open span: 120ft; length: 227ft 6in; max door height: 27ft (B1), 20ft 6in (B2). A MAP design used at many of Fighter Command's frontline stations and OTUs for the major servicing of aircraft. Steel construction with doors at each end.

'C' Type (1934)
'C' Type Gabled (1934) – Max door height: 35ft;
'C' Type Hipped (1938) – Max door height: 30ft.
Open span: 152ft; length: 300ft; max door height clearance: 35ft.
The width of the 'C' Type was standard although the length could vary according to local requirements. It was of brick and steel construction with steel plate doors at each end and came with either a gabled or hipped roof design. Single or

two-storey offices and workshops were built externally along the length of the hangar on either side.

'C1' Type (1939)
The same as the 'C', but making extensive use of asbestos sheeting instead of brickwork to save time and construction costs.

'D' Type (1936)
Open span: 150ft; length: 300ft; max door height: 30ft.
Constructed predominantly from reinforced concrete topped by a curved roof.

'F' Type
One of the earliest of the interwar period hangars, built of steel with side-opening doors.

'J' and 'K' Types (1939)
Open span: 150ft; length: 300ft; max door height: 30ft.
Predominantly of metal and brick construction with a curved roof of 0.25in steel plate. Offices and workshops built externally along the length of the hangar on either side.

'T' Types (1940/41/42)
The main types were the 'T2' and 'T2' (Home).
Open spans of 90ft or 97ft 2in; length: 239ft 7in; max door height: 25ft. Lengths could vary according to local requirements.
'T' stood for Transportable. The type was a transportable metal hangar which was quick to erect. 'T2's were by far the most ubiquitous type of hangar to be seen on wartime RAF airfields, superseding the prewar Bellman design.

The Airfields: An A to Z

Key

Opened: The date on which the airfield opened officially for flying operations during World War 2 (eg: Great Orton, 06/43) or, in the case of an old-established airfield or one which had seen almost continuous use up until then, the date on which it first saw use for flying (eg: Gatwick, 08/30).

Closed: The date on which operational flying from the airfield by the RAF ceased (eg: Gravesend, 06/56); or, in the case where military flying has continued since the war's end on a regular or semi-regular basis, or activities directly or closely related to flying are still undertaken, the current use of the airfield in 1992 (eg: Currently in use by RAF, USAF, Army, British Aerospace Plc, as civil airport, etc).

Elevation: The airfield's height in feet above mean sea level.

Pundit code: In order to identify airfields from the air a system of two-letter codes was adopted, usually taken from letters making up the airfield's name (eg: GE for Great Orton). However, with the proliferation of airfields during the war years the number of code permutations became exhausted and so new codes with apparently little or no connection to the airfields they represented were introduced (eg: QB for Harrowbeer or XQ for Coolham). These were displayed on the ground in 10ft-high white capital letters adjacent to the signals area or in the signals square near to the control tower. At night this method of airfield identification was obviously unworkable so a mobile beacon situated several miles away from the airfield, known as a Pundit, was used to flash in red light the identity letters in Morse code.

Formation: The controlling group within Fighter Command, Air Defence of Great Britain or 2nd Tactical Air Force.

Main contractor: The civil engineers and building contractors who undertook the majority of the construction work at the airfield. In some cases this was undertaken by a consortium of smaller contractors instead of one of the bigger firms like Laing or Costain.

Runways: The flying surfaces at individual airfields varied. Prewar stations used grass strips and it was not until well into the war that many had been replaced by concrete or tarmac runways, or a combination of the former material with a tarmac surfacing, on a compacted hardcore base. Some runways were also surfaced with wood or rubber chippings, or pine needles. Generally, they were laid to a triangular pattern with the main runway orientated roughly SW/NE to suit the prevailing wind.

Some satellite airfields and all of the Advanced Landing Grounds used a number of different types of steel matting for their flying surfaces which were quick to lay and equally quick to rip up again once the need for the airfield no longer existed.

Hangars: Large purpose-built weatherproof structures for aircraft storage and overhaul (see the earlier section on 'Hangar Designs Commonly Seen at Fighter Command Airfields').

User sqns/units: The RAF frontline squadrons (sqn) and secondline training units, ie: Operational Training Units (OTU), and their parent groups (Gp), permanently based at the airfield (not including squadrons and units on temporary detachment) and their dates of occupancy.

The notes following this entry refer to significant changes in the airfield's status during the war years, where known (eg: Poulton, opened in 81 (OTU) Gp as satellite to Hawarden, 03/43).

ACKLINGTON, Northumberland

Opened: 1938
Closed: 1972
Elevation: 120ft
Pundit code: AI
Formation: 13 Gp
Main contractor: Various
Runways: 3 tarmac
Hangars: F type (2), Bellman (1), Blister (16)
User sqns/units:

1 Sqn
08/07/42-09/02/43
Hurricane IIc, I, IIb; Typhoon Ib

25 Sqn
19/12/43-05/02/44
Mosquito II, XVII

32 Sqn
27/08-15/12/40
Hurricane I

43 Sqn
18/11/39-26/02/40
Hurricane I

46 Sqn
10/12/39-17/01/40
Hurricane I

56 Sqn
23/02-07/03/44
Typhoon Ib

72 Sqn
02/03-01/06/40
05/06-31/08/40
15/12/40-08/07/41
Gladiator I, II; Spitfire I, IIa, IIb

79 Sqn
13/07-27/08/40
Hurricane I

111 Sqn
27/10-07/12/39
Hurricane I

130 Sqn
21/12/43-04/01/44
Spitfire Vb

141 Sqn
29/01-23/06/42
Beaufighter If

152 Sqn
02/10/39-12/07/40
Gladiator I, II; Spitfire I

164 Sqn
08-16/03/44
Typhoon Ib

198 Sqn
09/02-24/03/43
Typhoon Ia, Ib

219 Sqn
23/06-21/10/42
Beaufighter If

222 Sqn
25/02-10/03/44
Spitfire LFIXb

258 Sqn
17/12/40-01/02/41
Hurricane I

266 Sqn
15-23/03/44
Typhoon Ib

315 Sqn
08/01-13/03/41
Hurricane I

316 Sqn
22/09/43-15/02/44
Spitfire LFVb

317 Sqn
19/02-29/04/41
Hurricane I

322 Sqn
10/03-24/04/44
Spitfire Vb, Vc

349 Sqn
25/08-22/10/43
Spitfire Va, LFVb

350 Sqn
13/03-08/06/43
20/07-25/08/43
Spitfire Vb

406 Sqn
05/05/41-01/02/42
Blenheim If, IVf; Beaufighter IIf

409 Sqn
23/02-19/12/43
05/02-01/03/44
Beaufighter VIf

410 Sqn
20/10/42-21/02/43
Beaufighter IIf; Mosquito II

1460 Flt ➤ 539 Sqn
15/12/41 (02/09/42)-25/01/43
Havoc I, II (Turbinlite); Boston III (Turbinlite)

607 Sqn
10/10-14/11/39
Gladiator I

609 Sqn
07-17/10/39
21/03-01/04/44
Spitfire I; Typhoon Ib

610 Sqn
31/08-15/12/40
Spitfire I

59 OTU
26/02-01/06/45
Typhoon I

To 13 Gp Fighter Command as satellite to Usworth 09/39
Closed for reconstruction 06/44-02/45
13 Gp Forward Sector Airfield 05/45

ALDERGROVE, Co Antrim, NI

Opened: 1918
Closed: Currently in use as Belfast Airport
Elevation: 294ft
Pundit code: JV
Formation: 13 Gp
Main contractor: Various
Runways: 2 concrete
Hangars: Various
User sqns/units:

245 Sqn
20/07/40-14/07/41
Hurricane I

To 13 Gp Fighter Command as Sector Station 07/40
To Coastal Command 07/41

ANDOVER, Hants

Opened: 08/17
Closed: Currently in use by Army
Elevation: 260ft
Pundit code: Not known
Formation: 22 (AC) Gp
Main contractor: Various
Runways: Grass
Hangars: Belfast Truss (7), GS (4), Blister (5)
User sqns/units:

No 2 School of Army Co-operation
21/10/39-01/07/41
Blenheim; Anson

To 22 (AC) Gp Fighter Command 05/39
To Army Cooperation Command 12/40
To USAAF 03/44

ANDREW'S FIELD (Great Saling), Essex

Opened: 07/42
Closed: 11/45
Elevation: 290ft
Formation: 11 Gp
Pundit code: GZ
Main contractor: US Pioneer Corps
Runways: 3 concrete/tarmac
Hangars: T2 (2)
User sqns/units:

19 Sqn
14/10/44-13/02/45
Mustang III

1. ACKLINGTON
Aircrew of No 406 (RCAF) Squadron climb out of a van behind a Beaufighter IIf on 15 September 1941. *Public Archives of Canada (PAC) PL-4644 via Chaz Bowyer*

2. ALDERGROVE
Hurricane Is of No 245 Squadron pictured in late 1940. *via Chaz Bowyer*

3. APPLEDRAM
Spitfire IXc MH819 of No 310 Squadron, June 1944. *via Chaz Bowyer*

ANDREW'S FIELD continued

65 Sqn
14/10/44-16/01/45
06-15/05/45
Mustang III, IV

122 Sqn
14/10/44-01/05/45
Mustang III

129 Sqn
11/10-11/12/44
Mustang III

303 Sqn
04/04-16/05/45
Mustang I, IV

306 Sqn
10/10/44-10/08/45
Mustang III

315 Sqn
10-24/10/44
16/01-08/08/45
Mustang III

316 Sqn
24/10/44-16/05/45
Mustang III

616 Sqn
28/02-31/03/45
Meteor III

Opened under USAAF control 04/43
To 11 Gp RAF Fighter Command as
Forward Airfield 09/44

ANGLE, Pembrokeshire

Opened: 12/41
Closed: 1945
Elevation: 182ft
Pundit code: AE
Formation: 10 Gp
Main contractor: Various
Runways: 3 tarmac
Hangars: Blister (4), T2 (1)
User sqns/units:

32 Sqn
01/06-27/11/41
Hurricane I, IIb

152 Sqn
16/08-27/09/42
Spitfire Vb

263 Sqn
18/04-15/08/42
Whirlwind I

312 Sqn
24/01-18/04/42
Spitfire Vb

412 Sqn
29/01-08/02/43
Spitfire Vb

421 Sqn
26/10-01/11/42
14-30/11/42
04/12/42-29/01/43
Spitfire Vb

615 Sqn
27/11/41-23/01/42
Hurricane IIb, IIc

Opened in 10 Gp Fighter Command as
Forward Airfield 12/41
To Royal Navy 05/43
To Coastal Command 09/43

ANNAN, Dumfries

Opened: 04/42
Closed: 1945
Elevation: 30ft
Pundit code: AG
Formation: 81 (OTU) Gp/9 Gp
Main contractor: John Laing & Son Ltd
Runways: 2
Hangars: Blister (8), T1 (3)
User sqns/units:

55 OTU ➡ 4 TEU ➡ 3 TEU
28/04/42 (26/01/44) (28/03/44)-17/07/44
Hurricane I, II; Master I; Typhoon

Opened in 81 (OTU) Gp Fighter Command
with full station status 04/42
To 9 Gp 06/43
To Maintenance Command 07/44

APPLEDRAM, Sussex

Opened: 05/43
Closed: 11/44
Elevation: 22ft
Pundit code: AO
Formation: 83 Gp/84 Gp, 2 TAF
Main contractor: RAF Airfield
Construction Service (RAFACS)
Runways: 2 steel matting
Hangars: Blister (4)
User sqns/units:

175 Sqn
02/06-01/07/43
Typhoon Ib

181 Sqn
02/06-03/07/43
Typhoon Ib

182 Sqn
02/06-02/07/43
Typhoon Ib

302 Sqn
28/06-16/07/44
Spitfire IXe

308 Sqn
28/06-16/07/44
Spitfire IX

310 Sqn
03/04-22/06/44
Spitfire LFIX

312 Sqn
04/04-22/06/44
Spitfire LFIXb

313 Sqn
04/04-22/06/44
Spitfire IX

317 Sqn
28/06-16/07/44
Spitfire IX

Advanced Landing Ground (ALG)

ASHBOURNE, Derby

Opened: 07/42
Closed: 1954
Elevation: 590ft
Pundit code: AS
Formation: 38 Wing/38 Gp
Main contractor: Various
Runways: 3 concrete
Hangars: T2 (4)
User sqns/units:

42 OTU (70/38 Gp)
26/10/42-20/03/45
Blenheim; Whitley V; Oxford; Anson;
Albemarle

Opened under 70 (Training) Gp Army Co-
operation Command 07/42
To 38 Wing Fighter Command 06/43
To 38 (Airborne Forces) Gp 09/43

ASHFORD, Kent

Opened: 03/43
Closed: 09/44
Elevation: 130ft
Pundit code: ZF
Formation: 83 Gp, 2 TAF
Main contractor: RAFACS/Royal Canadian
Engineers
Runways: 2 steel matting
Hangars: None
User sqns/units:

65 Sqn
05-15/10/43
Spitfire IX

122 Sqn
05-15/10/43
Spitfire IX

ALG
To USAAF 03/44

ASTON DOWN, Gloucs

Opened: 10/38
Closed: 1976
Elevation: 600ft
Pundit code: AD
Formation: 12 Gp/81 (OTU) Gp/9 Gp
Main contractor: Various
Runways: 3
Hangars: Various (50)
User sqns/units:

12 Gp Pool ➡ 5 OTU ➡ 55 OTU
23/08/39 (15/03/40) (01/11/40)-03/41
Harvard IIb; Gladiator; Blenheim I;
Spitfire; Hurricane I, II;
Defiant I; Battle; Master I, II, III

52 OTU
08/41-10/08/43
Spitfire II, V; Harvard; Master I, II

Fighter Leaders School
10/08/43-25/01/44
Spitfire Vb

3 Tactical Exercise Unit (TEU) ➡ 55 OTU
14/07/44-(15/12/44)-14/06/45
Typhoon Ib; Hurricane I, II; Master I, II,
III; Martinet; Harvard IIb

84 Group Support Unit (GSU)
14/02-13/07/44
Typhoon I; Tempest V; Spitfire IX;
Mustang I

To 12 Gp Fighter Command 09/39
To 81 (OTU) Gp 12/40
To 9 Gp 06/43

ATCHAM, Salop

Opened: 09/41
Closed: 04/46
Elevation: 200ft
Pundit code: AP
Formation: 9 Gp
Main contractor: Various
Runways: 3 tarmac
Hangars: Blister (8),Callender-Hamilton(3)
User sqns/units:

74 Sqn
25/03-10/04/42
Spitfire Vb

131 Sqn
27/09/41-09/02/42
Spitfire Ia, IIa, Vb

232 Sqn
10/04-16/05/42
Spitfire Vb

350 Sqn
19/02-05/04/42
Spitfire IIa

Opened as 9 Gp Group Sector Station
09/41
To USAAF 06/42
To RAF (non-operational) 03/45

AYR, Ayrshire

Opened: 04/41
Closed: 1946
Elevation: 50ft
Pundit code: AR
Formation: 13 Gp
Main contractor: Various
Runways: 3 tarmac/asphalt
Hangars: Bellman (3), Blister (17)
User sqns/units:

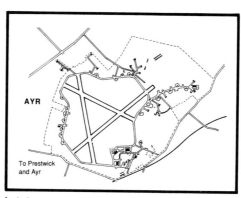

AYR

To Prestwick
and Ayr

1 Sqn
22-29/04/44
Typhoon Ib; Spitfire IXb

56 Sqn
30/03-07/04/44
Typhoon Ib

72 Sqn
12/08-26/09/42
Spitfire Vb

130 Sqn
16-30/11/43
Spitfire Vb

141 Sqn
29/04/41-29/01/42
Beaufighter If

165 Sqn
06/04-15/08/42
Spitfire Va, Vb

169 Sqn
01/10-08/12/43
Mosquito II

186 Sqn
03/08/43-07/01/44
Hurricane IV; Typhoon Ib

222 Sqn
22/10/42-27/03/43
Spitfire Vb

239 Sqn
30/09-10/12/43
Beaufighter If

312 Sqn
19/08/41-01/01/42
Hurricane IIb; Spitfire IIa, IIb, Vb

313 Sqn
10-20/01/44
Spitfire Vc

322 Sqn
25/02-01/03/44
Spitfire Vb, Vc

329 Sqn
03-22/01/44
16-24/03/44
Spitfire Vb, Vc, IX

340 Sqn
01/01-01/04/42
Spitfire IIa, Vb

345 Sqn
30/01-26/04/44
Spitfire Vb

402 Sqn
10/07-19/08/41
19/12/43-02/01/44
Hurricane IIb; Spitfire Vb, Vc

406 Sqn
01/02-16/06/42
Beaufighter IIf

410 Sqn
30/06-06/08/41
15/06-01/09/42
Defiant I; Beaufighter IIf

438 Sqn
10/01-18/03/44
Hurricane IV; Typhoon Ib

439 Sqn
08/01-18/03/44
Hurricane IV; Typhoon Ib

440 Sqn
08/02-18/03/44
Hurricane IV; Typhoon Ib

486 Sqn
21-29/03/44
Typhoon Ib

488 Sqn
01/09/42-03/08/43
Beaufighter IIf, VIf

602 Sqn
15/04-10/07/41
Spitfire I, IIa

611 Sqn
08-19/02/44
Spitfire LFVb

Opened in 13 Gp Fighter Command with
full station status 04/41

BAGINTON, Warks

Opened: 1934
Closed: Currently in use as Coventry
Airport
Elevation: 270ft
Pundit code: NG
Formation: 9 Gp
Main contractor: Various
Runways: 3 grass
Hangars: Bellman (2)
User sqns/units:

32 Sqn
19/10-25/11/42
Hurricane IIb

79 Sqn
24/12/41-04/03/42
Hurricane IIb

134 Sqn
26/03-10/04/42
Spitfire Vb

135 Sqn
15/08-04/09/41
Hurricane IIa

308 Sqn
25/09/40-31/05/41
Hurricane I; Spitfire I

403 Sqn
19/02-30/05/41
Tomahawk I,IIa; Spitfire I

457 Sqn
16/06-07/08/41
Spitfire I

605 Sqn
30/05-04/09/41
Hurricane IIa

No 1 Camouflage Unit
09/39-08/11/40
Reliant; Blenheim; Spitfire

Became 9 Gp Sector Station 09/40
Downgraded to satellite for Honiley 08/41

BALADO BRIDGE, Kinross

Opened: 03/42
Closed: 1957
Elevation: 420ft
Pundit code: Not known
Formation: 81 (OTU) Gp
Main contractor: Various
Runways: 2 concrete
Hangars: Blister (4), B1 (1), Super Robin (1)
User sqns/units:

58 OTU ➡ 2TEU
23/03/42 (17/10/43)-25/06/44
Spitfire I, II, V; Hurricane

Opened in 81 (OTU) Gp as satellite to Grangemouth 03/42
To War Dept 11/44

BALLYHALBERT, Co Down, NI

Opened: 06/41
Closed: 1946
Elevation: 26ft
Pundit code: YB
Formation: 13 Gp/82 Gp
Main contractor: Various
Runways: 3 tarmac
Hangars: Bellman (20, Blister (12)
User sqns/units:

25 Sqn
16/01-17/05/42
Beaufighter If

130 Sqn
30/04-05/07/43
Spitfire Vb

153 Sqn
24/10/41-18/12/42
Defiant I; Beaufighter If, VIf

245 Sqn
14/07-01/09/41
Hurricane I, IIb

303 Sqn
12/11/43-30/04/44
Spitfire LFVb

315 Sqn
06/07-13/11/43
Spitfire Vb

501 Sqn
19/10/42-30/04/43
Spitfire Vb

504 Sqn
26/08/41-12/01/42
19/06-19/10/42
Hurricane IIb; Spitfire IIa, IIb, Vb

Opened as 13 Gp Sector Station 06/41
To 82 Gp 09/41
To RN as HMS *Corncrake* 04/45

BEAULIEU, Hants

Opened: 08/42
Closed: 09/50
Elevation: 135ft
Pundit code: BQ
Formation: 2 TAF/10 Gp ADGB
Main contractor: Various
Runways: 3 tarmac
Hangars: Blister (1), T2 (2)
User sqns/units:

257 Sqn
20/01-03/02/44
Typhoon Ib

263 Sqn
23/01-06/03/44
Typhoon Ib

486 Sqn
31/01-28/02/44
Typhoon Ib; Tempest V

Opened in 19 Gp Coastal Command 08/42
To 2 TAF 01/44
To 10 Gp ADGB as Forward Airfield 03/44
To USAAF control 05/44
To RAF control 09/44

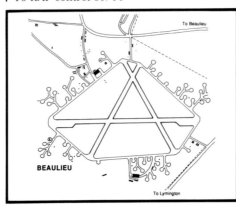

BEAULIEU

BENTWATERS, Suffolk

Opened: 04/44
Closed: Currently in use by USAF
Elevation: 80ft
Pundit code: BY
Formation: 11 Gp
Main contractor: Various
Runways: 3 concrete
Hangars: T2 (2)
User sqns/units:

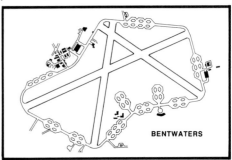

BENTWATERS

64 Sqn
29/12/44-15/08/45
Mustang III

118 Sqn
15/12/44-11/08/45
Spitfire IXc; Mustang III

126 Sqn
30/12/44-05/09/45
Mustang III, IV

129 Sqn
11/12/44-26/05/45
Mustang III

165 Sqn
15/12/44-29/05/45
Spitfire IXb; Mustang III

234 Sqn
17/12/44-01/05/45
Mustang III, IV

Opened in Bomber Command 04/44
To 11 Gp Fighter Command 12/44

BICESTER, Oxon

Opened: 1917
Closed: Currently in use by RAF, Army and USAF
Elevation: 271ft
Pundit code: BC
Formation: 9 Gp
Main contractor: Various
Runways: 3 grass
Hangars: A Type (2), C Type (2)
User sqns/units:

13 OTU
01/06/43-12/10/44
Blenheim I, V; Spitfire; Mosquito

To 9 Gp Fighter Command 6/43

5. BAGINTON
No 403 Squadron formed at Baginton on 19 February 1941 with Curtiss Tomahawk aircraft, which it flew until July when it re-equipped with the Spitfire IIa and Vb. *via Chaz Bowyer*

6. BIGGIN HILL
Blenheim Ifs of No 601 Squadron, Auxiliary Air Force, flew from Biggin Hill between September and December 1939. The nearest aircraft, UF-R, is piloted by Flg Off Roger Bushell who was later shot down and became a prisoner-of-war in Germany. He masterminded the mass escape from *Stalag Luft III* in March 1944 in which he and 49 other re-captured PoW escapers were murdered by the Gestapo on the direct orders of Adolf Hitler. *via Chaz Bowyer*

7. BIGGIN HILL
Hurricanes of No 32 Squadron return from combat on 15 August 1940. On this day, the squadron lost one Hurricane in combat with two more damaged. All three pilots escaped with their lives although Plt Off D.Grice suffered burns before baling out over the Channel when his Hurricane was attacked by Bf109s. *via Chaz Bowyer*

8. BLACKBUSHE
A trio of No 418 (RCAF) Squadron Mosquito FBVIs cross the English Channel. The squadron converted from the Mosquito II to the FBVI in November 1944. *PAC RE-14960 via Chaz Bowyer*

BIGGIN HILL, Kent

Opened: 02/17
Closed: 1992
Elevation: 377ft
Pundit code: GI
Formation: 11 Gp
Main contractor: Various
Runways: 3 asphalt
Hangars: Bessoneau (2), Blister (12)
User sqns/units:

1 Sqn
09/02-15/03/43
Typhoon Ib

3 Sqn
01/05-02/09/39
Gladiator I; Hurricane I

19 Sqn
01-07/07/42
Spitfire Vb

32 Sqn
27/03-26/05/40
04/06-27/08/40
Hurricane I

41 Sqn
21-28/05/43
Spitfire XII

64 Sqn
13-15/10/40
Spitfire I

66 Sqn
07/11/40-24/02/41
Spitfire I, IIa

72 Sqn
31/08-01/09/40
12/09-13/10/40
26/07-20/10/41
22/03-30/06/42
07/07-04/08/42
Spitfire I, IIb, Vb, Vc, IX

74 Sqn
15/10/40-20/02/41
Spitfire IIa

79 Sqn
08/03-10/05/40
21-27/05/40
05/06-01/07/40
27/08-08/09/40
Hurricane I

91 Sqn
07-29/10/44
Spitfire IXb

92 Sqn
08/09/40-09/01/41
20/02-24/09/41
Spitfire I, Vb

124 Sqn
17/11/41-03/05/42
Spitfire Va, Vb

133 Sqn
03/05-30/06/42
12-31/07/42
31/08-23/09/42
Spitfire Vb

154 Sqn
05/11/44-01/03/45
Spitfire VII; Mustang IV

213 Sqn
09-18/06/40
Hurricane I

242 Sqn
21/05-08/06/40
Hurricane I

264 Sqn
11/01-14/04/41
Defiant I

322 Sqn
31/10/44-03/01/45
Spitfire LFIXe, LFXVIe

340 Sqn
23/09/42-21/03/43
02/11-17/12/44
Spitfire Vb, IXb

341 Sqn
21/03-11/10/43
Spitfire IXb

345 Sqn
28/10-01/11/44
Spitfire HFIX

401 Sqn
20/10/41-19/03/42
03-14/08/42
21/08-24/09/42
13/10/43-08/04/44
Spitfire Vb, IX, IXb

411 Sqn
13/10/43-24/02/44
29/02-16/04/44
Spitfire IXb

412 Sqn
14/10/43-05/01/44
20/01-30/03/44
07-15/04/44
Spitfire Vb, IXb

485 Sqn
01/07-18/10/43
Spitfire IXb

601 Sqn
02/09-30/12/39
Blenheim If

602 Sqn
16-20/08/42
Spitfire Vb

609 Sqn
24/02-28/07/41
24/09-19/11/41
18/09-02/11/42
Spitfire IIa, Vb; Typhoon Ia, Ib

610 Sqn
10-27/05/40
08/07-31/08/40
Spitfire I

611 Sqn
23/09/42-01/07/43
Spitfire IX

11 Gp Sector Station 09/39
To Balloon Command 07/44
To ADGB 09/44
To 11 Gp Fighter Command 10/44

BLACKBUSHE (Hartfordbridge Flats), Hants

Opened: 11/42
Closed: 11/46
Elevation: 320ft
Pundit code: XB
Formation: 85 Gp, 2 TAF
Main contractor: Sir Alfred McAlpine Ltd
Runways: 3 concrete
Hangars: Bessoneau (2), Blister (6), T2 (3)
User sqns/units:

264 Sqn
07/05-26/07/44
Mosquito XIII

322 Sqn
4/04-20/06/44
Spitfire XIV

418 Sqn
21/11/44-15/03/45
Mosquito VI

605 Sqn
21/11/44-15/03/45
Mosquito VI

Opened in 70 Gp Army Co-operation
Command 11/42
To 2 Gp, 2 TAF 08/43
To 85 Gp, 2 TAF 11/43
Name changed from Hartfordbridge Flats
to Blackbushe 12/44
To 46 Gp Transport Command 03/45

BOGNOR, Sussex

Opened: 06/43
Closed: 01/45
Elevation: 23ft
Pundit code: OG
Formation: 84 Gp/83 Gp, 2 TAF
Main contractor: RAFACS
Runways: 2 steel matting
Hangars: Blister (4)
User sqns/units:

19 Sqn
06/06-02/07/43
Spitfire Vb

66 Sqn
31/03-22/04/44
25/04-08/05/44

14/05-22/06/44
Spitfire LFIXb

122 Sqn
01/06-01/07/43
Spitfire Vb

331 Sqn
31/03-22/06/44
Spitfire IXb

332 Sqn
31/03-21/06/44
Spitfire IXb

602 Sqn
01/06-01/07/43
Spitfire Vb

83 GSU
21/06-26/09/44
Mustang I; Spitfire IX, XI; Typhoon I

ALG

BOLT HEAD, Devon

Opened: 1941
Closed: 1947
Elevation: 420ft
Pundit code: OH
Formation: 10 Gp/11 Gp
Main contractor: Various
Runways: 2 steel matting
Hangars: Blister (2)
User sqns/units:

41 Sqn
29/04-16/05/44
24/05-19/06/44
Spitfire XII

234 Sqn
18/03-29/04/44
Spitfire Vb

263 Sqn
19/06-10/07/44
Typhoon Ib

266 Sqn
07-12/03/44
Typhoon Ib

610 Sqn
26/06-19/12/43
16-24/05/44
Spitfire Vb, Vc, XIV

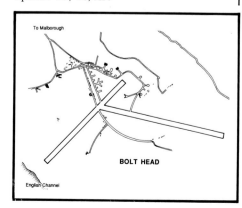
To Malborough
BOLT HEAD
English Channel

611 Sqn
17/07-30/08/44
Spitfire IX

Opened as Forward Operating Base (FOB)
for 10 and 11 Gps 1941
Upgraded to satellite for Exeter 04/42
To C&M 04/45

BOULMER, Northumberland

Opened: 03/43
Closed: Currently in use by RAF
Elevation: 44ft
Pundit code: BM
Formation: 81 (OTU) Gp/9 Gp
Main contractor: Various
Runways: 3 tarmac
Hangars: Blister (4)
User sqns/units:

57 OTU
01/03/43-06/06/45
Spitfire; Master

59 OTU
1943-44
Hurricane; Master

Opened as satellite to Eshott 03/43
Additionally used as satellite to Milfield
1943-44

BRADWELL BAY, Essex

Opened: 11/41
Closed: 1946
Elevation: 30ft
Pundit code: RB
Formation: 11 Gp
Main contractor: Various
Runways: 3 tarmac/asphalt
Hangars: Bellman (1), Blister (12)
User sqns/units:

3 Sqn
06/03-06/04/44
14-28/04/44
Typhoon Ib; Tempest V

23 Sqn
14-21/08/42
13/10-27/12/42
Havoc I; Boston III; Mosquito II

29 Sqn
13/05-03/09/43
Beaufighter VIf; Mosquito XXI, VI

56 Sqn
23/08-04/10/43
Typhoon Ib

64 Sqn
30/08-29/12/44
Spitfire IX; Mustang III

124 Sqn
23/04-26/07/44
Spitfire VII

126 Sqn
30/08-30/12/44
Spitfire IXb

151 Sqn
01/03-17/05/45
Mosquito XXX

157 Sqn
15/03-13/05/43
Mosquito II

198 Sqn
19-22/08/43
Typhoon Ib

219 Sqn
01/04-29/08/44
Mosquito XVII, XXX

247 Sqn
04/06-10/07/43
Typhoon Ib

310 Sqn
29/12/44-27/02/45
Spitfire LFIX

312 Sqn
03/10/44-27/02/45
Spitfire HFIX

313 Sqn
29/12/44-27/02/45
Spitfire IX

418 Sqn
15/04/42-15/03/43
Boston III

456 Sqn
16/03-15/06/45
Mosquito XXX

488 Sqn
03/09/43-03/04/44
Mosquito XII, XIII

501 Sqn
22/09/44-03/03/45
Tempest V

605 Sqn
06/10/43-07/04/44
Mosquito VI

611 Sqn
30/08-03/10/44
Spitfire IX

Opened in 11 Gp Fighter Command with
full station status 11/41

BRENZETT, Kent

Opened: 03/43
Closed: 12/44
Elevation: 9ft
Pundit code: ZT
Formation: 84 Gp, 2 TAF; 11 Gp
Main contractor: RAFACS
Runways: 2 steel matting
Hangars: Blister (5)

User sqns/units:

129 Sqn
08/07-11/10/44
Mustang III

306 Sqn
08/07-10/10/44
Mustang III

315 Sqn
10/07-10/10/44
Mustang III

ALG

BRUNTON, Northumberland

Opened: 08/42
Closed: 05/45
Elevation: 80ft
Pundit code: BN
Formation: 81 (OTU) Gp/9 Gp
Main contractor: Various
Runways: 3 tarmac
Hangars: Blister (4)
User sqns/units:

56 OTU
15/12/44-21/05/45
Typhoon Ib; Tempest

59 OTU
04/08/42-26/01/44
Hurricane; Typhoon Ib

Fighter Leaders School
26/01-27/12/44
Spitfire; Typhoon; Hurricane

Opened as satellite to Milfield 08/42

CAISTOR, Lincs

Opened: 1941
Closed: 1963
Elevation: 100ft
Pundit code: Not known
Formation: 81 (OTU) Gp/9 Gp
Main contractor: Various
Runways: 4 grass
Hangars: Blister (1)
User sqns/units:

53 OTU
17/05/43-15/05/45
Spitfire

Opened as RLG for Kirton-in-Lindsey 1941
RLG to Leconfield 05/42
RLG to Manby 12/42
To Kirton-in-Lindsey as RLG 1943

CASTLE CAMPS, Essex

Opened: 06/40
Closed: 01/46
Elevation: 417ft
Pundit code: CC

Formation: 11 Gp
Main contractor: Various and John Laing & Son Ltd
Runways: 3 tarmac
Hangars: Bellman (1), Blister (8)
User sqns/units:

25 Sqn
27/10/44-14/07/45
Mosquito XVII, XXX, VI

68 Sqn
23/06-28/10/44
Beaufighter VIf; Mosquito XVII, XIX

73 Sqn
05/09-06/11/40
Hurricane I

85 Sqn
03-05/09/40
Hurricane I

91 Sqn
29/02-17/03/44
Spitfire XII

151 Sqn
08/10-19/11/44
Mosquito XXX

157 Sqn
18/12/41-15/03/43
Mosquito II

307 Sqn
27/01-31/05/45
Mosquito XXX

410 Sqn
30/12/43-29/04/44
Mosquito XIII

486 Sqn
06-21/03/44
29/03-29/04/44
Typhoon Ib; Tempest V

605 Sqn
15/03-06/10/43
Mosquito II, VI

Opened in 11 Gp Fighter Command as satellite to Debden 06/40
Closed for rebuilding 11/40
Reopened 12/41
Assumed full station status 04/42

CASTLETOWN, Caithness

Opened: 05/40
Closed: 1945
Elevation: 90ft
Pundit code: AX
Formation: 13 Gp/14 Gp
Main contractor: Various
Runways: 3 asphalt
Hangars: Bellman (1), T3 (1)
User sqns/units:

1 (RCAF) Sqn
12/12/40-01/03/41
Hurricane I

3 Sqn
03-14/09/40
13/10/40-07/01/41
10/02-03/04/41
Hurricane I

17 Sqn
05/04-16/06/41
Hurricane IIa, I

54 Sqn
17/11/41-02/02/42
Spitfire IIb

66 Sqn
08-14/05/44
Spitfire LFIXb

118 Sqn
19/10/43-20/01/44
Spitfire Vb

123 Sqn
22/09/41-11/04/42
Spitfire IIa, Vb

124 Sqn
10/05-17/11/41
Spitfire I, IIb, Va, Vb

131 Sqn
22/01-26/06/43
Spitfire Vb, Vc

167 Sqn
01/06-14/10/42
Spitfire Vb

213 Sqn
18/02-11/05/41
Hurricane I

232 Sqn
18/09-13/10/40
Hurricane I

260 Sqn
22/11-05/12/40
07/01-10/02/41
Hurricane I

310 Sqn
26/06-19/09/43
Spitfire VI

331 Sqn
1/08-21/09/41
Hurricane IIb

504 Sqn
21/06-02/09/40
10/03-30/04/44
Hurricane I; Spitfire IXb, Vb

607 Sqn
27/07-20/08/41
Hurricane I, IIa, IIb

610 Sqn
15/10/42-20/01/43
Spitfire Vb, Vc

Opened in 13 Gp Fighter Command as a satellite to Wick 05/40

CATTERICK, Yorks

Opened: 1914
Closed: Currently in use by RAF
Elevation: 175ft
Pundit code: AK
Formation: 13 Gp
Main contractor: Various and John Laing & Son Ltd
Runways: 1 asphalt
Hangars: Blister (8), C Type (2)
User sqns/units:

17 Sqn
31/10-10/11/41
Hurricane IIb

41 Sqn
25/09/36-19/10/39
25/10/39-28/05/40
17/06-26/07/40
08/08-03/09/40
23/02-28/07/41
Demon; Fury II; Spitfire I, IIa

54 Sqn
28/05-04/06/40
28/07-08/08/40
03/09/40-23/02/41
Spitfire I

68 Sqn
07/01-23/04/41
Blenheim If

122 Sqn
31/08-06/10/41
Spitfire I, IIa

130 Sqn
18/09-10/11/43
Spitfire Vb

131 Sqn
10/07-06/08/41
Spitfire Ia

134 Sqn
07-30/12/41
Spitfire Va

145 Sqn
28/07/41-11/02/42
Spitfire IIb, Vb

219 Sqn
04/10/39-12/10/40
25/04-14/05/43
Blenheim If; Beaufighter If

222 Sqn
14-25/02/44
Spitfire LFIXb

256 Sqn
23/11/40-04/01/41
Defiant I

306 Sqn
30/05-11/08/43
Spitfire Vb

313 Sqn
10/05-01/07/41
Spitfire I

331 Sqn
21/07-21/08/41
Hurricane I

332 Sqn
15/01-19/06/42
Spitfire Va, Vb

401 Sqn
23/01-29/05/43
Spitfire Vb

403 Sqn
19/06-01/07/42
08/07/42-23/01/43
Spitfire Vb

504 Sqn
02-06/09/40
Hurricane I

600 Sqn
12/10/40-14/03/41
Beaufighter If

609 Sqn
27/08-07/10/39
Spitfire I

13 Gp Sector station 09/39

CHAILEY, Sussex

Opened: 06/43
Closed: 01/45
Elevation: 105ft
Pundit code: AJ
Formation: 84 Gp, 2 TAF; 11 Gp
Main contractor: RAFACS
Runways: 2 steel matting
Hangars: Blister (4)
User sqns/units:

302 Sqn
26/04-28/06/44
Spitfire IX, IXe

308 Sqn
28/04-28/06/44
Spitfire IX

317 Sqn
26/04-28/06/44
Spitfire IX

ALG
Not used for operational flying until 04/44

CHARMY DOWN, Somerset

Opened: 11/40
Closed: 10/46
Elevation: 690ft
Pundit code: CH
Formation: 10 Gp
Main contractor: Various
Runways: 3 tarmac
Hangars: Bellman (1), Blister (12)
User sqns/units:

87 Sqn
18/12/40-07/08/41
27/01-02/11/42
Hurricane I, IIc

125 Sqn
07/08-24/09/41
Defiant I

137 Sqn
20/02-08/11/41
Whirlwind I

234 Sqn
23-30/08/42
Spitfire Vb

245 Sqn
26/10/42-29/01/43
Hurricane IIc

263 Sqn
07/08-19/12/41
23/12/41-28/01/42
Whirlwind I

417 Sqn
27/11/41-26/01/42
Spitfire IIa

421 Sqn
30/11-04/12/42
Spitfire Vb

1454 Flt ➡ 533 Sqn
01/42 (08/09/42)-25/01/43
Havoc I, II (Turbinlite); Boston III (Turbinlite)

Fighter Leaders School
02/43-10/08/43
Spitfire Vb

Opened in 10 Gp Fighter Command as satellite to Colerne 11/40
To USAAF 02/44
To 23 Gp RAF Flying Training Command 10/44

CHARTER HALL, Berwickshire

Opened: 04/42
Closed: 03/46
Elevation: 368ft
Pundit code: KH
Formation: 81 (OTU) Gp/9 Gp
Main contractor: James Miller & Partners Ltd
Runways: 2 tarmac
Hangars: Bellman (4), Blister (7)
User sqns/units:

54 OTU
01/05/42-31/10/45
Blenheim I, IVf, V; Beaufort I; Beaufighter I, II, VI; Wellington XVIII; Mosquito II, III, VI, XII, XIII, XVII, XIX, 30

Opened in 81 (OTU) Gp Fighter Command with full station status 04/42
To 9 Gp 06/43

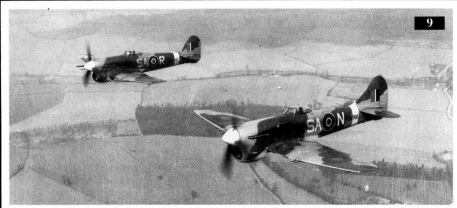

9. CASTLE CAMPS
Typhoon Ib and Tempest V of No 486 (NZ) Squadron at the time of the squadron's conversion to the latter, April 1944. *IWM CH13977 via Chaz Bowyer*

10. CATTERICK
Formed at Catterick on 7 January 1941 as a nightfighter unit equipped with Blenheim Ifs and IVfs, No 68 Squadron moved to High Ercall in April. Mk IVf Z5722 was the personal mount of Wg Cdr The Hon Max Aitken, OC No 68 Squadron. *via Chaz Bowyer*

11. CHARMY DOWN
Hurricane IIcs of No 87 Squadron were based at Colerne's satellite airfield of Charmy Down from January to November 1942, with spells on detachment to St Mary's, Scilly Isles. *via Chaz Bowyer*

12. Dornier Do217s, like this E-4 variant from 4/KG40, were the main bomber type used by the Luftwaffe in its *Baedeker* raids against Bath in April 1942. Nightfighters from Colerne and Charmy Down had no success in downing raiders on either of the two raids on 25/26 and 26/27 April. *Dornier*

CHEDWORTH, Gloucs

Opened: 04/42
Closed: 05/45
Elevation: 826ft
Pundit code: YW
Formation: 81 (OTU) Gp/9 Gp
Main contractor: Various
Runways: 2 tarmac
Hangars: Blister (2)
User sqns/units:

52 OTU ➡ *Fighter Command School of Tactics*
08/42-02/43
Spitfire I, II

3 Tactical Exercise Unit (TEU)
17/07-18/12/44
Mustang; Typhoon Ib

55 OTU
18/12/44-29/05/45
Typhoon Ib

Satellite to Aston Down 08/42
To Flying Training Command as satellite to South Cerney 02/43
To Fighter Command as satellite to Honiley 10/43
Satellite to Aston Down 07/44

CHILBOLTON, Hants

Opened: 09/40
Closed: 1961
Elevation: 290ft
Pundit code: CI
Formation: 10 Gp/9 Gp
Main contractor: Various
Runways: 3 concrete/tarmac
Hangars: Blister (3), T2 (2)
User sqns/units:

174 Sqn
01-11/03/43
Hurricane IIb

184 Sqn
01-11/03/43
Hurricane IId

238 Sqn
30/09/40-00/01/41
01/02-01/04/41
16/04-20/05/41
Hurricane I, IIa

245 Sqn
01/09-17/11/41
Hurricane IIb

308 Sqn
31/05-24/06/41
Spitfire IIa

501 Sqn
25/06-05/08/41
Spitfire IIa

504 Sqn
11-26/08/41
Hurricane IIb

41 OTU
23/03-26/05/45
Hurricane; Spitfire; Master; Martinet

Opened in 10 Gp Fighter Command as a Relief Landing Ground to Middle Wallop 09/40
Achieved full satellite status 04/42
To 70 (Training) Gp 11/42
To 10 Gp Fighter Command 06/43
To USAAF 12/43
To RAF Fighter Command 03/45

CHRISTCHURCH, Hants

Opened: 1935
Closed: 1967
Elevation: 20ft
Pundit code: XC
Formation: 10 Gp/11 Gp
Main contractor: Various
Runways: 5 grass/steel matting/concrete
Hangars: Bellman (1), Bessoneau (1), Blister (3)
User sqns/units: No fighter units based

To 10 Gp Fighter Command as satellite to Hurn 08/41
To 11 Gp as satellite to Ibsley 11/44
To 46 Gp Transport Command 03/45

CHURCH FENTON, Yorks

Opened: 06/37
Closed: Currently in use by RAF
Elevation: 27ft
Pundit code: CF
Formation: 11 Gp/12 Gp/81 (OTU) Gp
Main contractor: Various
Runways: 3 concrete/tarmac
Hangars: Bellman (1), Blister (10), C Type (2), T2 (1)
User sqns/units:

25 Sqn
17/05/42-19/12/43
Beaufighter If; Mosquito II, VI

46 Sqn
28/02-01/03/41
Hurricane I

64 Sqn
24/08/39-01/05/40
Blenheim If; Spitfire I

68 Sqn
16/03-20/04/45
Mosquito XXX

71 Sqn
19/09-23/11/40
Buffalo I

72 Sqn
01/06/37-17/10/39
01/11-01/12/39
13/01-02/03/40
Gladiator I; Spitfire I

73 Sqn
18/06-05/09/40
Hurricane I

85 Sqn
05/09-23/10/40
Hurricane I

87 Sqn
24/05-05/07/40

96 Sqn
06/08-04/09/43
Beaufighter VIf

124 Sqn
18/03-23/04/44
Spitfire VII

125 Sqn
24/04-20/11/45
Mosquito XXX

183 Sqn
01/11/42-01/03/43
12-24/03/43
Hurricane I; Typhoon Ia, Ib

234 Sqn
22/05-18/06/40
26/06-08/07/43
31/12/43-28/01/44
Spitfire I, Vb

242 Sqn
30/10/39-21/05/40
Blenheim I; Battle; Hurricane I

249 Sqn
16-17/05/40
08/07-14/08/40
Hurricane I, II; Spitfire I

264 Sqn
18/12/43-07/05/44
Mosquito II, XII

306 Sqn
29/08-07/11/40
Hurricane I

307 Sqn
06/05/44-27/01/45
Mosquito XII

308 Sqn
29/04-05/07/43
Spitfire Vb

456 Sqn
31/12/44-16/03/45
Mosquito XVII, XXX

488 Sqn
25/06-01/09/42
Beaufighter IIf

600 Sqn
02/09-18/11/42
Beaufighter VIf

604 Sqn
25/04-03/05/44
Mosquito XII, XIII

4 OTU ➡ *54 OTU*
16/12/40 (21/12/40)-01/05/42
Blenheim; Beaufighter; Defiant; Master;
Havoc; Oxford

13 Gp station 09/39
To 12 Gp 08/40
To 81 (OTU) Gp 12/40
To 12 Gp 05/42

CLEAVE, Cornwall

Opened: 05/39
Closed: 11/45
Elevation: 400ft
Pundit code: Not known
Formation: 10 Gp
Main contractor: Various
Runways: 2 grass
Hangars: Bellman (2), Blister (1)
User sqns/units: No fighter units based

Anti-Aircraft Co-operation Unit (AACU)
Opened in 22 Gp (Army Co-operation)
05/40
To 10 Gp Fighter Command 06/43

COLEBY GRANGE, Lincs

Opened: 1940
Closed: 1963
Elevation: 200ft
Pundit code: CG
Formation: 12 Gp
Main contractor: Various
Runways: Grass
Hangars: Blister (15), T1 (1)
User sqns/units:

68 Sqn
05/02-01/03/44
Beaufighter VIf

264 Sqn
07/11-18/12/43
Mosquito II

307 Sqn
02/03-06/05/44
Mosquito II, XII

409 Sqn
26/07/41-23/02/43
19/12/43-05/02/44
Defiant I; Beaufighter IIf, VIf

410 Sqn
21/02-20/10/43
Mosquito II, VI

Opened as RLG for Cranwell in Flying
Training Command 03/40
To 12 Gp Fighter Command as satellite to
Digby 05/41

COLERNE, Wilts

Opened: 01/40
Closed: Currently in use by Army and
MOD (Navy)
Elevation: 577ft
Pundit code: CQ

Formation: 10 Gp
Main contractor: Various
Runways: 3 tarmac
Hangars: Blister (1), J Type (1), K Type
(3), L Type (5), Robin (6)
User sqns/units:

19 Sqn
23-31/07/42
Spitfire Vb

29 Sqn
22/02-11/05/45
Mosquito XXX

87 Sqn
28/11-18/12/40
07/08/41-27/01/42
Hurricane I, IIc

89 Sqn
25/09-19/11/41
Beaufighter If

118 Sqn
07-09/04/41
Spitfire IIa

125 Sqn
16/06-07/08/41
25/01-14/05/42
Defiant I, II; Beaufighter IIf

131 Sqn
10-22/02/44
29/02-24/03/44
Spitfire IX

137 Sqn
02/01-04/02/44
Typhoon Ib

151 Sqn
30/04-16/08/43
17/11/43-25/03/44
Mosquito II, XII, XIII

165 Sqn
10/02-01/03/44
07-10/03/44
Spitfire IXb

175 Sqn
08/04-29/05/44
Typhoon Ib

183 Sqn
24/03-08/04/43
30/05-05/06/43
Typhoon Ib

184 Sqn
01/12/42-01/03/43
Hurricane IId

256 Sqn
06/02-26/03/41
Defiant I

263 Sqn
28/01-10/02/42
15/08-13/09/42
Whirlwind I

264 Sqn
01/05/42-30/04/43
30/11-01/12/44
Defiant II; Mosquito II, XIII

307 Sqn
26/03-26/04/41
Defiant I

316 Sqn
18/06-02/08/41
Hurricane I, IIa, IIb

317 Sqn
26-27/06/41
Hurricane I

402 Sqn
04-17/03/42
Hurricane IIb

406 Sqn
17/09-27/11/44
Mosquito XXX

410 Sqn
28/07-09/09/44
Mosquito XIII, XXX

417 Sqn
26/01-24/02/42
Spitfire IIa

456 Sqn
17/08-17/11/43
Mosquito II, VI

488 Sqn
03-12/05/44
29/07-09/10/44
Mosquito XIII

501 Sqn
09/04-25/06/41
Spitfire I

504 Sqn
28/03-10/08/45
Meteor III

1454 Flt
04/07/41-00/01/42
Havoc I (Turbinlite)

1457 Flt
15/09-00/11/41
Havoc I (Turbinlite)

600 Sqn
27/04-18/06/41
27/06-06/10/41
Beaufighter If, IIf

604 Sqn
13-25/07/44
28/07-06/08/44
Mosquito XIII

616 Sqn
17/01-28/02/45
Meteor III

Became a 10 Gp Fighter Command Sector
Station 05/40

13

13. COLEBY GRANGE
Flt Lt M.A.Cybulski RCAF and Flg Off
H.H.Ladbrook of No 410 (RCAF)
Squadron with their scorched Mosquito,
DZ757:Q, after destroying a Dornier
Do217 on 27 September 1944. *via
Chaz Bowyer*

14

14. COLERNE
Beaufighter NFIs of No 600 Squadron
were stationed at Colerne for the night
defence of the west of England from
April to October 1941, with a short spell
on detachment to Fairwood Common
and Predannack in June. *IWM CH17265
via Chaz Bowyer*

15. COLTISHALL
Merlin-engined Beaufighter IIf of No
255 Squadron is seen here in September
1941. This aircraft later served with No
410 Squadron. *Bristol via Chaz Bowyer*

15

COLLYWESTON, Northants

Opened: 05/40
Closed: Currently in use by RAF
Elevation: 282ft
Pundit code: WI
Formation: 12 Gp
Main contractor: Various
Runways: 4 grass
Hangars: Blister (4)
User sqns/units:

23 Sqn
31/05-16/08/40
Blenheim If

133 Sqn
28/09-03/10/41
Hurricane IIb

152 Sqn
27-30/09/40
Spitfire I

266 Sqn
03-24/10/41
Spitfire Vb

349 Sqn
08-29/06/43
Spitfire Va

Opened in 12 Gp Fighter Command as a
satellite to Wittering 05/40
To 21 Gp Flying Training Command
04/45

COLTISHALL, Norfolk

Opened: 05/40
Closed: Currently in use by RAF
Elevation: 57ft
Pundit code: CS
Formation: 12 Gp
Main contractor: Various
Runways: 3 steel matting
Hangars: Blister (8), C Type (4)
User sqns/units:

1 Sqn
08/04-14/05/45
Spitfire IXb

25 Sqn
05/02-27/10/44
Mosquito XVII, XXX

64 Sqn
15/10-11/11/40
25/09/43-21/01/44
02/02-29/04/44
Spitfire I, Vc

66 Sqn
29/05-03/09/40
Spitfire I

68 Sqn
08/03/42-05/02/44
28/10/44-08/02/45
27/02-16/03/45
Beaufighter If, VIf

72 Sqn
20-30/10/40
02-29/11/40
Spitfire I

74 Sqn
09/09-15/10/40
Spitfire I, IIa

80 Sqn
20-29/09/44
Tempest V

118 Sqn
17/01-15/08/43
Spitfire Vb

124 Sqn
10/02-07/04/45
Spitfire HFIXe

125 Sqn
18/10/44-24/04/45
Mosquito XVII, XXX

133 Sqn
31/07-15/08/41
Hurricane IIb

137 Sqn
08-31/11/41
Whirlwind I

152 Sqn
17/12/41-17/01/42
Spitfire IIa

154 Sqn
12/03-05/04/42
Spitfire IIa, IIb, Va, Vb

195 Sqn
21/08-24/09/43
Typhoon Ib

222 Sqn
11/11/40-06/06/41
Spitfire I, IIa, IIb

229 Sqn
01/07-25/09/44
02/12/44-10/01/45
Spitfire IX, LFXVIe

234 Sqn
28/01-18/03/44
Spitfire Vb

242 Sqn
18/06-26/10/40
30/11-16/12/40
Hurricane I

255 Sqn
20/09/41-02/03/42
Defiant I; Beaufighter IIf

257 Sqn
16/12/40-07/11/41
Hurricane I, IIb, IIc

274 Sqn
20-29/09/44
Tempest V

303 Sqn
25/09/44-04/04/45
Spitfire LFVb, IXc, XVI

312 Sqn
11/07-27/08/44
Spitfire HFIX

315 Sqn
24/10-01/11/44
16/01-08/08/45
Mustang III

316 Sqn
28/04-04/07/44
27/08-24/10/44
Mustang III

453 Sqn
30/09-18/10/44
Spitfire IXb

602 Sqn
30/09-18/10/44
19-23/02/45
05/04-15/05/45
Spitfire IXb, XVI

603 Sqn
10/01-24/02/45
05-28/04/45
Spitfire LFXVIe

611 Sqn
04/08-06/09/43
13/09-08/10/43
13/10-19/11/43
23/11/43-08/02/44
19/02-30/04/44
Spitfire LFVb

616 Sqn
03-09/09/40
Spitfire I

Opened in 12 Gp Fighter Command with
full station status 05/40

COOLHAM, Sussex

Opened: 04/44
Closed: 01/45
Elevation: 55ft
Pundit code: XQ
Formation: 84 Gp, 2 TAF
Main contractor: RAFACS
Runways: 2 steel matting
Hangars: Blister (5)
User sqns/units:

129 Sqn
03/04-22/06/44
Mustang III

222 Sqn
30/06-04/07/44
Spitfire LFIXb

306 Sqn
01/04-22/06/44
Mustang III

315 Sqn
01/04-22/06/44
Mustang III

349 Sqn
30/06-04/07/44
Spitfire LFIXe

485 Sqn
30/06-03/07/44
Spitfire IXb, IXe

ALG

CRANAGE, Cheshire

Opened: 10/40
Closed: 06/45
Elevation: 165ft
Pundit code: RG
Formation: 9 Gp
Main contractor: Various
Runways: 3 steel matting
Hangars: Bellman (8), Blister (4)
User sqns/units:

96 Sqn
16/12/40-21/10/41
Hurricane I, IIc; Defiant I

Opened in Flying Training Command
10/40
To 9 Gp Fighter Command 12/40
To Flying Training Command 10/41

CRANFIELD, Beds

Opened: 06/37
Closed: Currently in use as Institute of
Technology
Elevation: 340ft
Pundit code: CX
Formation: 81 (OTU) Gp/9 Gp
Main contractor: John Laing & Son Ltd
Runways: 3 concrete
Hangars: Blister (9), C Type (4), T3 (1)
User sqns/units:

181 Sqn
01-08/03/43
Typhoon Ib

183 Sqn
01-08/03/43
Typhoon Ib

51 OTU
17/08/41-14/06/45
Blenheim I, IV, V; Beaufighter I, II, VI;
Hudson III; Havoc I, II;
Beaufort I, II; Mosquito II, III, VI, XII;
Wellington XVII, XVIII;
Hurricane IIc, IV

Opened in 1 Gp Bomber Command with
full station status 06/37
To 81 (OTU) Gp Fighter Command 05/41

CROSBY-ON-EDEN, Cumberland

Opened: 02/41
Closed: Currently in use as Carlisle
Airport
Elevation: 164ft
Pundit code: KX
Formation: 81 (OTU) Gp
Main contractor: Various
Runways: 3 tarmac
Hangars: Bellman (3), Blister (5), T2 (3)
User sqns/units:

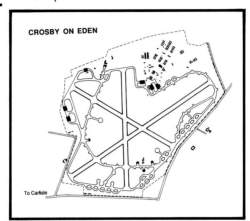

59 OTU
20/02/41-08/08/42
Hurricane I

Opened in 81 (OTU) Gp Fighter Command
02/41
To 17 Gp Coastal Command 08/42

CROYDON, Surrey

Opened: 01/16
Closed: 1955
Elevation: 217ft
Pundit code: CO
Formation: 11 Gp
Main contractor: Various
Runways: 3 grass
Hangars: Blister (4)
User sqns/units:

1 Sqn
07/04-01/05/41
Hurricane I, IIa, IIb

1 (RCAF) Sqn
07-08/40
Hurricane I

3 Sqn
02-10/09/39
17/09-12/10/39
13/11/39-28/01/40
Hurricane I

17 Sqn
02-09/09/39
26/02-01/04/41
Hurricane I, IIa

72 Sqn
01-12/09/40
Spitfire I

85 Sqn
19/08-03/09/40
Hurricane I

92 Sqn
30/12/39-09/05/40
Blenheim If; Spitfire I

111 Sqn
04/06-19/08/40
03-08/09/40
Hurricane I

145 Sqn
10/10/39-09/05/40
Blenheim If

302 Sqn
30/06-07/07/42
Spitfire Vb

317 Sqn
30/06-07/07/42
Spitfire Vb

501 Sqn
21/06-04/07/40
Hurricane I

605 Sqn
07/09/40-25/02/41
Hurricane I, IIa

607 Sqn
14-15/11/39
22/05-04/06/40
Gladiator I; Hurricane I

615 Sqn
02/09-15/11/39
Gladiator I, II

Satellite to Kenley in 11 Gp Fighter
Command 09/39
To Transport Command 03/43

CULMHEAD (Church Stanton), Somerset

Opened: 08/41
Closed: 08/46
Elevation: 864ft
Pundit code: UC
Formation: 10 Gp
Main contractor: Various
Runways: 3 asphalt
Hangars: Blister (10), T2 (1)
User sqns/units:

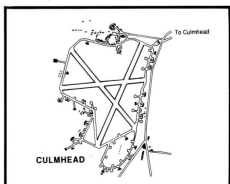

CULMHEAD continued

66 Sqn
28/06-10/08/43
Spitfire Vb, Vc

126 Sqn
22/05-03/07/44
Spitfire IXb

131 Sqn
17/09/43-10/02/44
Spitfire IX

154 Sqn
07/05-07/06/42
Spitfire Vb

165 Sqn
17/09/43-10/02/44
Spitfire IXb

302 Sqn
07/08-05/09/41
Hurricane IIb

306 Sqn
12/12/41-03/05/42
Spitfire Vb

312 Sqn
10/10/42-20/02/43
14/03-24/06/43
Spitfire Vb, Vc

313 Sqn
08/06/42-28/06/43
Spitfire Vb, Vc

316 Sqn
02/08-13/12/41
Hurricane IIa, IIb; Spitfire IIa, Vb

504 Sqn
30/06-14/08/43
Spitfire Vb, Vc

610 Sqn
07-23/04/44
30/04-16/05/44
Spitfire XIV

616 Sqn
16/05-21/07/44
Spitfire VII; Meteor I

Opened in 10 Gp Fighter Command as
Church Stanton 08/41
Renamed Culmhead 12/43
To 23 Gp Flying Training Command
12/44

DARLEY MOOR, Derbys

Opened: 07/42
Closed: 02/45
Elevation: 580ft
Pundit code: DM
Formation: 38 Gp
Main contractor: Various
Runways: 3 concrete
Hangars: None
User sqns/units:

42 OTU
12/06/43-20/03/45
Blenheim IV; Whitley V; Albemarle I, II;
Oxford II; Anson I;
Martinet I; Lysander III

Opened in 38 Wing Army Co-operation
Command as a satellite
to Ashbourne 07/42
To 38 Gp Fighter Command 06/43

DEANLAND, Sussex

Opened: 04/44
Closed: 01/45
Elevation: 77ft
Pundit code: XB
Formation: 84 Gp, 2 TAF
Main contractor: RAFACS/Royal
Engineers Airfield Construction Group
Runways: 2 steel matting
Hangars: Blister (4)
User sqns/units:

64 Sqn
29/04-26/06/44
Spitfire Vc

91 Sqn
21/07-07/10/44
Spitfire XIV, IXb

234 Sqn
29/04-19/06/44
Spitfire Vb

302 Sqn
01-12/04/44
14-26/04/44
Spitfire IX

308 Sqn
01-28/04/44
Spitfire IX

317 Sqn
01-26/04/44
Spitfire IX

322 Sqn
21/07-10/10/44
Spitfire XIV, LFIXe

345 Sqn
16/08-10/10/44
Spitfire Vb, HFIX

611 Sqn
30/04-24/06/44
Spitfire LFVb

ALG

DEBDEN, Essex

Opened: 04/37
Closed: 1975
Elevation: 395ft
Pundit code: DB
Formation: 11 Gp
Main contractor: W & C French Ltd
Runways: 2 concrete/tarmac

Hangars: Bellman (1), Blister (11), C Type (3)
User sqns/units:

17 Sqn
09/09-16/12/39
24-30/12/39
08-13/01/40
20-30/01/40
11-22/02/40
27/02-05/03/40
12-23/03/40
27/03-05/04/40
13-23/04/40
30/04-07/05/40
22-25/05/40
19/06-19/08/40
02/09-09/10/40
Hurricane I

25 Sqn
08/10-27/12/40
Blenheim If; Beaufighter If

29 Sqn
22/11/37-04/04/40
10/05-27/06/40
Demon; Blenheim If

41 Sqn
08/07-01/08/42
Spitfire Vb

54 Sqn
11-13/06/41
Spitfire Va

65 Sqn
22/12/41-14/04/42
Spitfire Vb

71 Sqn
02/05-14/08/42
20/08-29/09/42
Spitfire Vb

85 Sqn
04/11/38-09/09/39
23/05-19/08/40
01/01-03/05/41
Hurricane I; Defiant I; Havoc I

87 Sqn
07/06/37-04/09/39
22-24/05/40
Gladiator I; Hurricane I

111 Sqn
19/08-03/09/40
01/11-15/12/41
22/12/41-30/06/42
07-28/07/42
Hurricane I; Spitfire Vb

121 Sqn
23-29/09/42
Spitfire Vb

124 Sqn
29/07-25/09/42
Spitfire VI

129 Sqn
01/11-22/12/41
Spitfire Vb

No 17 Squadron's Hurricane I N2359:J
with Plt Off L.W.Stevens and LACs
McEvoy and Jaquest, in August 1940.
via Chaz Bowyer

17 DIGBY

With two erks hanging onto the
tailplane to keep it down, groundcrew
run up the engine of No 401 Squadron's
Hurricane IIb Z3658:N on 24 July 1941.
*Public Archives of Canada DND-PL-4478
via Chaz Bowyer*

DEBDEN continued

157 Sqn
15-18/12/41
No aircraft

257 Sqn
15/08-05/09/40
Hurricane I

258 Sqn
03/10-01/11/41
Hurricane IIa

264 Sqn
27/11-31/12/40
Defiant I

303 Sqn
05-12/03/43
Spitfire Vb

350 Sqn
15/04-30/06/42
Spitfire Vb

403 Sqn
25/08-03/10/41
Spitfire IIa,Vb

418 Sqn
15/11/41-15/04/42
Boston III

504 Sqn
09/10-24/12/39
30/12/39-08/01/40
13-20/01/40
30/01-11/02/40
22-27/02/40
05-12/03/40
18-27/03/40
04-13/04/40
23-30/04/40
07-12/05/40
21-22/05/40
Hurricane I

531 Sqn
02-09/10/42
Havoc I (Turbinlite); Boston III (Turbinlite)

601 Sqn
19/08-02/09/40
Hurricane I

51 OTU
26/07-17/08/41
Blenheim; Beaufighter; Havoc; Hudson

52 OTU
01/02-15/08/41
Hurricane; Master; Battle

11 Gp Fighter Command Sector Station
09/39
To USAAF 09/42

DETLING, Kent

Opened: 09/38
Closed: 10/59
Elevation: 530ft

Pundit code: DQ
Formation: 11 Gp/83 Gp, 2 TAF
Main contractor: Various
Runways: 3 grass
Hangars: Bellman (1), Bessoneau (1), Blister (14)
User sqns/units:

1 Sqn
22/06-11/07/44
10/08-18/12/44
Spitfire IXb

80 Sqn
19/05-22/06/44
Spitfire IX

118 Sqn
20-23/01/44
05/02-10/03/44
12/07-09/08/44
Spitfire IXc, Vb, VII, IXc

124 Sqn
26/07-09/08/44
Spitfire HFIXe

132 Sqn
10-13/03/44
19/03-18/04/44
Spitfire IXb

165 Sqn
22/06-12/07/44
10/08-15/12/44
Spitfire IXb

184 Sqn
12/10/43-06/03/44
Hurricane IV

229 Sqn
19/05-22/06/44
Spitfire IX

274 Sqn
19/05-22/06/44
Spitfire IX

453 Sqn
19-21/01/44
04/02-13/03/44
19/03-18/04/44
Spitfire IXb

504 Sqn
12/07-13/08/44
Spitfire IXe

602 Sqn
12/10/43-17/01/44
12-13/03/44
20/03-18/04/44
Spitfire IXb, LFVb

Opened in 6 Gp Bomber Command 09/38
To 16 Gp Coastal Command 11/38
To Army Co-operation Command 01/43
To 11 Gp Fighter Command 06/43
To 83 Gp, 2 TAF 11/43
To ADGB 05/44
To C&M 01/45

DIGBY, Lincs

Opened: 03/18
Closed: Currently in use by RAF
Elevation: 67ft
Pundit code: DJ
Formation: 12 Gp
Main contractor: Various
Runways: 3 grass
Hangars: Blister (10), C Type (2)
User sqns/units:

19 Sqn
17/05-04/06/43
Spitfire Vb

29 Sqn
27/06-27/07/40
Blenheim If

46 Sqn
15/11/37-10/12/39
17/01-09/05/40
13/06-01/09/40
14/12/40-28/02/41
Gauntlet II; Hurricane I

56 Sqn
31/05-05/06/40
Hurricane I

73 Sqn
09/11/37-09/09/39
Gladiator I; Hurricane I

79 Sqn
27/05-05/06/40
Hurricane I

92 Sqn
20/10/41-12/02/42
Spitfire Vb

111 Sqn
21-30/05/40
Hurricane I

151 Sqn
01/09-28/11/40
Hurricane I

167 Sqn
13-18/05/43
Spitfire Vb,Vc

198 Sqn
07/12/42-23/01/43
Typhoon Ia, Ib

222 Sqn
10-23/05/40
Spitfire I

229 Sqn
04/10/39-26/06/40
Blenheim If; Hurricane I

242 Sqn
01/09-30/10/42
Spitfire Vb

310 Sqn
11/07-28/08/44
Spitfire Vb

349 Sqn
16-25/08/43
Spitfire Va

350 Sqn
25/08-07/09/43
19/09-01/10/43
Spitfire Vb

1 (RCAF) Sqn ➡ 401 Sqn
22/02-(01/03/41)-20/10/41
Hurricane I, IIa; Spitfire IIa

2 (RCAF) Sqn ➡ 402 Sqn
11/12/40 (01/03/41)-23/06/41
21/03-07/08/43
19/09-19/12/43
02/01-12/02/44
Hurricane I, IIa, IIb; Spitfire Vb, Vc

409 Sqn
16/06-26/07/41
Defiant I

411 Sqn
16/06-19/11/41
30/03-05/06/42
07/06-05/08/42
08/08/42-01/03/43
12-22/03/43
Spitfire I, IIa, Vb

412 Sqn
30/06-20/10/41
Spitfire IIa

416 Sqn
07/06-09/08/43
02/10/43-12/02/44
Spitfire Vb, Vc, IXb

421 Sqn
06/04-03/05/42
Spitfire Va

438 Sqn
10/11-19/12/43
Hurricane IV

441 Sqn
08/02-18/03/44
Spitfire Vb

442 Sqn
08/02-18/03/44
Spitfire Vb

443 Sqn
08/02-18/03/44
Spitfire Vb

504 Sqn
27/08-09/10/39
30/04-11/07/44
Gauntlet II; Hurricane I; Spitfire Vb

601 Sqn
25/03-10/04/42
Spitfire Vb

609 Sqn
19/11/41-30/03/42
Spitfire Vb

611 Sqn
10/10/39-13/12/40
Spitfire I, IIa

12 Gp Fighter Command Sector Station
09/39

DREM, East Lothian

Opened: 1917
Closed: 03/46
Elevation: 36ft
Pundit code: DE
Formation: 13 Gp
Main contractor: Various
Runways: 3 grass
Hangars: Bellman (3), Blister (14)
User sqns/units:

29 Sqn
04/04-10/05/40
01/03-01/05/44
Blenheim If; Mosquito XII, XIII

43 Sqn
12/12/40-22/02/41
01/03-04/10/41
Hurricane I, IIa, IIb

64 Sqn
17/05-06/08/41
04/10-16/11/41
Spitfire IIa

65 Sqn
26/09-02/10/42
11/10/42-03/01/43
10/01-29/03/43
Spitfire Vb

72 Sqn
01/12/39-12/01/40
Spitfire I, Vb, Vc

91 Sqn
17/03-23/04/44
Spitfire XIV

96 Sqn
04/09-08/11/43
Beaufighter VIf; Mosquito XIII

111 Sqn
07/12/39-27/02/40
08/09-12/10/40
Hurricane I

123 Sqn
06/08-22/09/41
Spitfire I, IIa

124 Sqn
29/12/42-21/01/43
Spitfire VI

130 Sqn
30/03-30/04/43
Spitfire Vb

137 Sqn
02-11/08/42
Whirlwind I

141 Sqn
15-22/10/40
Defiant I

145 Sqn
14-31/08/40
Hurricane I

186 Sqn
27/04-03/08/43
No aircraft

197 Sqn
25/11/42-28/03/43
Typhoon Ia, Ib

222 Sqn
10-15/08/42
21/08-22/10/42
Spitfire Vb

232 Sqn
24/10-11/11/40
Hurricane I

242 Sqn
01/06-11/08/42
Spitfire Vb

245 Sqn
12/05-05/06/40
Hurricane I

258 Sqn
04-17/12/40
Hurricane I

260 Sqn
16/04-19/05/41
Hurricane I

263 Sqn
10-28/06/40
02/09-28/11/40
Hurricane I; Whirlwind I

307 Sqn
09/11/43-02/03/44
Mosquito II, XII

340 Sqn
20/12/41-01/01/42
30/04-09/11/43
17/12/44-30/01/45
Spitfire IIa, Vb, IXb

410 Sqn
06/08/41-15/06/42
Defiant I; Beaufighter IIf

453 Sqn
09/06-25/09/42
Spitfire Vb

488 Sqn
03/08-03/09/43
Beaufighter VIf; Mosquito XII

600 Sqn
14/03-27/04/41
Beaufighter If

18. DREM
No 453 (RAAF) Squadron's Spitfire Vbs are pictured with their air and groundcrews shortly after the squadron was re-formed in the UK on 9 June 1942. The squadron moved south to Hornchurch in late September the same year. *J. Barrien via K. Merrick*

19. DREM
Beaufighter VIf V8748:R of No 96 Squadron. The squadron was based at Drem for two months in the autumn during which time it discarded its Beaufighters in favour of the more potent Mosquito NFXIII. *IWM CE24 via Chaz Bowyer*

20. DUXFORD
Bell Airacobras of No 601 Squadron lined up at Duxford in the late summer of 1941. The aircraft's unorthodox design featured an engine installed below and behind the pilot's seat, coupled to the propeller by means of an extension shaft and gearbox. It was also one of the first fighters in the world to have a tricycle undercarriage.

After trials as a ground attack aircraft, the Airacobra was found to be unsuitable and withdrawn from RAF service, undelivered aircraft being taken over by the USAAF for training duties. *via Chaz Bowyer*

21. DUXFORD
Spitfire Vb AA927:O of the Air Fighting Development Unit (AFDU), probably in 1942. The unit used a handful of Spitfires and Hurricanes for tactical development work, but its main task was to test the fighting potential of new aircraft types. *via Author*

DREM continued

602 Sqn
13/10/39-14/04/40
22/05-13/08/40
Spitfire I

603 Sqn
14/04-05/05/40
13/12/40-27/02/41
07/05-14/06/45
Spitfire I, IIa, LFXVIe

605 Sqn
28/05-07/09/40
Hurricane I

607 Sqn
08/11-12/12/40
02/03-16/04/41
Hurricane I

609 Sqn
17/10-05/12/39
10/01-20/05/40
Spitfire I

611 Sqn
12/11/41-03/06/42
Spitfire IIa, IIb, Vb

Re-opened in Flying Training Command 1939
To 13 Gp Fighter Command 10/39
To RN as HMS *Nighthawk* 04/45

DUNSFOLD, Surrey

Opened: 12/42
Closed: Currently in use by British Aerospace Plc
Elevation: 168ft
Pundit code: DT
Formation: 11 Gp
Main contractor: Royal Canadian Engineers
Runways: 3 concrete
Hangars: Blister (11), T2 (2)
User sqns/units: No fighter units based

To 11 Gp ADGB 05/44
Satellite to Odiham 01/45

DUXFORD, Cambs

Opened: 1919
Closed: 07/61
Elevation: 97ft
Pundit code: DX
Formation: 12 Gp
Main contractor: Various
Runways: 3 grass
Hangars: Belfast (4), Blister (8)
User sqns/units:

19 Sqn
16-25/05/40
05-25/06/40
03-24/07/40
01/11/40-06/02/41
Spitfire I, Ib, IIa

56 Sqn
26/06/41-30/03/42
Hurricane IIb; Typhoon Ia

66 Sqn
20/07/36-16/05/40
Gauntlet II; Spitfire I

133 Sqn
15/08-28/09/41
Hurricane IIb

181 Sqn
25/08-10/12/42
Hurricane I; Typhoon Ia, Ib

195 Sqn
15-19/11/42
Typhoon Ib

222 Sqn
04/10/39-10/05/40
Blenheim If; Spitfire I

242 Sqn
26/10-30/11/40
Hurricane I

264 Sqn
10/05-03/07/40
Defiant I

266 Sqn
29/01-02/08/42
11/08-21/09/42
Spitfire Vb; Typhoon Ia, Ib

310 Sqn
10/07/40-26/06/41
Hurricane I, IIa

312 Sqn
29/08-26/09/40
Hurricane I

601 Sqn
16/08/41-06/01/42
Hurricane IIb; Airacobra I

609 Sqn
30/03-26/08/42
30/08-18/09/42
Spitfire Vb; Typhoon Ia, Ib

611 Sqn
13/08-10/10/39
Spitfire I

AFDU
12/40-03/43
Spitfire; Hurricane; Various

12 Gp Fighter Command Sector Station
09/39
To USAAF 04/43

DYCE, Aberdeenshire

Opened: 07/34
Closed: Currently in use as Aberdeen Airport
Elevation: 234ft
Pundit code: DY
Formation: 13 Gp
Main contractor: Various
Runways: 3 concrete/tarmac
Hangars: Bellman (4), Blister (12), T3 (2)
User sqns/units:

111 Sqn
12/10/40-20/07/41
Hurricane I; Spitfire I, IIa

141 Sqn
22-30/08/40
Defiant I

145 Sqn
31/08-09/10/40
Hurricane I

310 Sqn
20/07-24/12/41
Hurricane IIa, IIb; Spitfire IIa, Vb

331 Sqn
22/04-22/05/45
Spitfire IXe

332 Sqn
22/04-22/05/45
Spitfire IXe

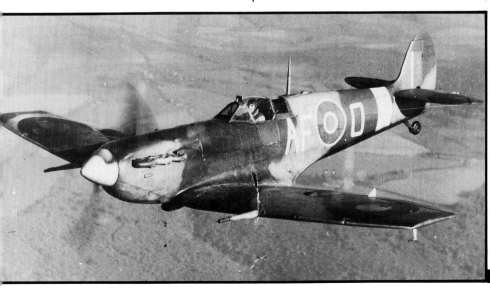

416 Sqn
14/03-03/04/42
Spitfire Vb

602 Sqn
14/04-22/05/40
Spitfire I

603 Sqn
17/01-14/04/40
15/12/41-14/03/42
Spitfire I, Vb

Opened in Coastal Command 10/39
To 13 Gp Fighter Command 01/40
To Coastal Command 07/42

EARLS COLNE, Essex

Opened: 08/42
Closed: 03/46
Elevation: 222ft
Pundit code: EC
Formation: 38 Gp
Main contractor: US Army
Runways: 3 concrete/tarmac
Hangars: T2 (2)
User sqns/units:

296 Sqn
29/09/44-23/01/46
Albemarle II, V, VI; Halifax V, III, VII

297 Sqn
30/09/44-01/04/46
Albemarle II, V, VI; Halifax V, III, VII

Opened in 3 Gp Bomber Command 08/42
To USAAF 05/43
To 38 Gp RAF Fighter Command 09/44

EAST FORTUNE, East Lothian

Opened: 1916
Closed: 1961
Elevation: 97ft
Pundit code: EF
Formation: 81 (OTU) Gp
Main contractor: Various
Runways: 3 tarmac
Hangars: Blister (8), Callender-Hamilton (3), T2 (1)
User sqns/units:

60 OTU ➡ *132 OTU*
04/06/41-
(Transferred to Coastal Command as 132 OTU 24/11/42)
Defiant; Blenheim; Oxford; Beaufighter

Satellite to Drem 06/40
To 17 Gp Coastal Command 11/42

EASTCHURCH, Kent

Opened: 1911
Closed: 1946
Elevation: 47ft
Pundit code: EA

Formation: 11 Gp/83 Gp, 2 TAF
Main contractor: Various
Runways: 3 grass
Hangars: Bellman (3)
User sqns/units:

65 Sqn
14-20/08/42
Spitfire Vb

122 Sqn
18/05-01/06/43
Spitfire Vb

124 Sqn
30/06-05/07/42
Spitfire Vb

132 Sqn
05/04-18/05/43
Spitfire Vb

165 Sqn
15-20/08/42
Spitfire Vb

174 Sqn
21/01-04/02/44
Typhoon Ib

175 Sqn
24/02-08/03/44
Typhoon Ib

181 Sqn
06-21/02/44
Typhoon Ib

182 Sqn
05-23/01/44
Typhoon Ib

183 Sqn
14-25/07/44
Typhoon Ib

184 Sqn
05/04-31/05/43
11/03-03/04/44
Hurricane IId, IV; Typhoon Ib

245 Sqn
25-30/04/44
12-22/05/44
Typhoon Ib

247 Sqn
01-24/04/44
Typhoon Ib

263 Sqn
23/07-06/08/44
Typhoon Ib

266 Sqn
29/06-13/07/44
Spitfire I; Typhoon Ib

401 Sqn
03-28/07/42
Spitfire Vb

To 16 Gp Coastal Command 11/38
To Technical Training Command 06/41

To 11 Gp Fighter Command, as Forward Operating Base (FOB) for Gravesend 06/42
To 72 Gp Army Co-operation Command 10/42
To 11 Gp Fighter Command 04/43
To 54 Gp Flying Training Command (but continued in use as FOB) 05/43

EGLINTON, Co Londonderry, NI

Opened: 04/41
Closed: 09/66
Elevation: 26ft
Pundit code: QN
Formation: 13 Gp/82 Gp
Main contractor: Various
Runways: 3 tarmac
Hangars: Blister (12)
User sqns/units:

41 Sqn
22-30/09/42
Spitfire Vb

133 Sqn
08/10/41-02/01/42
Hurricane IIb; Spitfire IIa

134 Sqn
30/12/41-26/03/42
Spitfire Va, IIa, Vb; Hurricane IIb

152 Sqn
17/01-16/08/42
Spitfire IIa, Vb

Opened with full station status in 13 Gp Fighter Command 04/41
To RN as HMS *Gannet* 05/43

ESHOTT, Northumberland

Opened: 11/42
Closed: 06/45
Elevation: 151ft
Pundit code: Not known
Formation: 81 (OTU) Gp/9 Gp
Main contractor: Various
Runways: 3 concrete
Hangars: Blister (8), T3 (1)
User sqns/units:

57 OTU
10/11/42-06/06/45
Spitfire

Opened as satellite to Boulmer 11/42

EXETER, Devon

Opened: 05/37
Closed: Currently in use as Exeter Airport
Elevation: 100ft
Pundit code: EX
Formation: 10 Gp
Main contractor: John Laing & Son Ltd
Runways: 3 asphalt

Hangars: Blister (10), RAF 7 (1)
User sqns/units:

66 Sqn
24/02-27/04/41
Spitfire I, IIa

87 Sqn
05/07-28/11/40
Hurricane I

125 Sqn
15/04-14/11/43
Beaufighter VIf

131 Sqn
26/06-16/08/43
Spitfire Vb, Vc

165 Sqn
30/07-08/08/43
Spitfire Vb, VC

213 Sqn
18/06-07/09/40
Hurricane I

247 Sqn
17/05-21/09/42
Hurricane I, IIc

263 Sqn
28/11/40-24/02/41
Whirlwind I

266 Sqn
08/01-07/09/43
10-21/09/43
Typhoon Ib

307 Sqn
26/04/41-15/04/43
Defiant I; Beaufighter IIf, VIf; Mosquito II

308 Sqn
01/04-07/05/42
Spitfire Vb

310 Sqn
07/05-01/07/42
07/07-16/08/42
21/08/42-26/06/43
Spitfire Vb, Vc

317 Sqn
21/07/41-01/04/42
Hurricane IIb; Spitfire Vb

406 Sqn
15/11/43-14/04/44
Beaufighter VIf

421 Sqn
29/06-08/07/42
Spitfire Vb

504 Sqn
18/12/40-21/07/41
Hurricane I

601 Sqn
07/09-17/12/40
Hurricane I

610 Sqn
04/01-07/04/44
Spitfire Vb, Vc, XIV

616 Sqn
17/09-16/11/43
01/12/43-18/03/44
Spitfire VI, VII

Opened with full station status in 10 Gp 07/40
To USAAF 04/44
To 23 Gp, RAF Flying Training Command 01/45

FAIRFORD, Gloucs

Opened: 01/44
Closed: Currently in use by USAF
Elevation: 256ft
Pundit code: FA
Formation: 38 Gp
Main contractor: Sir Alfred McAlpine Ltd
Runways: 3 concrete/asphalt
Hangars: T2 (2)
User sqns/units:

190 Sqn
25/03-14/10/44
Stirling IV

620 Sqn
18/03-18/10/44
Stirling IV

Opened in 38 Gp with full station status 01/44
To 23 Gp Flying Training Command 10/44

FAIRLOP, Essex

Opened: 11/41
Closed: 08/46
Elevation: 85ft
Pundit code: FP
Formation: 11 Gp
Main contractor: Various
Runways: 3 concrete/asphalt
Hangars: Blister (8)
User sqns/units:

64 Sqn
08/09-14/11/42
02/01-15/03/43
Spitfire IX

65 Sqn
18-31/05/43
Spitfire Vb

81 Sqn
17/07-01/09/42
Spitfire Vb

122 Sqn
08-29/06/42
06-17/07/42
16/11-09/12/42
Spitfire Vb, IX

154 Sqn
27/07-10/08/42
15/08-01/09/42
Spitfire Vb

164 Sqn
22/09/43-04/01/44
13/01-11/02/44
Hurricane IV; Typhoon Ib

182 Sqn
05-29/04/43
Typhoon Ib

193 Sqn
20/02-16/03/44
Typhoon Ib

195 Sqn
24/09/43-15/02/44
Typhoon Ib

239 Sqn
21-27/06/43
Mustang I

245 Sqn
28/05-02/06/43
Typhoon Ib

247 Sqn
05/04-29/05/43
Typhoon Ib

302 Sqn
19/08-18/09/43
Spitfire Vb, Vc

313 Sqn
29/04-28/06/42
Spitfire Vb

317 Sqn
21/08-21/09/43
Spitfire Vb

350 Sqn
15-23/03/43
Spitfire Vb, Vc

602 Sqn
29/04-01/06/43
Spitfire Vb

603 Sqn
12/11-15/12/41
Spitfire Va, Vb

Opened in 11 Gp as satellite to Hornchurch 11/41
To Balloon Command as 24 Balloon Centre 09/44

FAIRWOOD COMMON, Glamorgan

Opened: 06/41
Closed: Currently in use as Swansea airport
Elevation: 268ft
Pundit code: FC
Formation: 10 Gp
Main contractor: Various

22. FAIRFORD
The airborne squadrons of No 38 Group came under the operational control of Fighter Command. They flew mainly Halifax and Stirling aircraft carrying paratroops, SOE agents, supplies to the Resistance. They also towed gliders to their drop zones in Europe on D-Day and afterwards. No 620 Squadron air and groundcrew are pictured at Fairford during September 1944. Standing behind them are some of the squadron's Short Stirling IVs. *R. Seeley*

23. FAIRLOP
Spitfire Vb's of No 122 Squadron scramble in the summer of 1942. *via Chaz Bowyer*

24. FAIRLOP
No 64 Squadron pilots and senior ground staff pictured in March 1943. Astride the nose of the Spitfire IX is Wg Cdr 'Bill' Crawford-Compton. *via Chaz Bowyer*

FAIRWOOD continued

Runways: 3 tarmac
Hangars: Blister (8), Bellman (3)
User sqns/units:

33 Sqn
10-18/08/44
Spitfire LFIXe

41 Sqn
16-24/05/44
Spitfire XII

66 Sqn
20/02-16/03/45
Spitfire LFXVIe

68 Sqn
01/03-23/06/44
Beaufighter VIf

79 Sqn
14/06-24/12/41
Hurricane I, IIb

125 Sqn
24/09/41-25/01/42
14/05/42-15/04/43
Defiant I, II; Beaufighter IIf, VIf

127 Sqn
20/02-17/03/45
Spitfire XVI

164 Sqn
29/01-08/02/43
12-26/12/44
Typhoon Ib

193 Sqn
18/09-06/10/44
Typhoon Ib

197 Sqn
25/11-12/12/44
Typhoon Ib

198 Sqn
06-21/11/44
Typhoon Ib

257 Sqn
11-12/04/44
11-30/08/44
Typhoon Ib

263 Sqn
10/02-18/04/42
05-23/01/44
13/01-10/02/45
Whirlwind I; Typhoon Ib

264 Sqn
07-12/08/43
Mosquito II

266 Sqn
25/04-04/06/45
Typhoon Ib

302 Sqn
02-19/12/43
30/08-16/09/44
Spitfire IX, IXe

307 Sqn
15/04-07/08/43
Mosquito II

312 Sqn
01-24/01/42
18-20/04/42
24/02-02/05/42
Spitfire Vb

317 Sqn
27/06-21/07/41
Hurricane I

322 Sqn
10-31/10/44
Spitfire LFIXe

331 Sqn
19/09-06/10/44
Spitfire IXb

332 Sqn
11-31/12/44
Spitfire IXb

345 Sqn
16/03-02/04/45
Spitfire HFIX

401 Sqn
08-18/04/44
Spitfire IXb

402 Sqn
17/03-14/05/42
Spitfire Vb

403 Sqn
23/09-03/10/44
Spitfire IXb

412 Sqn
08/02-01/03/43
08-13/04/43
13/03-07/04/44
Spitfire Vb, IXb

421 Sqn
03/05-14/06/42
28-29/06/42
08/07-16/08/42
22/08-06/10/42
11-26/10/42
Spitfire Vb

456 Sqn
17/11/43-29/02/44
Mosquito II, XVII

504 Sqn
21/07-11/08/41
Hurricane IIb

536 Sqn
27/10/42-25/01/43
Havoc II (Turbinlite)

600 Sqn
18-27/06/41
Beaufighter If, IIf

609 Sqn
06-20/02/44
Typhoon Ib

610 Sqn
19/12/43-04/01/44
23-30/04/44
Spitfire Vb, Vc, XIV

615 Sqn
23/01-17/03/42
Hurricane IIb, IIc

616 Sqn
24/04-16/05/44
Spitfire VII

Opened with full station status in 10 Gp 06/41
Upgraded to Sector Station 10/41

FILTON, Bristol

Opened: 1911
Closed: Currently in use by British Aerospace Plc
Elevation: 210ft
Pundit code: Not known
Formation: 11 Gp/10 Gp
Main contractor: Various
Runways: 2
Hangars: B Type (2), Various (23)
User sqns/units:

25 Sqn
15/09-04/10/39
Blenheim If

118 Sqn
20/02-07/04/41
Spitfire I

145 Sqn
09-10/05/40
Blenheim If; Hurricane I

263 Sqn
02/10/39-24/04/40
10/04-07/08/41
Gladiator I, II; Whirlwind I

501 Sqn
14/06/29-27/11/39
17/12/40-09/04/41
DH9A; Wapiti; Wallace; Hart; Hind; Hurricane I

504 Sqn
26/09-18/12/40
Hurricane I

Under 11 Gp control 09/39
To 10 Gp 07/40
To 44 Gp Transport Command 12/41

FINMERE, Bucks

Opened: 08/42
Closed: 07/45
Elevation: 390ft
Pundit code: FI
Formation: 9 Gp/12 Gp
Main contractor: Various
Runways: 3 concrete
Hangars: B1 (1), T2 (1)
User sqns/units:

25. FILTON
Only two RAF squadrons, Nos 137 and 263, operated the single-seat twin-engined Westland Whirlwind fighter-bomber. Every one of the 114 Whirlwinds produced saw operational service – 56 with No 263 Squadron, 26 with No 137, and 32 saw service with both squadrons at different times. No 263 Squadron flew Whirlwinds from Filton between April and August 1941. *via Chaz Bowyer*

26. FORD
Mosquito NFXVII, DZ659:H of the Fighter Interception Unit, pictured here in October 1944. *via Chaz Bowyer*

27. FORD
No 602 Squadron's Spitfire IX MH705:D about to take off for a 'Ramrod' operation on 27 April 1944. *via Chaz Bowyer*

13 OTU
01/11/43-01/03/45
Mosquito; Boston

Opened as satellite to Bicester 08/42
To 9 Gp Fighter Command 06/43

Satellite to Harwell in 12 Gp

FORD, Sussex

Opened: 1918
Closed: 11/58
Elevation: 23ft
Pundit code: FD
Formation: 11 Gp; 83 Gp/84 Gp, 2 TAF
Main contractor: Various
Runways: 2 tarmac
Hangars: Blister (20), Bellman (5), GP (1)
User sqns/units:

19 Sqn
15/04-12/05/44
15-25/06/44
Mustang III

23 Sqn
12/09/40-06/08/42
Blenheim If; Havoc I; Boston III; Mosquito II

29 Sqn
03/09/43-01/03/44
Mosquito XII, XIII

65 Sqn
15/04-14/05/44
Mustang III

66 Sqn
12-20/08/44
Spitfire LFIXb

96 Sqn
20/06-24/09/44
Mosquito XIII

122 Sqn
15/04-14/05/44
15-26/06/44
Mustang III

127 Sqn
12-20/08/44
Spitfire HFIX

129 Sqn
24/06-08/07/44
Mustang III

132 Sqn
18/04-25/06/44
Spitfire IXb

141 Sqn
10/08/42-18/02/43
Beaufighter If

256 Sqn
24/04-25/08/43
Beaufighter VIf; Mosquito XII

302 Sqn
16/07-04/08/44
Spitfire IXe

306 Sqn
27/06-08/07/44
Mustang III

308 Sqn
16/07-04/08/44
Spitfire IX

315 Sqn
25/06-10/07/44
Mustang III

317 Sqn
16/07-04/08/44
Spitfire IX

331 Sqn
13-30/08/44
Spitfire IXb

332 Sqn
12-20/08/44
Spitfire IXb

418 Sqn
15/03/43-08/04/44
Boston III; Mosquito II

441 Sqn
13/05-15/06/44
Spitfire IXb

442 Sqn
15/05-15/06/44
Spitfire IXb

443 Sqn
15/05-15/06/44
Spitfire IXb

453 Sqn
18/04-25/06/44
Spitfire IXb

456 Sqn
29/02-31/12/44
Mosquito II, XVII

602 Sqn
18/04-25/06/44
Spitfire IXb

604 Sqn
18/02-24/03/43
Beaufighter If

605 Sqn
07/06/42-15/03/43
Havoc I, II; Boston III; Mosquito II

Fighter Interception Unit (FIU)
01/02/41-04/44
➡ Fighter Interception Development Squadron (FIDS)/Night Fighter Development Wing (NFDW)
23/08/44-07/45
Blenheim; Beaufighter; Mosquito

Under RN control as HMS *Peregrine* 09/39

To 11 Gp Fighter Command 10/40
To 2 TAF 04/44
To 11 Gp Fighter Command 10/44

FOWLMERE, Cambs

Opened: 06/40
Closed: 10/45
Elevation: 100ft
Pundit code: FW
Formation: 12 Gp
Main contractor: Various
Runways: 2 steel matting
Hangars: Blister (7), T2 (1)
User sqns/units:

19 Sqn
25/06-03/07/40
24/07-01/11/40
Spitfire I, Ib, IIa

133 Sqn
03-08/10/41
Hurricane IIb

154 Sqn
17/11/41-12/03/42
05/04-07/05/42
Spitfire IIa, IIb, Va, Vb

174 Sqn
09-12/07/42
Hurricane IIb

111 Sqn
27/09-20/10/42
Spitfire Vb

264 Sqn
03-23/07/40
Defiant I

411 Sqn
05-12/03/43
Spitfire Vb

Opened in 12 Gp Fighter Command as satellite to Duxford 06/40
To USAAF 04/44

FRISTON, Sussex

Opened: 05/40
Closed: 04/46
Elevation: 355ft
Pundit code: FX
Formation: 11 Gp
Main contractor: Various
Runways: 2 grass
Hangars: Blister (2)
User sqns/units:

32 Sqn
14/06-07/07/42
14-20/08/42
Hurricane I, Ib, IIc

41 Sqn
28/05-21/06/43
11/03-29/04/44
Spitfire XII

64 Sqn
06-19/08/43
Spitfire Vb

131 Sqn
28/08-31/10/44
Spitfire VII

253 Sqn
14/06-07/07/42
16-20/08/42
Hurricane I, IIa, IIb, IIc

306 Sqn
19/08-22/09/43
Spitfire Vb

316 Sqn
11/07-27/08/44
Mustang III

349 Sqn
22-26/10/43
10/11/43-11/03/44
Spitfire LFVb, Vc, LFIXe

350 Sqn
25/04-03/07/44
Spitfire Vb, Vc

412 Sqn
21/06-14/07/43
Spitfire Vb

501 Sqn
30/04-02/07/44
Spitfire Vb

610 Sqn
02/07-12/09/44
Spitfire XIV

Designated as 11 Gp Fighter Command
ELG for Kenley 05/40
Upgraded as satellite to Kenley 05/41
Satellite to Tangmere 04/44
Downgraded to ELG 11/44

FUNTINGTON, Sussex

Opened: 09/43
Closed: 13/12/44
Elevation: 115ft
Pundit code: FJ
Formation: 11 Gp; 83 Gp/84 Gp, 2 TAF
Main contractor: Various
Runways: 2 steel matting
Hangars: Blister (4)
User sqns/units:

19 Sqn
20/05-15/06/44
Mustang III

33 Sqn
17/07-06/08/44
Spitfire LFIXe

65 Sqn
14-28/05/44
Mustang III

66 Sqn
06-12/08/44
Spitfire LFIXb

122 Sqn
14-21/05/44
28/05-15/06/44
Mustang III

127 Sqn
06-12/08/44
Spitfire LFIXe

164 Sqn
18-22/06/44
Typhoon Ib

183 Sqn
18/06-01/07/44
Typhoon Ib

198 Sqn
18-22/06/44
Typhoon Ib

222 Sqn
04/07-06/08/44
Spitfire LFIXb

329 Sqn
22/06-01/07/44
Spitfire IX

331 Sqn
06-13/08/44
Spitfire IXb

332 Sqn
06-12/08/44
Spitfire IXb

340 Sqn
22/06-01/07/44
Spitfire IXb

341 Sqn
22/06-01/07/44
Spitfire IXb

349 Sqn
04/07-06/08/44
Spitfire LFIXe

438 Sqn
03-19/04/44
Hurricane IV; Typhoon Ib

439 Sqn
02-19/04/44
Hurricane IV; Typhoon Ib

440 Sqn
03-20/04/44
Typhoon Ib

441 Sqn
23/04-13/05/44
Spitfire IXb

442 Sqn
23-25/04/44
01-15/05/44
Spitfire IXb

443 Sqn
22/04-15/05/44
Spitfire IXb

485 Sqn
03/07-07/08/44
Spitfire IXe

609 Sqn
18/06-01/07/44
Typhoon Ib

ALG

GATWICK, Surrey

Opened: 08/30
Closed: Currently in use as Gatwick
Airport
Elevation: 205ft
Pundit code: GK
Formation: 11 Gp/2 TAF
Main contractor: Various
Runways: Steel matting/grass

28. GATWICK
**Flt Lt Walter Dring poses for the
camera with his No 183 Squadron
Typhoon Ib, R8884:L, in April 1944.**
IWM CH9289 via Chaz Bowyer

28

GATWICK continued

Hangars: Bellman (1), Blister (6)
User sqns/units:

19 Sqn
15-24/10/43
Spitfire IX

65 Sqn
15-24/10/43
Spitfire IX

80 Sqn
27/06-05/07/44
Spitfire IX

141 Sqn
22/10-03/11/40
Defiant I

175 Sqn
09/12/42-14/01/43
Hurricane IIb

183 Sqn
08/04-03/05/43
Typhoon Ib

229 Sqn
28/06-01/07/44
Spitfire IX

274 Sqn
28/06-05/07/44
Spitfire IX

Under control of 11 Gp 09/39
To 71 Gp Army Co-operation Command 01/41
To 11 Gp Fighter Command as satellite to Biggin Hill 06/43
To 2 TAF 04/44
To 11 Gp 11/44

GOXHILL, Lincs

Opened: 06/41
Closed: 12/53
Elevation: 20ft
Pundit code: GX
Formation: 12 Gp
Main contractor: John Laing & Son Ltd
Runways: 3 tarmac
Hangars: Blister (4), J Type (1), T2 (2)
User sqns/units: No Fighter Command flying units based

Opened in 1 Gp Bomber Command 06/41
To 12 Gp Fighter Command 12/41
To USAAF control 06/42
To 12 Gp Fighter Command 01/45

GRANGEMOUTH, Stirlingshire

Opened: 05/39
Closed: 1945
Elevation: 13ft
Pundit code: GW
Formation: 13 Gp/14 Gp/81 (OTU) Gp/9 Gp

Main contractor: Various
Runways: 2 tarmac
Hangars: Blister (8)
User sqns/units:

141 Sqn
19/10/39-13/02/40
22/02-28/06/40
Gladiator I; Blenheim If; Defiant I

263 Sqn
28/06-02/09/40
Hurricane I; Whirlwind I

602 Sqn
07-13/10/39
Spitfire I

58 OTU ➡ *2 Tactical Exercise Unit (TEU)*
02/12/40 (17/10/43)-25/06/44
Spitfire I, II, V

Parent station in 13 Gp 09/39

GRAVESEND, Kent

Opened: 10/32
Closed: 06/56
Elevation: 240ft
Pundit code: GN
Formation: 11 Gp
Main contractor: Various
Runways: 2 grass
Hangars: Blister (8), T1 (1)
User sqns/units:

19 Sqn
06-20/06/43
24/10/43-15/04/44
Spitfire Vb; Mustang III

32 Sqn
03/01-08/03/40
22-27/03/40
Hurricane I

64 Sqn
19/08-06/09/43
Spitfire Vb

65 Sqn
29/07-14/08/42
20/08-26/09/42
24/10/43-15/04/44
Spitfire Vb, IX; Mustang III

66 Sqn
10/09-30/10/40
Spitfire I

71 Sqn
14-20/08/42
Spitfire Vb

72 Sqn
01-05/06/40
08-26/07/41
20/10/41-22/03/42
Spitfire I, IIa, IIb, Vb

74 Sqn
30/04-09/07/41
Spitfire IIa, Vb

85 Sqn
23/11/40-01/01/41
Hurricane I

92 Sqn
24/09-20/10/41
Spitfire Vb

111 Sqn
30/06-07/07/42
Spitfire Vb

122 Sqn
03/11/43-15/04/44
Spitfire IX; Mustang III

124 Sqn
03/05-30/06/42
13-29/07/42
Spitfire Vb, VI

132 Sqn
20/06-03/07/43
Spitfire Vb, Vc

133 Sqn
31/07-17/08/42
Spitfire Vb

141 Sqn
03/11/40-29/04/41
Defiant I

165 Sqn
20/08-02/11/42
Spitfire Vb

174 Sqn
05/04-12/06/43
Typhoon Ib

181 Sqn
24/03-05/04/43
Typhoon Ib

193 Sqn
17/08-18/09/43
Typhoon Ib

232 Sqn
14-20/08/42
Spitfire Vb

245 Sqn
30/03-28/05/43
Typhoon Ib

247 Sqn
29/05-04/06/43
Typhoon Ib

257 Sqn
12/08-17/09/43
Typhoon Ib

264 Sqn
31/12/40-11/01/41
Defiant I

266 Sqn
07-10/09/43
Typhoon Ib

306 Sqn
11-19/08/43
Spitfire Vb

350 Sqn
30/06-07/07/42
Spitfire Vb

401 Sqn
19/03-03/07/42
Spitfire Vb

501 Sqn
25/07-10/09/40
Hurricane I

604 Sqn
03-27/07/40
Blenheim If

609 Sqn
28/07-24/09/41
Spitfire Vb

610 Sqn
27/05-08/07/40
Spitfire I

421 Flt
07-30/10/43
Hurricane II

Satellite to Biggin Hill 09/39
Upgraded to full station status 11/40

GREAT DUNMOW, Essex

Opened: 07/43
Closed: 04/58
Elevation: 324ft
Pundit code: GD
Formation: 38 Gp
Main contractor: US Army
Runways: 3 concrete
Hangars: Blister (1), T2 (2)
User sqns/units:

190 Sqn
14/10/44-21/01/46
Stirling IV; Halifax III, VII

620 Sqn
18/10/44-15/01/46
Stirling IV; Halifax VII

Opened under USAAF control 07/43
To 38 Gp RAF 10/44

GREAT ORTON, Cumberland

Opened: 06/43
Closed: 1952
Elevation: 241ft
Pundit code: GE
Formation: 9 Gp
Main contractor: Various
Runways: 3 concrete/tarmac
Hangars: Blister (3)
User sqns/units:

55 OTU ➡ *4 TEU* ➡ *3 TEU*
20/10/43 (26/01/44)-28/03/44
07/04-10/05/44
Hurricane I, II; Typhoon I; Master I, II, III

Opened as satellite to Annan 06/43

GREAT SAMPFORD, Essex

Opened: 04/42
Closed: 08/44
Elevation: 342ft
Pundit code: GS
Formation: 11 Gp
Main contractor: Various
Runways: 2 steel matting
Hangars: Blister (4)
User sqns/units:

65 Sqn
14/04-09/06/42
15-30/06/42
07-29/07/42
Spitfire Vb

133 Sqn
23-29/09/42
Spitfire Vb

616 Sqn
29/07-14/08/42
20/08-01/09/42
07-23/09/42
Spitfire Vb, VI

Opened in 11 Gp as satellite to Debden 04/42

GRIMSETTER (KIRKWALL), Orkney

Opened: 10/40
Closed: Currently in use as Kirkwall Airport
Elevation: 30ft
Pundit code: Not known
Formation: 14 Gp
Main contractor: Various
Runways: 3 concrete
Hangars: Various (14)
User sqns/units:

129 Sqn
25/09/42-19/01/43
Spitfire Vb

132 Sqn
11/06-23/09/42
Spitfire Vb

234 Sqn
19/01-24/04/43
Spitfire Vb,IV,VI

Opened in 14 Gp as Fighter Sector Station as a satellite of Skeabrae 10/40
To RN control as HMS *Robin*, 07/43

HAMPSTEAD NORRIS, Berks

Opened: 09/40
Closed: 1945
Elevation: 376ft
Pundit code: HN
Formation: 38 Gp
Main contractor: Various
Runways: 3 concrete/tarmac
Hangars: T2 (1), B1 (1), Bessoneau (1)
User sqns/units:

Operational Refresher Training Unit (ORTU)
01/03/44-27/02/45
Whitley; Albemarle; Tiger Moth; Horsa

13 OTU
15/03-22/07/45
Mosquito II, III

Opened in 6 Gp Bomber Command as satellite to Harwell 09/40
To 38 Gp Fighter Command and upgraded to full station status 03/44
Downgraded to satellite to Harwell 02/45

HARROWBEER, Devon

Opened: 08/41
Closed: 1950
Elevation: 650ft
Pundit code: QB
Formation: 10 Gp
Main contractor: Various
Runways: 3 asphalt
Hangars: Bellman (2), Blister (8)
User sqns/units:

1 Sqn
20-22/06/44
Spitfire IXb

64 Sqn
26/06-30/08/44
Spitfire Vc, IX

126 Sqn
03/07-30/08/44
Spitfire IXb

130 Sqn
25/10-30/11/41
Spitfire IIa, Vb, Vc

131 Sqn
24/03-24/05/44
Spitfire VII

165 Sqn
20-22/06/44
Spitfire IXb

175 Sqn
10/10-09/12/42
Hurricane IIb

183 Sqn
05/06-04/08/43
Typhoon Ib

HARROWBEER continued

193 Sqn
18/12/42-17/08/43
18/09/43-20/02/44
Hurricane II; Typhoon Ib

263 Sqn
20/02-15/03/43
19/03-19/06/44
Whirlwind I; Typhoon Ib

266 Sqn
07-10/09/43
21/09/43-07/03/44
12-15/03/44
Typhoon Ib

302 Sqn
01/11/41-27/04/42
Spitfire Vb

312 Sqn
02-19/05/42
31/05-01/07/42
08/07-16/08/42
20/08-10/10/42
Spitfire Vb, Vc

610 Sqn
24/05-19/06/44
Spitfire XIV

611 Sqn
24/06-03/07/44
Spitfire LFVb

Opened in 10 Gp as a satellite to Exeter
08/41
To C&M 08/44
Re-opened as parent station in 10 Gp
01/45

HARWELL, Oxon

Opened: 02/37
Closed: Currently in use as Atomic Energy
Research Establishment
Elevation: 384ft
Pundit code: HW

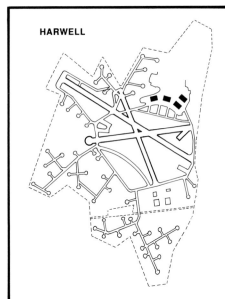

Formation: 38 Gp/12 Gp
Main contractor: John Laing & Son Ltd
Runways: 3 concrete
Hangars: C Type (4)
User sqns/units:

295 Sqn
15/03-11/10/44
Albemarle I, V; Stirling IV

570 Sqn
14/03-08/10/44
Albemarle I, II, V; Stirling IV

13 OTU
12/10/44-01/03/45
Mosquito I, III

Opened with full station status in Bomber
Command 02/37
To 38 Gp Fighter Command 04/44
To 12 Gp 10/44
To 2 Gp Bomber Command 03/45

HAWARDEN, Flintshire

Opened: 1939
Closed: Currently in use by British
Aerospace Plc
Elevation: 15ft
Pundit code: HK
Formation: 12 Gp/81 (OTU) Gp/9 Gp/70
(OTU) Gp
Main contractor: Various and Gerrard Ltd
Runways: 3 concrete
Hangars: J Type (1), K Type (3), L Type
(6), T2 (6)

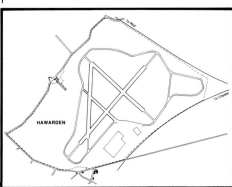

User sqns/units:

7 OTU ➡ 57 OTU
15/06/40 (28/12/40)-10/11/42
Spitfire

41 OTU
14/11/42-23/03/45
Mustang I

Opened in 12 Gp with full station status
1939

HAWKINGE, Kent

Opened: 1915
Closed: 01/62
Elevation: 540ft
Pundit code: VK
Formation: 11 Gp
Main contractor: Various

Runways: 3 grass
Hangars: Blister (6), GS (4)
User sqns/units:

17 Sqn
07-22/05/40
Hurricane I

25 Sqn
10-12/05/40
Blenheim If

41 Sqn
30/06-08/07/42
12/04-21/05/43
Spitfire XII

65 Sqn
30/06-07/07/42
Spitfire Vb

79 Sqn
01-11/07/40
Hurricane I

91 Sqn
09/01/41-02/10/42
09/10-23/11/42
11/01-20/04/43
21/05-28/06/43
Spitfire IIa, Vb, XII

124 Sqn
07-10/04/45
Spitfire HFIXe

313 Sqn
21/08-18/09/43
Spitfire Vb

322 Sqn
31/12/43-25/02/44
01-10/03/44
Spitfire Vb, Vc

350 Sqn
01-12/10/43
31/10-30/12/43
10-14/03/44
08/08-29/09/44
Spitfire Vb, Vc, IXb, XIV

402 Sqn
08/08-30/09/44
Spitfire IX, XIVe

416 Sqn
14-20/08/42
Spitfire Vb

441 Sqn
01/10-30/12/44
Spitfire IXb

451 Sqn
02/12/44-11/02/45
03-17/05/45
Spitfire IXb, XVI

453 Sqn
02/05-14/06/45
Spitfire LFXVI

29. HAWARDEN
Spitfire I X4595? JZ-D of No 57 OTU,
1940-41. *N. D. Welch/MAP*

30. HAWKINGE
Pilots of No 501 Squadron at readiness,
August 1940. Standing left to right, are:
Flg Off S.Witorzenc, Flt Lt G.Stoney (KIA
18/08/40), Sgt F.Kozlowski. Sitting left

to right, are: Flg Off R.Dafforn, Sgt
P.Farnes, Plt Off K.Lee, Flt Lt J.Gibson,
Sgt H.Adams (KIA 06/09/40). *via
Chaz Bowyer*

HAWKINGE continued

501 Sqn
21/06/43-21/01/44
04/02-30/04/44
Spitfire Vb, IX

504 Sqn
25-26/02/45
28/02-28/03/45
Spitfire IXe

605 Sqn
21-28/05/40
Hurricane I

611 Sqn
31/12/44-03/03/45
Spitfire IX

616 Sqn
14-20/08/42
Spitfire VI

421 Flt
15/11/40-09/01/41
Spitfire IIa

To 11 Gp Fighter Command 02/40

HEADCORN, Kent

Opened: 07/43
Closed: 09/44
Elevation: 107ft
Pundit code: ED
Formation: 11 Gp
Main contractor: RAFACS
Runways: 2 steel matting
Hangars: None
User sqns/units:

403 Sqn
20/08-14/10/43
Spitfire IXb

421 Sqn
20/08-14/10/43
Spitfire IX

ALG
Opened as HQ, No 17 Fighter Wing RCAF 07/43
To USAAF control 10/43

HESTON, Middlesex

Opened: 07/29
Closed: 1946
Elevation: 100ft
Pundit code: HS
Formation: 11 Gp/81 (OTU) Gp
Main contractor: Various
Runways: 2 grass
Hangars: Blister (6), T2 (6)
User sqns/units:

129 Sqn
16-30/03/44
Spitfire IX; Mustang III

302 Sqn
07/07-21/09/42
29/09/42-01/02/43
01-20/06/43
Spitfire Vb

303 Sqn
05/02-05/03/43
12-26/03/43
08/04-01/06/43
Spitfire Vb

306 Sqn
22/09-19/12/43
01/01-15/03/44
20/03-01/04/44
Spitfire Vb

308 Sqn
30/07-15/09/42
21/09-29/10/42
21/09-11/11/43
Spitfire Vb

315 Sqn
13/11-19/12/43
01/01-24/03/44
28/03-01/04/44
Spitfire Vb; Mustang III

316 Sqn
23/04-30/07/42
Spitfire Vb

317 Sqn
01-21/06/43
Spitfire Vb

350 Sqn
01-05/03/43
Spitfire Vb, Vc

515 Sqn
29/10/42-01/06/43
Defiant II

53 OTU
18/02-01/07/41
Spitfire I, II; Master III

61 OTU
01/07/41-15/04/42
Spitfire

Heston Special Flight ➡ *No 2 Camouflage Unit*
➡ *No 1 Photographic Development Unit (PDU)*
22/03/39-18/06/40
Blenheim IV; Spitfire I; Hudson

1422 (Turbinlite) Flt
12/05/41-25/01/43
Boston; Havoc; Spitfire; Hurricane

Became satellite to Northolt 09/39
To 81 (OTU) Gp 12/40
To 11 Gp 04/42
Forward Airfield in Tangmere Sector 02/44
Satellite to Northolt 06/44
To MAP 01/45

HIBALDSTOW, Lincs

Opened: 05/41
Closed: 05/45
Elevation: 33ft
Pundit code: HE
Formation: 12 Gp/81 (OTU) Gp/9 Gp
Main contractor: Various
Runways: 3 tarmac
Hangars: Bellman (1), Blister (12)
User sqns/units:

253 Sqn
21/09/41-24/05/42
30/05-14/06/42
07/07-16/08/42
20/08-13/11/42
Hurricane IIa, IIb, IIc, I

255 Sqn
15/05-20/09/41
Defiant I; Hurricane I; Beaufighter IIf

532 Sqn
09/11/42-25/01/43
Havoc I (Turbinlite); Boston III (Turbinlite)

1459 Flt ➡ *538 Sqn*
09/41 (02/09/42)-25/01/43
Havoc I, II (Turbinlite); Boston III (Turbinlite)

53 OTU
09/05/43-15/05/45
Spitfire I, II, V, IX; Master III

Opened as satellite to Kirton-in-Lindsey 05/41
To 81 (OTU) Gp as RLG for Kirton-in-Lindsey 05/43

HIGH ERCALL, Salop

Opened: 04/41
Closed: 02/62
Elevation: 220ft
Pundit code: HC
Formation: 9 Gp/81 (OTU) Gp/9 Gp
Main contractor: G. Walker & Slater Ltd
Runways: 3 concrete
Hangars: Blister (12), J Type (1), K Type (3), L Type (8), T2 (2)
User sqns/units:

41 Sqn
25/02-12/04/43
Spitfire Vb, XII

68 Sqn
23/04/41-08/03/42
Blenheim If; Beaufighter If

247 Sqn
21/09/42-28/02/43
Hurricane IIb; Typhoon Ib

255 Sqn
02/03-06/06/42
Beaufighter IIf, VIf

257 Sqn
06/06-21/09/42
Hurricane IIb, IIa, IIc, I; Typhoon Ia, Ib

1456 Flt ➡ 535 Sqn
00/06/42 (02/09)-25/01/43
Havoc I,II (Turbinlite); Boston III
(Turbinlite)

60 OTU
17/05/43-11/03/45
Mosquito II, III

Opened with full station status in 9 Gp
04/41
Upgraded to Sector Station 05/43
To Maintenance Command 03/45

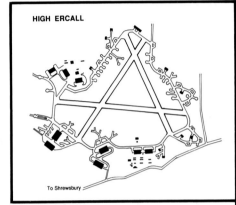

HIGH ERCALL

To Shrewsbury

HOLMSLEY SOUTH, Hants

Opened: 09/42
Closed: 10/46
Elevation: 20ft
Pundit code: Not known
Formation: 10 Gp
Main contractor: John Laing & Son Ltd
Runways: 3 tarmac
Hangars: T2 (5)
User sqns/units:

129 Sqn
22-24/06/44
Mustang III

174 Sqn
01/04-17/06/44
Typhoon Ib

175 Sqn
01/04-20/06/44
Typhoon Ib

184 Sqn
14-20/05/44
17-27/06/44
Typhoon Ib

245 Sqn
01-25/04/44
30/04-12/05/44
22/05-27/06/44
Typhoon Ib

306 Sqn
22-27/06/44
Mustang III

315 Sqn
22-25/06/44
Mustang III

418 Sqn
08/04-14/07/44
Mosquito II

441 Sqn
18/03-01/04/44
Spitfire IXb

442 Sqn
18/03-01/04/44
Spitfire IXb

443 Sqn
18-27/03/44
Spitfire IXb

Opened in Coastal Command 09/42
To 10 Gp Fighter Command 01/44
To USAAF 06/44
To 116 Wing RAF Transport Command
10/44

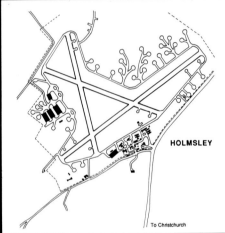

HOLMSLEY

To Christchurch

HONILEY, Warks

Opened: 08/41
Closed: 03/58
Elevation: 426ft
Pundit code: HY
Formation: 9 Gp
Main contractor: John Laing & Son Ltd
Runways: 3 tarmac
Hangars: Blister (12), Bellman (3)
User sqns/units:

32 Sqn
10/09-19/10/42
Hurricane IIb, IIc

91 Sqn
20/04-09/05/43
Spitfire Vb, XII

96 Sqn
20/10/42-06/08/43
Beaufighter IIf, VIf

130 Sqn
05/07-05/08/43
Spitfire Vb

Honiley – *Ingredients for a Fighter Station*

Honiley in Warwickshire was a fighter station in No 9 Group developed from an intended bomber OTU station, the main contractor for which was the building and engineering firm of John Laing & Son Ltd of Mill Hill in northwest London. To give an idea of what was physically involved in the construction of a wartime airfield, the following facts and figures make interesting reading:

Contract Value
£588,042

Buildings Contract
No of bricks used: 3,500,000
Length of soil drains: 3.5 miles
Length of surface water drains: 2.75 miles
Length of water main: 4 miles
Area of concrete roads, aprons etc: 66,000sq yd

Runways Contract
Area of top concrete laid; 353,000sq yd
Vol of all concrete laid: 60,000cu yd
Vol of excavation of virgin ground: 150,000cu yd
Length of perimeter track: 3.25 miles
Length of surface water drains: 14 miles
Length of French drains: 8.5 miles
Tarmac area laid: 7,000sq yd
Area of asphalt surfacing: 338,000sq yd
Vol of ashes used as filling: 75,000cu yd

Other Interesting Figures
Length of hedgerow uprooted: 1.75 miles
No of trees uprooted: 5,000
Sectional huts erected, if placed end to end, length would be: 1 mile

(Source: John Laing Plc)

135 Sqn
04/09-10/11/41
Hurricane IIa

219 Sqn
15-26/03/44
Mosquito XVII

234 Sqn
08/07-05/08/43
Spitfire Vb

255 Sqn
06/06-15/11/42
Beaufighter VIf

257 Sqn
07/11/41-06/06/42
Hurricane IIa, IIb, IIc, I; Spitfire Vb

605 Sqn
04/09-01/11/41
Hurricane IIb

31. HIGH ERCALL
Beaufighter If X7842:P 'Birmingham
Civil Defence' of No 68 Squadron. This
nightfighter squadron was based at
High Ercall from April 1941 until March
1942, when it moved to Coltishall.
Z. Hurt via Chaz Bowyer

32. HORNCHURCH
Hornchurch Wing, spring 1942. Seated:
fifth from left, J. H. L. Hallowes; eighth
from left, H.Broadhurst; ninth from left,
Duncan-Smith. *via Chaz Bowyer*

1456 Flt
24/11/41-06/42
Havoc I, II (Turbinlite); Boston III
(Turbinlite)

63 OTU (AI Training)
17/08/43-21/03/44
Beaufighter II; Beaufort II; Blenheim V;
Wellington XI

Opened in 9 Gp as Sector Station 08/41
To 26 (Signals) Gp Bomber Command
07/44

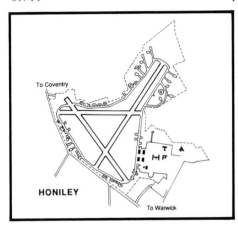

HONILEY

HORNCHURCH, Essex

Opened: 04/28
Closed: 07/62
Elevation: 60ft
Pundit code: HO
Formation: 11 Gp
Main contractor: Various
Runways: 3 grass
Hangars: Blister (12), A Type (2), C Type (1)
User sqns/units:

19 Sqn
25/05-05/06/40
Spitfire I

41 Sqn
28/05-17/06/40
26/07-08/08/40
03/09/40-23/02/41
Spitfire I, IIa

54 Sqn
15/01/30-28/10/39
03-17/11/39
02-16/12/39
29/12/39-16/01/40
14/02-23/03/40
20/04-28/05/40
04-25/06/40
24-28/07/40
08/08-03/09/40
23/02-31/03/41
20/05-11/06/41
13/06-04/08/41
25/08-17/11/41
Siskin IIIa; Bulldog IIa; Gauntlet II;
Gladiator I; Spitfire I, IIa, Va, Vb

64 Sqn
11/11/40-27/01/41
31/03-09/05/41

15-16/05/41
16/11/41-06/02/42
22/02-31/03/42
01/05-19/07/42
27/07-08/09/42
14/11-09/12/42
15-28/03/43
Spitfire I, IIa, Vb, IX

65 Sqn
01/08/34-02/10/39
28/03-28/05/40
05/06-27/08/40
Demon; Gauntlet II; Gladiator I; Spitfire I

66 Sqn
08-16/11/43
01/12/43-22/02/44
Spitfire Vb, Vc, LFIXb

74 Sqn
21/09/36-22/10/39
29/10-03/11/39
14/11-02/12/39
16-29/12/39
16/01-14/02/40
23/03-20/04/40
26/06-14/08/40
Demon; Gauntlet II; Spitfire I, IIa

80 Sqn
05-19/05/44
Spitfire IX

81 Sqn
14/05-17/07/42
Spitfire Vb

92 Sqn
09-18/06/40
Spitfire I

122 Sqn
01/04-08/06/42
17/07-29/09/42
03/10-16/11/42
09/12/42-18/05/43
Spitfire Vb, IX

129 Sqn
28/06/43-17/01/44
Spitfire IX

132 Sqn
02-09/10/42
Spitfire Vb

154 Sqn
07/06-27/07/42
Spitfire Vb

167 Sqn
18-21/05/43
Spitfire Vb, Vc

222 Sqn
28/05-04/06/40
29/08-11/11/40
29/04-20/12/43
27-30/12/43
10/03-04/04/44
Spitfire I, Vb, IX, LFIXb

229 Sqn
24/04-19/05/44
Spitfire IX

239 Sqn
15/08-30/09/43
Mustang I

264 Sqn
22-29/08/40
Defiant I

266 Sqn
14-21/08/40
Spitfire I

274 Sqn
24/04-19/05/44
Spitfire IX

313 Sqn
15/12/41-06/02/42
07/03-29/04/42
Spitfire Vb

340 Sqn
28/07-23/09/42
Spitfire Vb

349 Sqn
11/03-06/04/44
Spitfire LFIXe

350 Sqn
07/12/42-01/03/43
13-15/03/43
19/02-10/03/44
Spitfire Vb, Vc, IXb

403 Sqn
04-25/08/41
Spitfire IIa, Vb

411 Sqn
19/11/41-07/03/42
Spitfire Vb

453 Sqn
25/09-02/10/42
27/03-28/06/43
Spitfire Vb, IXb

485 Sqn
18/10-21/11/43
28/02-21/03/44
07/04-07/05/44
Spitfire IXb

504 Sqn
19-28/01/44
04/02-10/03/44
Spitfire IXb

600 Sqn
02-16/10/39
20/10-27/12/39
24/08-12/09/40
Blenheim If, IV

603 Sqn
28/08-03/12/40
16/05-16/06/41
09/07-12/11/41
Spitfire I, IIa, Va, Vb

HORNCHURCH continued

611 Sqn
27/01-20/05/41
14/06-12/11/41
Spitfire I, IIa, Va, Vb

Opened with full station status 04/28
De-commissioned as fighter Sector Station
06/44

HORNE, Surrey

Opened: 04/44
Closed: 07/44
Elevation: 190ft
Pundit code: OR
Formation: 11 Gp
Main contractor: RAFACS
Runways: 2 steel matting
Hangars: Blister (4)
User sqns/units:

130 Sqn
30/04-19/06/44
Spitfire Vb

303 Sqn
30/04-19/06/44
Spitfire LFVb

402 Sqn
30/04-19/06/44
Spitfire Vb, Vc

ALG
Used by ADGB squadrons

HUCKNALL, Notts

Opened: 1916
Closed: 1971
Elevation: 300ft
Pundit code: Not known
Formation: 12 Gp
Main contractor: John Laing & Son Ltd
Runways: 2 grass
Hangars: Blister (5); Various (6)
User sqns/units: No Fighter Command
flying units based here

Under 12 Gp Fighter Command control
09/39
To 1 Gp Bomber Command 06/40

HUNSDON, Herts

Opened: 02/41
Closed: 07/47
Elevation: 254ft
Pundit code: HD
Formation: 11 Gp/2 TAF
Main contractor: Various
Runways: 2 asphalt
Hangars: Bellman (1), Blister (16)
User sqns/units:

3 Sqn
09/08/41-14/05/43
Hurricane IIb, IIc; Typhoon Ib

21 Sqn
31/12/43-17/04/44
Mosquito VI

29 Sqn
19/06/44-22/02/45
Mosquito XIII, XXX

85 Sqn
03/05/41-13/05/43
Havoc I, II; Mosquito II, XV, XII

151 Sqn
19/11/44-01/03/45
Mosquito XXX

154 Sqn
01-19/03/45
Mustang IV

157 Sqn
13/05-09/11/43
Mosquito II, VI

219 Sqn
29/08-10/10/44
Mosquito XVII, XXX

264 Sqn
26/07-11/08/44
Mosquito XIII

409 Sqn
01/03-14/05/44
19/06-25/08/44
Beaufighter VIf; Mosquito XIII

410 Sqn
08/11-30/12/43
29/04-18/06/44
09-22/09/44
Mosquito II, VI, XIII, XXX

418 Sqn
28/08-21/11/44
Mosquito II

441 Sqn
29/04-17/05/45
Spitfire IX; Mustang III

442 Sqn
23/03-17/05/45
Mustang III

464 Sqn
31/12/43-25/03/44
09-17/04/44
Mosquito VI

487 Sqn
31/12/43-18/04/44
Mosquito VI

488 Sqn
09/10-15/11/44
Mosquito XXX

501 Sqn
03/03-20/04/45
Tempest V

515 Sqn
01/06-15/12/43
Defiant II; Beaufighter IIf

1451 Flt ➡ 530 Sqn
22/05/41 (08/09/42)-25/01/43
Havoc II (Turbinlite); Boston III
(Turbinlite)

611 Sqn
03/03-07/05/45
Mustang IV

Opened with full station status 02/41

HURN, Hants

Opened: 07/41
Closed: Currently in use as Bournemouth
airport
Elevation: 34ft
Pundit code: KU
Formation: 11 Gp
Main contractor: Various
Runways: 3 concrete
Hangars: Bellman (3), Blister (10), T2 (4)
User sqns/units:

125 Sqn
25/03-31/07/44
Mosquito XVII

164 Sqn
22/06-17/07/44
Typhoon Ib

181 Sqn
01/04-20/06/44
Typhoon Ib

182 Sqn
01/04-20/06/44
Typhoon Ib

183 Sqn
01-14/07/44
Typhoon Ib

193 Sqn
03-11/07/44
Typhoon Ib

197 Sqn
03-20/07/44
Typhoon Ib

198 Sqn
22/06-01/07/44
Typhoon Ib

247 Sqn
24/04-20/06/44
Typhoon Ib

257 Sqn
02-08/07/44
Typhoon Ib

263 Sqn
10-23/07/44
Typhoon Ib

266 Sqn
13-20/07/44
Typhoon Ib

33a. HUNSDON
Nightfighter crews of No 29 Squadron at readiness, September 1944. *via Chaz Bowyer*

33b. HUNSDON
Mosquito NFXIII HK382:T of No 29 Squadron, late 1944/early 1945. HK382 was used mainly on 'Night Ranger' operations until it was destroyed in a crash on 16 March 1945. *Hawker Siddeley via Chaz Bowyer*

33c. HUNSDON
A summer dawn at dispersal, August 1943. *Hawker Siddeley Neg No: DH17588K via Chaz Bowyer*

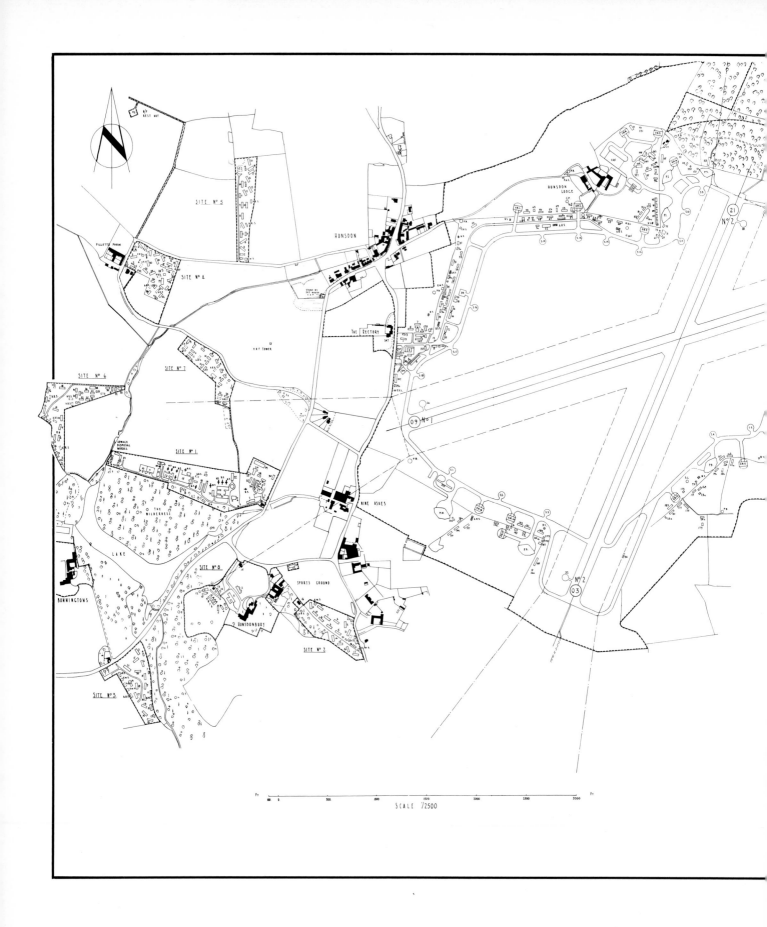

SCALE 1/2500

50

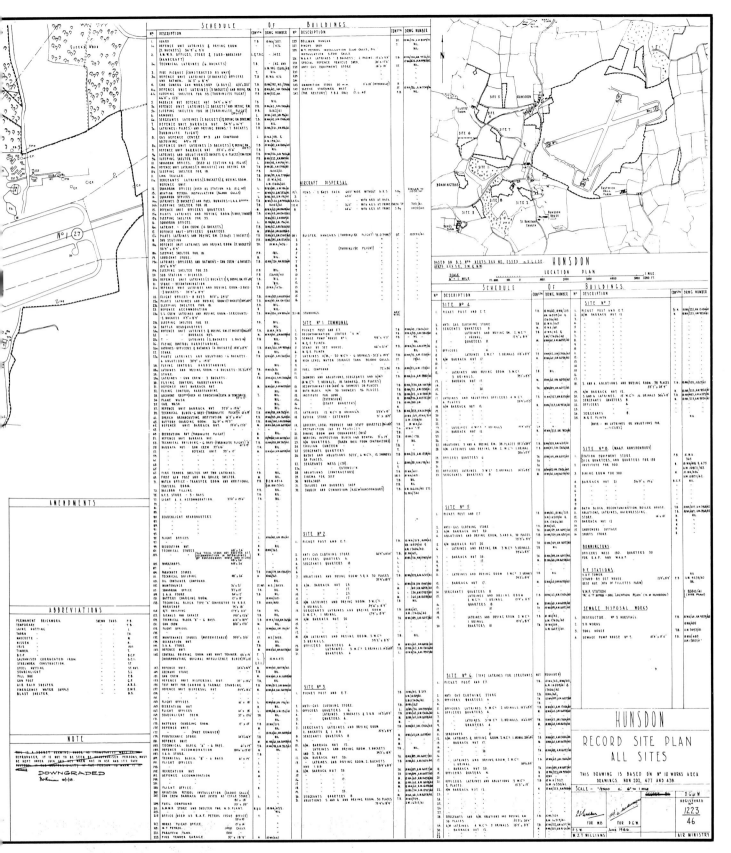

Crown Copyright RAF Museum

33d

33e

34

33d. HUNSDON
Working at dispersal on No 464 Squadron's Mosquito FBVI HX977. No 464 Squadron began converting to the Mosquito from the Ventura in August 1943 and continued operating the same mark until disbandment in September 1945. *Hawker Siddeley Neg No: 17588E via Chaz Bowyer*

33e. HUNSDON
A Mosquito NFXIII of No 29 Squadron burns after crashing on its return from a sortie in 1944. Thankfully, the crew were unhurt. *via Chaz Bowyer*

34. HURN
Mosquito NFXIII of No 604 Squadron takes off from Hurn in July 1944. In the background can be seen Typhoons of No 183 Squadron. *via Author*

HURN continued

412 Sqn
01-06/03/43
Spitfire Vb

418 Sqn
14-29/07/44
Mosquito II

438 Sqn
18/03-03/04/44
19/04-27/06/44
Hurricane IV; Typhoon Ib

439 Sqn
18/03-02/04/44
19/04-11/05/44
20/05-27/06/44
Hurricane IV; Typhoon Ib

440 Sqn
18/03-03/04/44
20/04-28/06/44
Hurricane IV; Typhoon Ib

604 Sqn
03/05-13/07/44
Mosquito XIII

Opened as a satellite to Ibsley 07/41
To 38 Wing 06/42
To 11 Gp 03/44
To USAAF 08/44
To BOAC 10/44

HUTTON CRANSWICK, Yorks

Opened: 01/42
Closed: 06/46
Elevation: 107ft
Pundit code: CK
Formation: 12 Gp
Main contractor: Various
Runways: 3 tarmac
Hangars: Blister (8), T Type (1)
User sqns/units:

19 Sqn
04/04-06/05/42
Spitfire Vb

91 Sqn
08-20/02/44
Spitfire XII

124 Sqn
10/04-15/07/45
Spitfire HFIXe

195 Sqn
19/11/42-12/02/43
Typhoon Ib

234 Sqn
15/10-31/12/43
Spitfire Vb

302 Sqn
17/04-01/06/43
Spitfire Vb

306 Sqn
12/03-30/05/43
Spitfire Vb

308 Sqn
07/05-01/07/42
07-30/07/42
05/07-07/09/43
13-21/09/43
02-18/12/43
Spitfire Vb, IX

310 Sqn
21-25/02/44
Spitfire Vc

315 Sqn
02/06-06/07/43
Spitfire Vb

316 Sqn
30/07/42-12/03/43
Spitfire Vb

403 Sqn
24-29/02/44
Spitfire IXb

412 Sqn
05-20/01/44
Spitfire IXb

439 Sqn
11-20/05/44
Typhoon Ib

441 Sqn
12-23/04/44
Spitfire IXb

442 Sqn
25/04-01/05/44
Spitfire IXb

443 Sqn
27/03-08/04/44
Spitfire IXb

610 Sqn
14/01-04/04/42
Spitfire Vb

Opened with full station status 01/42

IBSLEY, Hants

Opened: 02/41
Closed: 1947
Elevation: 80ft
Pundit code: IB
Formation: 10 Gp/11 Gp
Main contractor: Various
Runways: 3 tarmac
Hangars: Bellman (2), Blister (12)
User sqns/units:

32 Sqn
16/02-17/04/41
Hurricane I

66 Sqn
27/04-03/07/42
07/07-16/08/42
20-24/08/42

23/12/42-09/02/43
Spitfire Vb, Vc

118 Sqn
18/04/41-23/02/42
07/03-03/07/42
07/07-16/08/42
23/12/42-03/01/43
Spitfire IIa, IIb, Vb

129 Sqn
13-28/02/43
13/03-28/06/43
Spitfire Vb

165 Sqn
30/06-30/07/43
Spitfire Vb, Vc

234 Sqn
05-24/11/41
31/12/41-23/03/42
04-27/04/42
Spitfire Vb

263 Sqn
05/12/43-05/01/44
Typhoon Ib

302 Sqn
11/10-01/11/41
Spitfire IIa, Vb

310 Sqn
19/09-02/12/43
Spitfire Vb, Vc

312 Sqn
21/09-02/12/43
18/12/43-19/02/44
Spitfire Vc, LFIXb

313 Sqn
18/09/43-06/01/44
20/01-20/02/44
Spitfire Vb, Vc, IX

421 Sqn
16-22/08/42
Spitfire Vb

453 Sqn
28/06-20/08/43
Spitfire Vb, Vc

501 Sqn
05/08/41-25/01/42
07/02-03/07/42

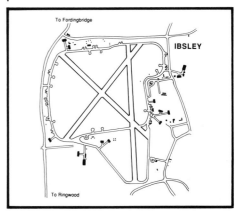

IBSLEY continued

07/07-24/08/42
Spitfire IIa, Vb, Vc

504 Sqn
30/12/42-30/06/43
Spitfire Vb

616 Sqn
02/01-15/03/43
18/03-17/09/43
Spitfire VI

Opened in 10 Gp as a satellite to Middle
Wallop 02/41
To USAAF 06/42
To 10 Gp RAF Fighter Command 12/42
To USAAF 01/44
To 11 Gp RAF 10/44
To 46 Gp Transport Command 03/45

IPSWICH, Suffolk

Opened: 06/30
Closed: Currently in use as Ipswich
Airport
Elevation: 123ft
Pundit code: Not known
Formation: 12 Gp
Main contractor: Various
Runways: 2 grass
Hangars: Not known
User sqns/units:

340 Sqn
20-26/07/42
Spitfire Vb

Under control of 2 Gp Bomber Command
09/39
To 12 Gp Fighter Command as satellite to
Martlesham Heath 03/42
Upgraded to full station status,
transferred to 70 (Training) Gp Army
Co-operation Command 03/43

KEEVIL, Wilts

Opened: 07/42
Closed: 1965
Elevation: 188ft
Pundit code: KV
Formation: 38 Gp
Main contractor: Various
Runways: 3 concrete
Hangars: Blister (9), T2 (2)
User sqns/units:

196 Sqn
14/03-09/10/44
Stirling IV

299 Sqn
15/03-09/10/44
Stirling IV

Opened with full station status in Army
Co-operation Command 07/42
To USAAF 09/42
To 70 (AC) Gp RAF 11/42
To USAAF 08/43

To 38 Gp RAF Fighter Command 02/44
To 23 Gp Flying Training Command
10/44

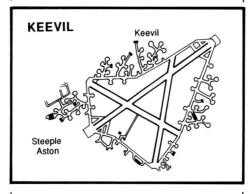

KEEVIL

Keevil

Steeple
Aston

KENLEY, Surrey

Opened: 1917
Closed: Currently in use by Army
Elevation: 524ft
Pundit code: KE
Formation: 11 Gp
Main contractor: Constable, Hart & Co Ltd
Runways: 2 concrete
Hangars: Belfast Truss (1), Blister (8)
User sqns/units:

1 Sqn
05/01-07/04/41
01-14/06/41
Hurricane I, IIa, IIb

3 Sqn
28/01-10/05/40
20-30/05/40
Hurricane I

17 Sqn
25/05-08/06/40
Hurricane I

64 Sqn
16/05-19/08/40
Spitfire I

66 Sqn
03-10/09/40
13/08-17/09/43
Spitfire I, Vb, Vc

111 Sqn
28/07-21/09/42
Spitfire Vb

165 Sqn
08/08-17/09/43
Spitfire Vb, Vc

253 Sqn
08-24/05/40
29/08/40-03/01/41
Hurricane I

258 Sqn
22/04-01/06/41
14/06-10/07/41
Hurricane IIa

302 Sqn
07/04-29/05/41
Hurricane IIa

312 Sqn
29/05-20/07/41
Hurricane IIb

350 Sqn
16-31/07/42
Spitfire Vb

401 Sqn
24/09/42-23/01/43
Spitfire IX, Vb

402 Sqn
14-31/05/42
13/08/42-21/03/43
Spitfire Vb, IX

403 Sqn
23/01-07/08/43
14/10/43-24/02/44
29/02-18/04/44
Spitfire IXb

411 Sqn
22/03-08/04/43
Spitfire Vb

412 Sqn
02/11/42-29/01/43
Spitfire Vb

416 Sqn
01/02-29/05/43
12/02-17/04/44
Spitfire Vb, IXb

421 Sqn
06-11/10/42
29/01-01/03/43
13-23/03/43
17/05-06/08/43
14/10/43-02/03/44
08/03-18/04/44
Spitfire Vb, IX, IXb

452 Sqn
21/07-21/10/41
14/01-23/03/42
Spitfire IIa, Vb

485 Sqn
21/10/41-08/07/42
Spitfire Vb

501 Sqn
10/09-17/12/40
Hurricane I

602 Sqn
10/07/41-14/01/42
04/03-13/05/42
Spitfire IIa, Vb

611 Sqn
03/06-13/07/42
14-20/08/42
Spitfire Vb, IX

615 Sqn
22/05-29/08/40

35. KENLEY
Spitfire Vbs of No 350 (Belgian) Squadron spent a couple of weeks at Kenley during July 1942 before moving on to Redhill. *via Chaz Bowyer*

36. KIRTON-IN-LINDSEY
Defiants of No 264 Squadron in late July 1940. *IWM CH873 via Chaz Bowyer*

37. KIRTON-IN-LINDSEY
Pilots of No 121 Squadron, the second of the RAF's USA 'Eagle' squadrons, pictured in November 1941. On 29 September 1942 the squadron was disbanded and redesignated as 335th Squadron, 4th Fighter Group, USAAF. *via Chaz Bowyer*

16/12/40-21/04/41
Hurricane I, IIa

616 Sqn
19/08-03/09/40
08-29/07/42
Spitfire I, VI

11 Gp Sector Station 09/39
Reduced to non-operational status 04/44

KING'S CLIFFE (Wansford), Northants

Opened: 10/41
Closed: 01/59
Elevation: 251ft
Pundit code: KC
Formation: 12 Gp
Main contractor: George Wimpey & Co Ltd
Runways: 3
Hangars: Blister (4), T2 (2), other (8)
User sqns/units:

93 Sqn
08/09-20/10/42
Spitfire Vb

266 Sqn
24/10/41-29/01/42
Spitfire IIa, Vb

349 Sqn
29/06-05/08/43
Spitfire Va

485 Sqn
08/07-16/08/42
22/08-24/10/42
13/11/42-02/01/43
Spitfire Vb

616 Sqn
30/01-03/07/42
Spitfire Vb, VI

Opened as satellite to Wittering 10/41
To USAAF 01/43
To RAF 04/43
To USAAF 09/43

KINGSNORTH, Kent

Opened: 07/43
Closed: 01/45
Elevation: 125ft
Pundit code: IN
Formation: 83 Gp, 2 TAF
Main contractor: RAFACS
Runways: 2 steel matting
Hangars: Blister
User sqns/units:

19 Sqn
18/08-29/09/43
Spitfire IX

65 Sqn
01/07-05/10/43
Spitfire Vb, IX

122 Sqn
01/07-05/10/43
Spitfire Vb, IX

184 Sqn
14-18/08/43
Hurricane IV

602 Sqn
01/07-13/08/43
Spitfire Vb

ALG
Opened 07/43
To USAAF 03/44

KINGSTON BAGPUIZE, Berks

Opened: 1942
Closed: 1954
Elevation: 300ft
Pundit code: KB
Formation: Fighter Command
Main contractor: Various
Runways: 2 steel matting
Hangars: Butler (2), Blister (3), T2 (2)
User sqns/units:
(uncertain)

OTU satellite to Harwell

KINNELL, Angus

Opened: 1942
Closed: 1945
Elevation: 150ft
Pundit code: KL
Formation: 81 (OTU) Gp/9 Gp
Main contractor: Various
Runways: 2 asphalt
Hangars: Blister (4)
User sqns/units:

56 OTU ➡ *1 Combat Training Wing (CTW)* ➡ *1 Tactical Exercise Unit (TEU)*
29/03/42 (05/10/43)-31/07/44
Hurricane; Spitfire

Opened as satellite to Tealing 1942
To Flying Training Command 08/44

KIRKISTOWN, Co Down, NI

Opened: 07/41
Closed: 1952
Elevation: 20ft
Pundit code: IK
Formation: 13 Gp/82 Gp
Main contractor: Various
Runways: 3 tarmac
Hangars: Blister (4)
User sqns/units:

485 Sqn
24/10-05/11/42
Spitfire Vb

504 Sqn
12/01-19/06/42
Spitfire IIa, IIb, Vb

Opened as satellite to Ballyhalbert 07/41
To RAF Northern Ireland 03/44

KIRTON-IN-LINDSEY, Lincs

Opened: 05/40
Closed: Currently in use by Army
Elevation: 200ft
Pundit code: Not known
Formation: 12 Gp/81 (OTU) Gp/9 Gp
Main contractor: John Laing & Son Ltd
Runways: 2 grass
Hangars: Blister (4), C Type (3)
User sqns/units:

43 Sqn
01/09-28/10/42
Hurricane IIc

65 Sqn
28/05-05/06/40
26/02-28/09/41
03-07/10/41
Spitfire I, IIa, IIb

71 Sqn
23/11/40-05/04/41
Hurricane I, IIa

74 Sqn
21/08-09/09/40
Spitfire I, IIa

85 Sqn
23/10-23/11/40
Hurricane I

121 Sqn
05/05-28/09/41
03/10-16/12/41
Hurricane I, IIb; Spitfire IIa, Vb

133 Sqn
02/01-03/05/42
Spitfire Va, Vb

136 Sqn
20/08-09/11/41
Hurricane IIa, IIb

222 Sqn
23-28/05/40
28/05-04/06/40
Spitfire I

253 Sqn
24/05-21/07/40
Hurricane I

255 Sqn
23/11/40-15/05/41
Defiant I; Hurricane I

264 Sqn
23/07-22/08/40
29/08-29/10/40
Defiant I

302 Sqn
01/02-17/04/43
Spitfire Vb

303 Sqn
16/06-15/08/42
20/08/42-02/02/43
Spitfire Vb

306 Sqn
03/05-16/06/42
Spitfire Vb

307 Sqn
05/09-07/11/40
Defiant I

317 Sqn
13/02-29/04/43
Spitfire Vb

452 Sqn
08/04-21/07/41
Spitfire I, IIa

457 Sqn
31/05-18/06/42
Spitfire Vb

486 Sqn
03/03-09/04/42
Hurricane IIb

616 Sqn
09/09/40-26/02/41
06/10/41-30/01/42
Spitfire I, IIb, Vb

53 OTU
09/05/43-15/05/45
Spitfire I, II, V, IX; Master III

Opened in 12 Gp as Sector Station 05/40

LASHAM, Hants

Opened: 11/42
Closed: 10/48
Elevation: 600ft
Pundit code: LQ
Formation: 10 Gp/11 Gp
Main contractor: Sir Alfred McAlpine Ltd
Runways: 3 concrete
Hangars: T2 (4)
User sqns/units:

175 Sqn
11-13/03/43
29/05-02/06/43
Hurricane IIb; Typhoon Ib

181 Sqn
05/04-02/06/43
Typhoon Ib

182 Sqn
29/04-02/06/43
Typhoon Ib

183 Sqn
03-30/05/43
Typhoon Ib

412 Sqn
07/03-08/04/43
Spitfire Vb

602 Sqn
14-29/04/43
Spitfire Vb

Forward Airfield
Opened in Army Co-operation Command 11/42
To 10 Gp Fighter Command 06/43
To 2 Gp, 2 TAF 08/43
To 11 Gp Fighter Command 11/44
Satellite to Blackbushe 01/45

LASHENDEN, Kent

Opened: 08/43
Closed: 01/45
Elevation: 72ft
Pundit code: XL
Formation: 83 Gp, 2 TAF
Main contractor: RAFACS
Runways: 2 steel matting
Hangars: None
User sqns/units:

403 Sqn
07-20/08/43
Spitfire IXb

421 Sqn
06-20/08/43
Spitfire IX

ALG
To USAAF 04/44

LECONFIELD, Yorks

Opened: 12/36
Closed: Currently in use by RAF
Elevation: 25ft
Pundit code: LC
Formation: 13 Gp
Main contractor: Various
Runways: 3 concrete
Hangars: C Type (5)
User sqns/units:

64 Sqn
19/08-13/10/40
Spitfire I

72 Sqn
17/10-01/11/39
12-13/01/40
13-20/10/40
Spitfire I

74 Sqn
27/05-06/06/40
Spitfire I

81 Sqn
28/07-12/08/41
Hurricane IIb

129 Sqn
16/06-29/08/41
Spitfire I

134 Sqn
28/07-12/08/41
Hurricane IIb

213 Sqn
29/11/40-15/01/41
Hurricane I

234 Sqn
30/10/39-22/05/40
Battle; Blenheim If; Gauntlet II; Spitfire I

245 Sqn
30/10/39-12/05/40
Blenheim If; Battle; Hurricane I

249 Sqn
17/05-08/07/40
Spitfire I; Hurricane I

253 Sqn
03/01-10/02/41
Hurricane I

258 Sqn
22/11-01/12/40
Hurricane I

302 Sqn
13/07-11/10/40
Hurricane I

303 Sqn
11/10/40-03/01/41
Hurricane I

313 Sqn
01/07-26/08/41
Spitfire I

485 Sqn
21/04-01/07/41
Spitfire I, IIa

610 Sqn
29/08/41-14/01/42
Spitfire IIa, Vb

616 Sqn
23/10/39-27/05/40
06/06-19/08/40
Gauntlet II; Battle; Spitfire I

60 OTU
28/04-04/06/41
Blenheim; Defiant; Oxford

Opened in Bomber Command 12/36
To 13 Gp Fighter Command 10/39
To 4 Gp Bomber Command 12/41

LEICESTER EAST, Leics

Opened: 10/43
Closed: 12/47
Elevation: 455ft
Pundit code: LE
Formation: 38 Gp
Main contractor: Various

Runways: 3 concrete
Hangars: T2 (4)
User sqns/units:

190 Sqn
05/01-25/03/44
Stirling IV

196 Sqn
18/11/43-07/01/44
Stirling III, IV

620 Sqn
22/11/43-18/03/44
Stirling III

Opened in 38 Gp Fighter Command with full station status 10/43
To Transport Command 05/44

LLANBEDR, Merioneth

Opened: 06/41
Closed: Currently in use by RAE
Elevation: 18ft
Pundit code: QD
Formation: 9 Gp
Main contractor: Various
Runways: 2 concrete
Hangars: Blister (4), T2 (2)
User sqns/units:

41 Sqn
11-17/08/42
20/08-22/09/42
30/09-05/10/42
11/10/42-25/02/43
Spitfire Vb

66 Sqn
22/02-01/03/44
Spitfire LFIXb

74 Sqn
03/10/41-24/01/42
Spitfire IIa

129 Sqn
30/03-03/04/44
Spitfire IX; Mustang III

131 Sqn
09/02-04/03/42
16/04-14/05/42
Spitfire Vb

193 Sqn
06-11/04/44
Typhoon Ib

232 Sqn
16/05-03/08/42
Spitfire Vb

302 Sqn
01-07/03/44
Spitfire IX

306 Sqn
19/12/43-01/01/44
15-20/03/44
Spitfire Vb

312 Sqn
02-18/12/43
Spitfire Vc

331 Sqn
05-21/01/44
Spitfire IXb

340 Sqn
15-19/05/44
Spitfire IXb

609 Sqn
22-30/04/44
Typhoon Ib

Opened as satellite to Valley 06/41

LLANDOW, Glamorgan

Opened: 1937
Closed: 1957
Elevation: 290ft
Pundit code: Not known
Formation: 81 (OTU) Gp
Main contractor: Various
Runways: 3 tarmac
Hangars: Various (38)
User sqns/units:

53 OTU
01/07/41-09/05/43
Spitfire I, II, V, IX; Master III

To 81 (OTU) Gp Fighter Command 07/41
To Maintenance Command 07/43

LONGTOWN, Cumberland

Opened: 07/41
Closed: 04/46
Elevation: 100ft
Pundit code: IO
Formation: 13 Gp/81 (OTU) Gp/9 Gp
Main contractor: Various
Runways: 3 concrete
Hangars: Blister (2), T2 (1)
User sqns/units:

41 Sqn
01-11/08/42
Spitfire Vb

55 OTU
28/04/42-10/43
Hurricane I, II; Master I, II, III

59 OTU
07/41-08/42
Hurricane

Opened in 13 Gp as satellite to Crosby-on-Eden 07/41
Satellite to Annan 08/42
To 17 Gp Coastal Command 10/43

LUDHAM, Norfolk

Opened: 10/41
Closed: 10/45
Elevation: 40ft
Pundit code: LU
Formation: 12 Gp
Main contractor: Richard Costain Ltd
Runways: 3 concrete/tarmac
Hangars: Blister (4), T2 (2)
User sqns/units:

19 Sqn
01/12/41-04/04/42
Spitfire Vb

91 Sqn
08/04-14/07/45
Spitfire IXb, XXI

167 Sqn
14/10/42-01/03/43
13/03-13/05/43
Spitfire Vb, Vc

195 Sqn
13/05-31/07/43
Typhoon Ib

602 Sqn
23/02-05/04/45
Spitfire XVI

603 Sqn
24/02-05/04/45
Spitfire LFXVIe

610 Sqn
04/04-16/08/42
21/08-15/10/42
Spitfire Vb, Vc

611 Sqn
31/07-04/08/43
Spitfire LFVb

Opened in 12 Gp as a satellite to Coltishall 10/41
Closed. To AMWD 08/43
To RN control 08/44
To 12 Gp RAF Fighter Command 02/45

LYDD, Kent

Opened: 06/43
Closed: 01/45
Elevation: 0ft
Pundit code: LD
Formation: 83 Gp, 2 TAF
Main contractor: RAFACS
Runways: 2 steel matting
Hangars: Blister (5)
User sqns/units:

174 Sqn
01/07-10/10/43
Typhoon Ib

175 Sqn
01/07-09/10/43
Typhoon Ib

245 Sqn
01/07-10/10/43
Typhoon Ib

Reserve ALG

LYMPNE, Kent

Opened: 1916
Closed: 05/45
Elevation: 340ft
Pundit code: PY
Formation: 11 Gp
Main contractor: Various
Runways: 3 grass
Hangars: Blister (4)
User sqns/units:

1 Sqn
15/03/43-15/02/44
11/07-10/08/44
Typhoon Ib; Spitfire IXb

33 Sqn
17/05-03/07/44
Spitfire LFIXe

41 Sqn
11/07-05/12/44
Spitfire XXI, XIV

65 Sqn
02-11/10/42
Spitfire Vb

72 Sqn
30/06-07/07/42
Spitfire Vb

74 Sqn
15/05-03/07/44
Spitfire LFIXe

91 Sqn
02-09/10/42
23/11/42-11/01/43
Spitfire Vb

127 Sqn
16/05-04/07/44
Spitfire HFIX

130 Sqn
05-30/04/44
11/08-30/09/44
Spitfire Vb, XIV

133 Sqn
30/06-12/07/42
17-22/08/42
Spitfire Vb

137 Sqn
14/12/43-02/01/44
04/02-01/04/44
Hurricane IV; Typhoon Ib

165 Sqn
12/07-10/08/44
Spitfire IXb

186 Sqn
01/03-05/04/44
Spitfire Vb

310 Sqn
01-11/07/44
Spitfire LFIX

312 Sqn
04-11/07/44
Spitfire HFIX

313 Sqn
04-11/07/44
Spitfire IX

350 Sqn
29/09-03/12/44
Spitfire XIV

401 Sqn
14-21/08/42
Spitfire IX

451 Sqn
06/04-03/05/45
Spitfire XVI

453 Sqn
06/04-02/05/45
Spitfire LFXVI

504 Sqn
11-12/07/44
Spitfire Vb

609 Sqn
18/08-14/12/43
Typhoon Ib

610 Sqn
12/09-04/12/44
Spitfire XIV

Became forward satellite to Biggin Hill in
11 Gp 06/40
Upgraded to full satellite status 1942

MACMERRY, East Lothian

Opened: 1929
Closed: 1953
Elevation: 300ft
Pundit code: VC
Formation: 13 Gp/81 (OTU) Gp
Main contractor: Various
Runways: 3 grass
Hangars: Blister (8), T2 (1)
User sqns/units:

607 Sqn
16/01-02/03/41
Hurricane I

60 OTU
06/41-11/42
Defiant; Blenheim; Beaufighter; Oxford

To 13 Gp Fighter Command as satellite to
Drem 01/41
Occasional use as satellite to East Fortune
1941-42
To Coastal Command 11/42

MANSTON, Kent

Opened: 1916
Closed: Currently in use by RAF
Elevation: 150ft
Pundit code: MQ
Formation: 11 Gp
Main contractor: Various and John Laing
& Son Ltd
Runways: Single emergency runway,
bitumen surface 3,000yd x 250yd,
with 500yd overshoots at each end
Hangars: Blister (7), Various (3)
User sqns/units:

1 Sqn
18/12/44-08/04/45
Spitfire IXb

3 Sqn
11/06-28/12/43
14/02-06/03/44
Typhoon Ib; Tempest V

23 Sqn
06-14/08/42
21/08-13/10/42
Boston III; Mosquito II

32 Sqn
08-22/03/40
27/11/41-05/05/42
Hurricane I, IIb, IIc

56 Sqn
29/05-01/06/42
22/07-06/08/43
15-23/08/43
Typhoon Ia, Ib

74 Sqn
20/02-30/04/41
Spitfire IIa

79 Sqn
12/11/39-08/03/40
Hurricane I

80 Sqn
29/08-20/09/44
Tempest V

91 Sqn
29/10/44-08/04/45
Spitfire IXb, XXI

92 Sqn
09/01-20/02/41
Spitfire I

118 Sqn
25/09-15/12/44
Spitfire IXc

124 Sqn
25/09/44-10/02/45
Spitfire HFIXe

137 Sqn
17/09/42-12/06/43
08/08-14/12/43
01/04-14/08/44
Whirlwind I; Hurricane IV; Typhoon Ib

59

38. LYMPNE
Flg Off Wusterfeld of No 350 Squadron poses for the camera in front of a line-up of Griffon-engined Spitfire XIVs (RB169:F is nearest) in October 1944. *via Chaz Bowyer*

39. MANSTON
These Gloster Meteor Is of No 616 Squadron are lined up at Manston early in 1945. In the foreground EE219:D is being refuelled. The Meteor was the RAF's first operational jet fighter, entering service with No 616 Squadron in July 1944. *via Chaz Bowyer*

40. MANSTON
No 609 Squadron Typhoon pilots at Manston. Wg Cdr Roland Beamont, OC No 609, is second from left at the rear. *via Chaz Bowyer*

MANSTON continued

164 Sqn
06/08-22/09/43
Hurricane IV

174 Sqn
03/03-09/07/42
12/07-01/09/42
21/09-06/12/42
Hurricane IIb

183 Sqn
15/03-01/04/44
Typhoon Ib

184 Sqn
12/06-14/08/43
Hurricane IV

193 Sqn
08-12/09/44
Typhoon Ib

197 Sqn
15/03-01/04/44
03-11/09/44
Typhoon Ib

198 Sqn
24/03-15/05/43
22/08/43-16/03/44
Typhoon Ia, Ib

222 Sqn
01-19/07/41
30/06-07/07/42
Spitfire IIb, Vb

229 Sqn
25/09-22/10/44
Spitfire IX

242 Sqn
19/07-16/09/41
14-20/08/42
Hurricane IIb; Spitfire Vb

253 Sqn
20/10/39-14/02/40
Battle; Hurricane I

263 Sqn
07-10/09/43
06-11/09/44
Whirlwind I; Typhoon Ib

274 Sqn
17/08-20/09/44
Tempest V

310 Sqn
27/02-07/08/45
Spitfire LFIX

312 Sqn
27/02-07/08/45
Spitfire HFIX

313 Sqn
27/02-07/08/45
Spitfire IX

331 Sqn
30/06-07/07/42
14-20/08/42
02-09/10/42
Spitfire Vb

332 Sqn
14-20/08/42
02-09/10/42
Spitfire Vb

403 Sqn
01-08/07/42
Spitfire Vb

406 Sqn
27/11/44-14/06/45
Mosquito XXX

451 Sqn
11-23/02/45
Spitfire XVI

501 Sqn
02/08-22/09/44
Tempest V

504 Sqn
20-21/05/40
13/08/44-25/02/45
Hurricane I; Spitfire IXe

600 Sqn
27/12/39-14/05/40
20/06-24/08/40
Blenheim If, IV

601 Sqn
01/05-30/06/41
Hurricane IIb

604 Sqn
15/05-20/06/40
Blenheim I; Gladiator I

605 Sqn
07/04-21/11/44
Mosquito VI

609 Sqn
02/11/42-22/07/43
04/12/43-06/02/44
20/02-16/03/44
Typhoon Ia, Ib

615 Sqn
11/09-27/11/41
Hurricane IIb, IIc

616 Sqn
21/07/44-17/01/45
Spitfire VII; Meteor I

To 11 Gp Fighter Command 11/39
FIDO-equipped emergency landing
ground under 11 Gp control

MARTLESHAM HEATH, Suffolk

Opened: 01/17
Closed: 1963
Elevation: 90ft
Pundit code: MH
Formation: 11 Gp
Main contractor: Various
Runways: 2 concrete/tarmac
Hangars: Blister (3), A Type (1), G Type (1), GS Type (1)
User sqns/units:

1 Sqn
15/02-03/04/44
Typhoon Ib

3 Sqn
03/04-23/06/41
Hurricane IIb, IIc

17 Sqn
16-24/12/39
30/12/39-08/01/40
13-20/01/40
30/01-11/02/40
22-27/02/40
05-12/03/40
19-20/03/40
23-27/03/40
05-13/04/40
23-30/04/40
09/10/40-26/02/41
01-05/04/41
Hurricane I

25 Sqn
12/06-02/09/40
Blenheim If

41 Sqn
15-30/06/42
Spitfire Vb

54 Sqn
04-25/08/41
Spitfire Va

56 Sqn
22/10/39-28/02/40
23-26/06/41
06-15/08/43
04/10/43-15/02/44
Hurricane I, IIb; Typhoon Ib

65 Sqn
09-15/06/42
Spitfire Vb

71 Sqn
05/04-23/06/41
14/12/41-02/05/42
Hurricane I, IIa; Spitfire Vb

111 Sqn
21-27/09/42
Spitfire Vb

151 Sqn
20/05-29/08/40
Hurricane I

MARTLESHAM continued

182 Sqn
25/08-07/12/42
30/01-01/03/43
Hurricane I; Typhoon Ia, Ib

198 Sqn
05/06-19/08/43
Typhoon Ib

222 Sqn
01-29/04/43
Spitfire Vb

242 Sqn
16/12/40-09/04/41
Hurricane I, IIb

257 Sqn
05/09-08/10/40
07/11-16/12/40
Hurricane I

258 Sqn
10/07-03/10/41
Hurricane IIa

264 Sqn
07/12/39-10/05/40
Defiant I

266 Sqn
01/03-14/05/40
Battle; Spitfire I

303 Sqn
26/03-08/04/43
Spitfire Vb

310 Sqn
26/06-20/07/41
Hurricane IIa, IIb

312 Sqn
20/07-19/08/41
Hurricane IIb

317 Sqn
29/04-01/06/43
Spitfire Vb

350 Sqn
07-16/07/42
07-15/09/42
Spitfire Vb

401 Sqn
28/07-03/08/42
21-31/07/43
Spitfire Vb

402 Sqn
23/06-10/07/41
03-09/08/42
Hurricane IIa; Spitfire IX

403 Sqn
03/10-22/12/41
03-19/06/42
Spitfire Vb

412 Sqn
01/05-04/06/42
Spitfire Vb

416 Sqn
16/07-14/08/42
20/08-23/09/42
08-24/11/42
Spitfire Vb

453 Sqn
24/11-07/12/42
Spitfire Vb

501 Sqn
17/05-05/06/43
Spitfire Vb

504 Sqn
24-30/12/39
08-13/01/40
20-30/01/40
11-22/02/40
27/02-05/03/40
12-18/03/40
27/03-04/04/40
13-23/04/40
30/04-07/05/40
Hurricane I

605 Sqn
25/02-31/03/41
Hurricane IIa

607 Sqn
20/08-10/10/41
Hurricane I,IIa,IIb

11 Gp 09/39
To USAAF 10/43

MATLASKE, Norfolk

Opened: 10/40
Closed: 10/45
Elevation: 165ft
Pundit code: MK
Formation: 12 Gp
Main contractor: Various
Runways: 2 grass
Hangars: Blister (5), D2 (1)
User sqns/units:

3 Sqn
21-28/09/44
Tempest V

19 Sqn
16/08-01/12/41
04-20/06/43
28/09-14/10/44
Spitfire IIa, Vb; Mustang III

56 Sqn
24/08/42-22/07/43
23-28/09/44
Typhoon Ia, Ib; Tempest V

65 Sqn
29/09-03/10/44
04-14/10/44
Mustang III

122 Sqn
28/09-14/10/44
Mustang III

137 Sqn
30/11/41-02/08/42
11-24/08/42
Whirlwind I

195 Sqn
31/07-21/08/43
Typhoon Ib

222 Sqn
06/06-01/07/41
Spitfire IIb

229 Sqn
22/10-20/11/44
Spitfire IX

266 Sqn
02-11/08/42
Typhoon Ia, Ib

453 Sqn
18/10-20/11/44
15/03-06/04/45
Spitfire IXb, LFXVI

486 Sqn
19-28/09/44
Tempest V

601 Sqn
30/06-16/08/41
Hurricane IIb

602 Sqn
18/10-20/11/44
Spitfire IXb

609 Sqn
22/07-18/08/43
Typhoon Ib

611 Sqn
01-31/07/43
Spitfire IX, LFVb

Opened in 12 Gp as a satellite to Coltishall 10/40
To C&M 08/43
Reopened in 12 Gp 09/44

MAYDOWN, Co Londonderry, NI

Opened: 07/42
Closed: 01/49
Elevation: 50ft
Pundit code: Not known
Formation: 13 Gp
Main contractor: Various
Runways: 2 concrete
Hangars: Blister (9), T1 (1)
User sqns/units:

No Fighter Command flying units based

Opened as satellite to Eglinton 07/42
Closed for rebuilding 01/43
To Royal Navy as HMS *Shrike* 05/43

MENDLESHAM, Suffolk

Opened: 12/43
Closed: 06/54
Elevation: 210ft
Pundit code: MZ
Formation: 12 Gp
Main contractor: Various
Runways: 3 concrete/tarmac
Hangars: T2 (2)
User sqns/units:

310 Sqn
19-21/02/44
25/02-28/03/44
Spitfire LFIX

312 Sqn
19-23/02/44
03/03-04/04/44
Spitfire LFIXb

313 Sqn
20/02-14/03/44
20/03-04/04/44
Spitfire IX

Opened with full station status 12/43
To USAAF control 04/44

MERRYFIELD, Somerset

Opened: 04/43
Closed: Currently in use by RN
Elevation: 110ft
Pundit code: HI
Formation: 10 Gp
Main contractor: John Laing & Son Ltd
Runways: 3 concrete/bitumen
Hangars: T2 (2)
User sqns/units: No Fighter Command
flying units based

Opened in 70 Gp Army Co-operation
Command with full station status 04/43
To 10 Gp Fighter Command 06/43
To USAAF 02/44
To 10 Gp RAF ADGB 08/44
To 47 Gp Transport Command 11/44

MERSTON, Sussex

Opened: 04/41
Closed: 11/45
Elevation: 50ft
Pundit code: XM
Formation: 11 Gp
Main contractor: Various
Runways: 2 steel matting
Hangars: Blister (6)
User sqns/units:

41 Sqn
28/07-16/12/41
01/04-15/06/42
Spitfire I, IIa, Vb

80 Sqn
22-27/06/44
Spitfire IX

118 Sqn
24/08-20/09/43
Spitfire Vb

130 Sqn
27/06-03/08/44
Spitfire Vb

131 Sqn
14/05-22/08/42
Spitfire Vb

145 Sqn
28/05-28/07/41
Spitfire IIa, IIb

174 Sqn
12/06-01/07/43
Typhoon Ib

181 Sqn
08/10-31/12/43
13/01-06/02/44
21/02-01/04/44
Typhoon Ib

182 Sqn
12/10-31/12/43
23/01-01/04/44
Typhoon Ib

184 Sqn
31/05-12/06/43
Hurricane IV

229 Sqn
24-28/06/44
Spitfire IX

247 Sqn
11-31/10/43
05/11-31/12/43
13/01-01/04/44
Typhoon Ib

274 Sqn
22-28/06/44
Spitfire IX

303 Sqn
27/06-09/08/44
Spitfire LFVb, IXc

329 Sqn
17/04-19/05/44
23/05-22/06/44
Spitfire IX

340 Sqn
17/04-15/05/44
19/05-22/06/44
Spitfire IXb

341 Sqn
14/04-11/05/44
16/05-22/06/44
Spitfire IXb

402 Sqn
07/08-19/09/43
27/06-08/08/44
Spitfire Vc, IX

412 Sqn
19/06-24/08/42
Spitfire Vb

416 Sqn
09/08-19/09/43
Spitfire Vb

485 Sqn
21/05-01/07/43
Spitfire Vb

Opened in 11 Gp as satellite to Tangmere
04/41
To USAAF 08/42
To 11 Gp Fighter Command 05/43

MIDDLE WALLOP, Hants

Opened: 04/40
Closed: Currently in use by Army
Elevation: 286ft
Pundit code: MW
Formation: 11 Gp/10 Gp
Main contractor: Various
Runways: 2 steel matting
Hangars: Blister (4), C Type (5)
User sqns/units:

1 (RCAF) Sqn
20/06-01/07/40
Hurricane I

19 Sqn
01-10/03/43
13/03-05/04/43
Spitfire Vb, Vc

32 Sqn
15/12/40-16/02/41
Hurricane I

56 Sqn
29/11-17/12/40
Hurricane I

420 Flt ➡ 93 Sqn
09/40 (07/12/40)-18/11/41
Havoc I; Wellington Ic; Boston I

125 Sqn
31/07-18/10/44
Mosquito XVII

151 Sqn
16/08-17/11/43
Mosquito XII

164 Sqn
08/02-20/06/43
Hurricane IId, IV
Hurricane IV

182 Sqn
01/03-05/04/43
Typhoon Ib

234 Sqn
14/08-11/09/40
Spitfire I

41

42a

42b

41. MENDLESHAM
Spitfire LFIXc MJ553:K of No 312
(Czech) Squadron is run up at its
dispersal early in 1944. *via Chaz Bowyer*

42a. MIDDLE WALLOP
Turbinlite Havoc of No 1458 Flt. All 10
Turbinlite flights were upgraded to full
squadron status in September 1942, No
1458 becoming No 537 Squadron.
W. Huntley via Chaz Bowyer

42b. MIDDLE WALLOP
Hurricanes of No 245 Squadron were
paired with Turbinlite Havocs of No
1458 Flt but, like all the rest of the
Turbinlite units, its operational record
was completely unsuccessful.
W. Huntley via Chaz Bowyer

MIDDLE WALLOP continued

238 Sqn
20/06-14/08/40
Hurricane I

245 Sqn
19/12/41-26/10/42
Hurricane IIb, IIc

247 Sqn
28/02-05/04/43
Hurricane IIb; Typhoon Ib

406 Sqn
08/12/42-31/03/43
Beaufighter VIf

418 Sqn
29/07-28/08/44
Mosquito II

456 Sqn
29/03-17/08/43
Mosquito II, VI

501 Sqn
04-25/07/40
24/08-08/10/42
Hurricane I; Spitfire Vb, Vc

504 Sqn
19/10-30/12/42
Spitfire Vb, Vc

Turbinlite Havoc Flights

Flight	Airfield	Associated Fighter Sqn
1451	Hunsdon, Herts	3
1452	West Malling	264, 32
1453	Wittering	151, 486
1454	Charmy Down	87
1455	Tangmere	3, 1
1456	Honiley	257
1457	Colerne	247
1458	Middle Wallop	93, 245
1459	Hibaldstow	253
1460	Acklington	43

All 10 Turbinlite Flights were raised to full squadron status on 2 September 1942, being numbered Nos 530-539 Squadrons as follows:
530 Sqn (1451 Flt) Hunsdon
531 Sqn (1452 Flt) West Malling, Debden
532 Sqn (1453 Flt) Wittering, Hibaldstow
533 Sqn (1454 Flt) Charmy Down
534 Sqn (1455 Flt) Tangmere
535 Sqn (1456 Flt) High Ercall
536 Sqn (1457 Flt) Predannack, Fairwood Common
537 Sqn (1458 Flt) Middle Wallop
538 Sqn (1459 Flt) Hibaldstow
539 Sqn (1460 Flt) Acklington

All 10 Turbinlite squadrons were disbanded on 25 January 1943.

1458 Flt ➡ *537 Sqn*
06/12/41 (08/09/42)-25/01/43
Havoc I (Turbinlite); Boston III (Turbinlite)

601 Sqn
01-17/06/40
Hurricane I

604 Sqn
27/07/40-12/08/42
23/08-07/12/42
Blenheim If; Beaufighter If

609 Sqn
06/07-02/10/40
Spitfire I

Opened in Flying Training Command 04/40
To 11 Gp Fighter Command 06/40
To 10 Gp as Sector Station 08/40
To USAAF 12/43
To 10 Gp RAF Fighter Command 07/44
To RN as HMS *Flycatcher* 02/45

MILFIELD, Northumberland

Opened: 08/42
Closed: 02/46
Elevation: 150ft
Pundit code: IL
Formation: 81 (OTU) Gp/9 Gp
Main contractor: Various
Runways: 3 concrete
Hangars: Blister (8), T2 (2)
User sqns/units:

59 OTU
06/08/42-26/01/44
Hurricane IV; Typhoon Ib

Fighter Leaders School
26/01-27/12/44
Spitfire; Hurricane; Typhoon Ib

56 OTU
15/12/44-14/02/46
Typhoon; Tempest; Hurricane; Master

Opened with full station status 08/42

MONTFORD BRIDGE, Salop

Opened: 04/42
Closed: 12/45
Elevation: 265ft
Pundit code: MD
Formation: 81 (OTU) Gp/9 Gp
Main contractor: Various
Runways: 3 tarmac
Hangars: Bessoneau (2), Blister (4)
User sqns/units:

61 OTU
04/42-06/45
Spitfire; Mustang III

Opened in 81 (OTU) Gp as satellite to Rednal 04/42

MORPETH, Northumberland

Opened: 01/42
Closed: 07/48
Elevation: 363ft
Pundit code: EP
Formation: 13 Gp
Main contractor: John Laing & Son Ltd
Runways: 3 tarmac
Hangars: Blister (17), T1 (3)
User sqns/units:

72 Sqn
04-12/08/42
Spitfire Vb, Vc, IX

80 OTU
23/04-07/45
Spitfire; Master

Opened in 29 Gp Flying Training Command 01/42
To 13 Gp Fighter Command 04/45

NEEDS OAR POINT, Hants

Opened: 04/44
Closed: 11/44
Elevation: 30ft
Pundit code: NI
Formation: 84 Gp, 2 TAF
Main contractor: RAFACS
Runways: 2 steel matting
Hangars: Blister (4)
User sqns/unit:

193 Sqn
11/04-03/07/44
Typhoon Ib

197 Sqn
10/04-03/07/44
Typhoon Ib

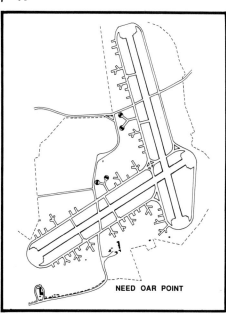

NEED OAR POINT

257 Sqn
10-11/04/44
12/04-02/07/44
Typhoon Ib

266 Sqn
10-27/04/44
06/05-29/06/44
Typhoon Ib

ALG

NEW ROMNEY, Kent

Opened: 03/43
Closed: 12/44
Elevation: 10ft
Pundit code: XR
Formation: 83 Gp, 2 TAF
Main contractor: RAFACS
Runways: 2 steel matting
Hangars: Blister (4)
User sqns/units:

181 Sqn
03/07-08/10/43
Typhoon Ib

182 Sqn
02/07-12/10/43
Typhoon Ib

247 Sqn
10/07-07/08/43
13/08-11/10/43
Typhoon Ib

Became Reserve ALG 10/43

NEWCHURCH, Kent

Opened: 07/43
Closed: 1945
Elevation: 0ft
Pundit code: XN
Formation: 83 Gp; 85 Gp, 2 TAF
Main contractor: RAFACS
Runways: 2 steel matting
Hangars: Blister (4)
User sqns/units:

3 Sqn
28/04-21/09/44
Tempest V

19 Sqn
02/07-18/08/43
Spitfire Vb, IX

56 Sqn
28/04-23/09/44
Typhoon Ib; Spitfire IX; Tempest V

132 Sqn
03/07-12/10/43
Spitfire Vb

184 Sqn
18/08-15/09/43
17/09-12/10/43
Hurricane IV

486 Sqn
29/04-19/09/44
Tempest V

602 Sqn
13/08-12/10/43
Spitfire Vb

ALG

NORTH WEALD, Essex

Opened: 1916
Closed: 09/64
Elevation: 270ft
Pundit code: NQ
Formation: 11 Gp
Main contractor: Various
Runways: 2 tarmac
Hangars: Blister (12), A Type (2)
User sqns/units:

1 Sqn
03-22/04/44
Typhoon Ib; Spitfire IXb

17 Sqn
23/05-02/09/39
Hurricane I

25 Sqn
16/01-10/05/40
12/05-19/06/40
02/09-08/10/40
Blenheim If; Beaufighter If

33 Sqn
23/04-17/05/44
Spitfire LFIXe

46 Sqn
08/11-14/12/40
Hurricane I

56 Sqn
12/10/27-22/10/39
22/02-31/05/40
05/06-01/09/40
17/12/40-23/06/41
Hurricane I, IIb

66 Sqn
01-31/03/44
Spitfire LFIXb

71 Sqn
23/06-14/12/41
Hurricane IIa; Spitfire IIa, Vb

74 Sqn
24/04-15/05/44
Spitfire IX

111 Sqn
30/05-04/06/40
20/07-01/11/41
15-22/12/41
Hurricane I; Spitfire I, IIa, Vb

121 Sqn
16/12/41-03/06/42
Spitfire Vb

124 Sqn
07/11-07/12/42
21-29/12/42
21/01-01/03/43
12/03-26/07/43
Spitfire VI, IX, Vb, VII

127 Sqn
23/04-16/05/44
Spitfire HFIX

151 Sqn
04/08/36-13/05/40
20/05-29/08/40
Gauntlet II; Hurricane I

222 Sqn
18/08/41-30/06/42
07/07-04/08/42
Spitfire Vb

234 Sqn
28/08-17/12/44
Spitfire Vb; Mustang III

242 Sqn
22/05-19/07/41
11-14/08/42
20/08-01/09/42
Hurricane IIb; Spitfire Vb

249 Sqn
01/09/40-21/05/41
Hurricane I, IIa

257 Sqn
08/10-07/11/40
Hurricane I

285 Sqn
04/01-20/06/45
Hurricane IIc; Mustang I

310 Sqn
28/08-29/12/44
Spitfire Vb, LFIX

312 Sqn
27/08-03/10/44
Spitfire HFIX

313 Sqn
04/10-29/12/44
Spitfire IX

331 Sqn
04/05-30/06/42
07/07-14/08/42
20/08-07/09/42
14/09-02/10/42
09/10/42-05/01/44
21/01-05/03/44
13-31/03/44
Spitfire Vb, IXb

332 Sqn
19/06-14/08/42
20/08-01/09/42
06/09-02/10/42
09/10/42-05/01/44
21/01-21/03/44
27-31/03/44
Spitfire Vb, IXb

43. NEWCHURCH
A No 3 Squadron Tempest is refuelled and rearmed in June 1944. In the background No 56 Squadron's dispersal can be seen. *IWM via Chaz Bowyer*

44. NORTH WEALD
No 249 Squadron's Hurricane pilots, summer 1940. From left to right, are: Flg Off Percy Burton (KIA 27/09/40), Flt Lt R.Barton, Plt Off A.Lewis, Plt Off Tom Neill, Plt Off H.J.Beazley, Sqn Ldr J.Grandy, Plt Off G.Barclay (KIA), Plt Off K.Lofts. *via Chaz Bowyer*

45. NORTH WEALD
No 257 Squadron's Hurricanes take off late in 1940, led by squadron CO Sqn Ldr Bob Stanford-Tuck in DT-A. *via Chaz Bowyer*

46. NORTHOLT
Spitfire Vbs scramble from Northolt in mid-1941. *IWM CH5762 via Chaz Bowyer*

47. NORTHOLT
Spitfire IXc BS459:T of No 306 (Polish) Squadron in October 1942. This aircraft and its pilot were posted missing in January 1943. *IWM HU4581 via Chaz Bowyer*

48. ODIHAM
Hurricane IIb BN795 *Our John* of No 174 Squadron with its pilot, Flt Lt J.R.Sterne DFC, 1 January 1943. *via Chaz Bowyer*

403 Sqn
22/12/41-02/05/42
Spitfire Vb

412 Sqn
04-19/06/42
Spitfire Vb

486 Sqn
27/09-10/10/42
Typhoon Ib

604 Sqn
02/09/39-16/01/40
Blenheim I

11 Gp Sector Station 09/39

NORTHOLT, Middx

Opened: 1915
Closed: Currently in use by RAF
Elevation: 120ft
Pundit code: NH
Formation: 11 Gp; 84 Gp, 2 TAF
Main contractor: Various and John Laing & Son Ltd
Runways: 3 asphalt
Hangars: Belfast Truss (1), C1 (2)
User sqns/units:

1 Sqn
18/06-23/07/40
01/08-09/09/40
15/12/40-05/01/41
Hurricane I

1 (RCAF) Sqn
00/08-09/10/40
Hurricane I

17 Sqn
26/08-02/09/40
Hurricane I

25 Sqn
22/08-15/09/39
04/10/39-16/01/40
Blenheim If

65 Sqn
02/10/39-28/03/40
Spitfire I

92 Sqn
09/05-09/06/40
Spitfire I

111 Sqn
12/07/34-27/10/39
13-21/05/40
Bulldog IIa; Gauntlet I, II; Hurricane I

124 Sqn
26/07-20/09/43
Spitfire VII

229 Sqn
09/09-15/12/40
Hurricane I

253 Sqn
14/02-08/05/40
Battle; Hurricane I

257 Sqn
04/07-15/08/40
Hurricane I

302 Sqn
11/10-23/11/40
21/09-02/12/43
19/12/43-01/03/44
07/03-01/04/44
Hurricane I; Spitfire IX

303 Sqn
22/07-11/10/40
03/01-15/07/41
07/10/41-16/06/42
02-05/02/43
01/06-12/11/43
Hurricane I; Spitfire I, IIa, Vb, IXc

306 Sqn
03/04-07/10/41
16/06/42-12/03/43
Hurricane IIa; Spitfire IIb, Vb, IXb

308 Sqn
24/06-12/12/41
29/10/42-29/04/43
11/11-02/12/43
18/12/43-08/03/44
15/03-01/04/44
Spitfire IIa, Vb, IX

315 Sqn
14/07/41-01/04/42
05/09/42-02/06/43
Spitfire IIa, IIb, Vb, IX

316 Sqn
13/12/41-23/04/42
12/03-22/09/43
Spitfire Vb, IX

317 Sqn
01/04-30/06/42
07/07-05/09/42
18/12/43-01/04/44
Spitfire Vb, IX

515 Sqn
01-29/10/42
Defiant II

600 Sqn
25/08-02/10/39
14/05-20/06/40
Blenheim If, IV

601 Sqn
17/12/40-01/05/41
Hurricane I, IIb

604 Sqn
16/01-15/05/40
20/06-03/07/40
Blenheim I; Gladiator I

609 Sqn
20/05-06/07/40
Spitfire I

615 Sqn
10/10-16/12/40
Hurricane I

11 Gp Sector Station 09/39

ODIHAM, Hants

Opened: 12/36
Closed: Currently in use by RAF
Elevation: 400ft
Pundit code: OI
Formation: 11 Gp
Main contractor: Lindsay Parkinson Ltd
Runways: 2 concrete
Hangars: Blister (6), C Type (3)
User sqns/units:

96 Sqn
24/09-12/12/44
Mosquito XIII

174 Sqn
06/12/42-01/03/43
Hurricane IIb

175 Sqn
14/01-01/03/43
13-19/03/43
Hurricane IIb

181 Sqn
31/12/43-13/01/44
Typhoon Ib

184 Sqn
06-11/03/44
03-23/04/44
Hurricane IV; Typhoon Ib

247 Sqn
31/12/43-13/01/44
Typhoon Ib

264 Sqn
01/12/44-09/01/45
Mosquito XIII

604 Sqn
05-31/12/44
Mosquito XIII

Opened with full station status 12/36
To 11 Gp Fighter Command 06/43

OUSTON, Northumberland

Opened: 03/41
Closed: Currently in use by Army
Elevation: 450ft
Pundit code: OS
Formation: 13 Gp/12 Gp/9 Gp
Main contractor: Various
Runways: 3 tarmac
Hangars: Blister (8), J Type (1)
User sqns/units:

72 Sqn
26/09-08/11/42
Spitfire Vb, Vc

OUSTON continued

81 Sqn
06/01-14/02/42
15-29/03/42
13/04-14/05/42
Spitfire Va, Vb

122 Sqn
26/06-31/08/41
Spitfire I

131 Sqn
30/06-10/07/41
Spitfire Ia

198 Sqn
23/01-09/02/43
Typhoon Ia, Ib

232 Sqn
21/07-11/11/41
Hurricane I, IIb

242 Sqn
15/05-01/06/42
Spitfire Vb

243 Sqn
01/06-02/09/42
Spitfire Vb

317 Sqn
29/04-26/06/41
Hurricane I

350 Sqn
08/06-20/07/43
Spitfire Vb

55 OTU
04/41-04/42
Hurricane

62 OTU
21/06/43-06/06/45
Anson; Wellington

Opened in 13 Gp as Sector Station 03/41
Also satellite to Usworth 04/41-04/42

PEMBREY,
Carmarthenshire

Opened: 05/40
Closed: Currently in use by RAF
Elevation: 17ft
Pundit code: Not known
Formation: 10 Gp
Main contractor: Various
Runways: 3 concrete/tarmac
Hangars: Blister (13), Cranwell (2), F Type (4), VR1 (3)
User sqns/units:

32 Sqn
17/04-01/06/41
Hurricane I

79 Sqn
08/09/40-14/06/41
Hurricane I

92 Sqn
18/06-08/09/40
Spitfire I

238 Sqn
01-16/04/41
Hurricane IIa

256 Sqn
04/01-06/02/41
Defiant I

316 Sqn
12/02-18/06/41
Hurricane I

Opened in 10 Gp as Sector Station 05/40
To Flying Training Command 06/41

PERRANPORTH,
Cornwall

Opened: 04/41
Closed: 04/46
Elevation: 320ft
Pundit code: PP
Formation: 10 Gp
Main contractor: Various
Runways: 3 tarmac
Hangars: Blister (6), Teesside (1)
User sqns/units:

19 Sqn
06/05-01/06/42
14/06-01/07/42
07-23/07/42
31/07-16/08/42
20/08/42-01/03/43
Spitfire Vb, Vc

65 Sqn
29/03-18/05/43
Spitfire Vb

66 Sqn
27/04-14/12/41
17/09-08/11/43
Spitfire IIa, Vb, Vc

130 Sqn
05/12/41-12/07/42
17/07-04/08/42
20/08-21/10/42
31/10/42-30/03/43
Spitfire Vb, Vc

132 Sqn
18/05-20/06/43
Spitfire Vb, Vc

183 Sqn
18/09-14/10/43
Typhoon Ib

234 Sqn
28/10-26/11/42
26/12/42-19/01/43
Spitfire Vb, IV

302 Sqn
20/06-19/08/43
Spitfire Vb, Vc

310 Sqn
24/12/41-09/02/42
11/02-08/03/42
21/03-07/05/42
Spitfire IIa, Vb

317 Sqn
21/06-21/08/43
Spitfire Vb

329 Sqn
22/01-16/03/44
24/03-17/04/44
Spitfire Vb, Vc, IX

340 Sqn
09/11/43-17/04/44
Spitfire Vb, IXb

341 Sqn
11/10/43-14/04/44
Spitfire Vb, IXb

412 Sqn
13/04-21/06/43
Spitfire Vb

453 Sqn
20/08-15/10/43
Spitfire Vb, Vc

602 Sqn
20/01-14/04/43
Spitfire Vb, Vc

610 Sqn
30/04-26/06/43
Spitfire Vc

Opened in 10 Gp as a satellite to Portreath 04/41
To 19 Gp Coastal Command 04/44
To 46 Gp Transport Command 11/44

PETERHEAD,
Aberdeenshire

Opened: 07/41
Closed: 08/45
Elevation: 150ft
Pundit code: PH
Formation: 14 Gp/13 Gp
Main contractor: Various
Runways: 3 tarmac
Hangars: Blister (8), Teesside (5)
User sqns/units:

19 Sqn
13/02-23/05/45
Mustang III, IV

65 Sqn
03-04/10/44
16-28/01/45
01/02-06/05/45
Mustang III, IV

118 Sqn
20/09-19/10/43
23/01-05/02/44
09-29/08/44
Spitfire VI, IXc, Vb, VII

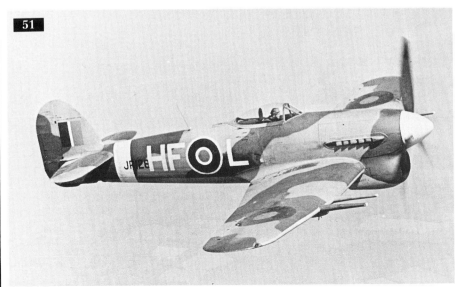

49. OUSTON
No 243 Squadron was re-formed at Ouston on 1 June 1942 with the Spitfire Vb. It moved north to Turnhouse in September before being posted to North Africa in November. *via Chaz Bowyer*

50. PEMBREY
No 256 Squadron and its Defiant NFIs were based at Pembrey briefly in early 1941 for the night defence of South Wales. *Real Photographs*

51. PERRANPORTH
Typhoon JR128:L served with No 183 Squadron at Perranporth and at Predannack in late 1943. *via Author*

PETERHEAD continued

122 Sqn
01/05-03/07/45
Mustang IV

129 Sqn
17/01-16/03/44
Spitfire IX

132 Sqn
07/07/41-16/02/42
Spitfire I, IIb

164 Sqn
06/04-05/05/42
10/09/42-29/01/43
Spitfire Va, Vb

165 Sqn
29/03-30/06/43
Spitfire Vb

234 Sqn
01/05-03/07/45
Mustang IV

245 Sqn
29/01-30/03/43
Typhoon Ib

313 Sqn
28/06-21/08/43
Spitfire Vb, Vc, VI

315 Sqn
01/11/44-16/01/45
Mustang III

350 Sqn
14/03-25/04/44
Spitfire Vb, Vc

416 Sqn
22/11/41-14/03/42
03/04-25/06/42
07-16/07/42
Spitfire IIa, Vb

504 Sqn
18/10/43-19/01/44
Spitfire Vb, VI, IXb

602 Sqn
17/07-16/08/42
20/08-10/09/42
Spitfire Vb

603 Sqn
14/03-13/04/42
Spitfire Vb

Opened as 14 Gp Sector Station 07/41

PORTREATH, Cornwall

Opened: 03/41
Closed: Currently in use by RAF
Elevation: 295ft
Pundit code: PA
Formation: 10 Gp
Main contractor: Richard Costain Ltd
Runways: 4 tarmac

Hangars: Blister (8), T2 (4)
User sqns/units:

66 Sqn
14/12/41-08/02/42
22/02-27/04/42
Spitfire IIa, Va, Vb, Vc

130 Sqn
16/06-25/10/41
Spitfire IIa

152 Sqn
09/04-25/08/41
Spitfire IIa

153 Sqn
18-20/12/42
Beaufighter If, VIf

234 Sqn
27/04-23/08/42
30/08-28/10/42
26/11-26/12/42
Spitfire Vb, IV

247 Sqn
10/05-18/06/41
Hurricane I, IIa

263 Sqn
18/03-10/04/41
Whirlwind I

313 Sqn
26/08-23/11/41
29/11-15/12/41
Spitfire IIa, Vb

Opened in 10 Gp with full station status 03/41
Became 10 Gp Sector Station 05/41
To 44 Gp Transport Command 05/45

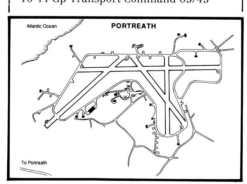

POULTON, Cheshire

Opened: 03/43
Closed: 08/45
Elevation: 50ft
Pundit code: PU
Formation: 81 (OTU) Gp/9 Gp
Main contractor: George Wimpey & Co Ltd
Runways: 3 concrete
Hangars: Bessoneau (1), Blister (8)
User sqns/units:

41 OTU
01/03/43-03/45
Hurricane II; Harvard

3 TEU
11/43-28/03/44
Hurricane

Opened in 81 (OTU) Gp as satellite to Hawarden 03/43

PREDANNACK, Cornwall

Opened: 05/41
Closed: Currently in use by RN
Elevation: 293ft
Pundit code: PD
Formation: 10 Gp
Main contractor: Various
Runways: 4 tarmac
Hangars: Bellman (1), Blister (12)
User sqns/units:

1 Sqn
29/04-20/06/44
Spitfire IXb

33 Sqn
15/12/44-21/02/45
Spitfire LFIXe; Tempest V

64 Sqn
09/12/42-02/01/43
Spitfire IX

141 Sqn
18/02-30/04/43
Beaufighter If

151 Sqn
25/03-08/10/44
Mosquito VI, XIII, XXX

157 Sqn
09/11/43-26/03/44
Mosquito II, VI

165 Sqn
02/04-20/06/44
Spitfire IXb

183 Sqn
14/10/43-01/02/44
Typhoon Ib

222 Sqn
15/12/44-21/02/45
Spitfire LFIXb; Tempest V

234 Sqn
19/06-28/08/44
Spitfire Vb

247 Sqn
18/06/41-17/05/42
Hurricane I, IIa, IIb, IIc

264 Sqn
30/04-07/08/43
12/08-07/11/43
25/09-30/11/44
Mosquito II, VI, XIII

307 Sqn
07/08-09/11/43
Mosquito II, VI

349 Sqn
16/02-19/04/45
Tempest V

406 Sqn
04/09-08/12/42
Beaufighter VIf

485 Sqn
25/02-19/04/45
Tempest V; Typhoon Ib

1457 Flt ➡ 536 Sqn
11/41 (08/09/42)-27/10/42
Havoc II (Turbinlite)

600 Sqn
06/10/41-02/09/42
Beaufighter IIf, VIf

604 Sqn
07/12/42-18/02/43
24/09-05/12/44
Beaufighter If; Mosquito XIII

611 Sqn
03-17/07/44
Spitfire LFVb, IX

Opened in 10 Gp as a satellite to Portreath 05/41

PRESTWICK, Ayrshire

Opened: 02/36
Closed: Currently in use as Prestwick airport
Elevation: 35ft
Pundit code: PW
Formation: 13 Gp
Main contractor: Various
Runways: 2 concrete
Hangars: Bellman (2), B1 (4)
User sqns/units:

1 (RCAF) Sqn
09/10-08/12/40
Hurricane I

141 Sqn
13-22/02/40
25/07-22/08/40
Gladiator I; Blenheim If; Defiant I

253 Sqn
23-29/08/40
Hurricane I

602 Sqn
17/12/40-15/04/41
Spitfire I

603 Sqn
16/12/39-17/01/40
Spitfire I

610 Sqn
04/04-10/05/40
Spitfire I

615 Sqn
29/08-10/10/40
Hurricane I

Temporary Forward Airfield in Turnhouse Sector 12/39
To Ferry Command 04/41

REDHILL, Surrey

Opened: 07/37
Closed: Currently in use by Bristow Helicopters Ltd
Elevation: 205ft
Pundit code: RI
Formation: 11 Gp
Main contractor: Various
Runways: 2 steel matting
Hangars: Blister (8)
User sqns/units:

1 Sqn
01/05-01/06/41
14/06-01/07/41
Hurricane IIa, IIb

66 Sqn
10-13/08/43
Spitfire Vb, Vc

131 Sqn
16/08-17/09/43
Spitfire Vb, Vc

219 Sqn
12/10-10/12/40
Blenheim If; Beaufighter If

258 Sqn
01-15/06/41
Hurricane IIa

303 Sqn
15-20/08/42
Spitfire Vb

308 Sqn
01-07/07/42
Spitfire Vb

310 Sqn
01-07/07/42
16-20/08/42
Spitfire Vb, Vc

312 Sqn
01-08/07/42
16-20/08/42
Spitfire Vb

340 Sqn
01-07/04/42
Spitfire Vb

350 Sqn
31/07-07/09/42
15-23/09/42
Spitfire Vb

401 Sqn
29/05-21/07/43
31/07-07/08/43
Spitfire Vb

402 Sqn
31/05-29/06/42
01/07-03/08/42

09-13/08/42
Spitfire Vb, IX

411 Sqn
08/04-07/08/43
Spitfire Vb

412 Sqn
23/09-01/11/42
14/07-08/08/43
Spitfire Vb

416 Sqn
23/09-08/11/42
24/11/42-01/02/43
Spitfire Vb

421 Sqn
23/03-10/04/43
22/04-17/05/43
Spitfire Vb

452 Sqn
21/10/41-14/01/42
Spitfire Vb

457 Sqn
23/03-31/05/42
Spitfire Vb

485 Sqn
01/07-21/10/41
Spitfire IIa, Vb

504 Sqn
14/08-19/09/43
Spitfire Vb, Vc

600 Sqn
12/09-12/10/40
Blenheim If; Beaufighter If

602 Sqn
14/01-04/03/42
13/05-17/07/42
Spitfire Vb

611 Sqn
20-27/07/42
01-14/08/42
20/08-23/09/42
Spitfire Vb, IX

To 11 Gp Fighter Command as a satellite to Biggin Hill 06/40

REDNAL, Salop

Opened: 04/42
Closed: 1945
Elevation: 300ft
Pundit code: Not known
Formation: 81 (OTU) Gp/9 Gp
Main contractor: Various
Runways: 3 tarmac
Hangars: Bellman (3), Blister (8)
User sqns/units:

61 OTU
15/04/42-16/06/45
Spitfire; Mustang III

Opened with full station status 04/42

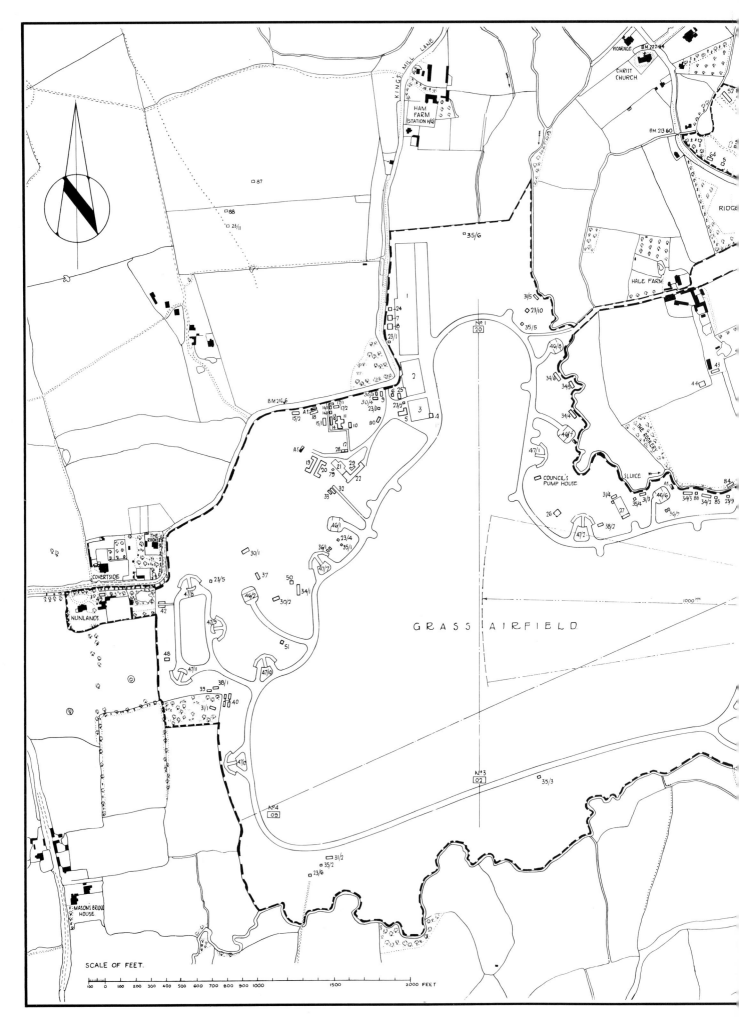

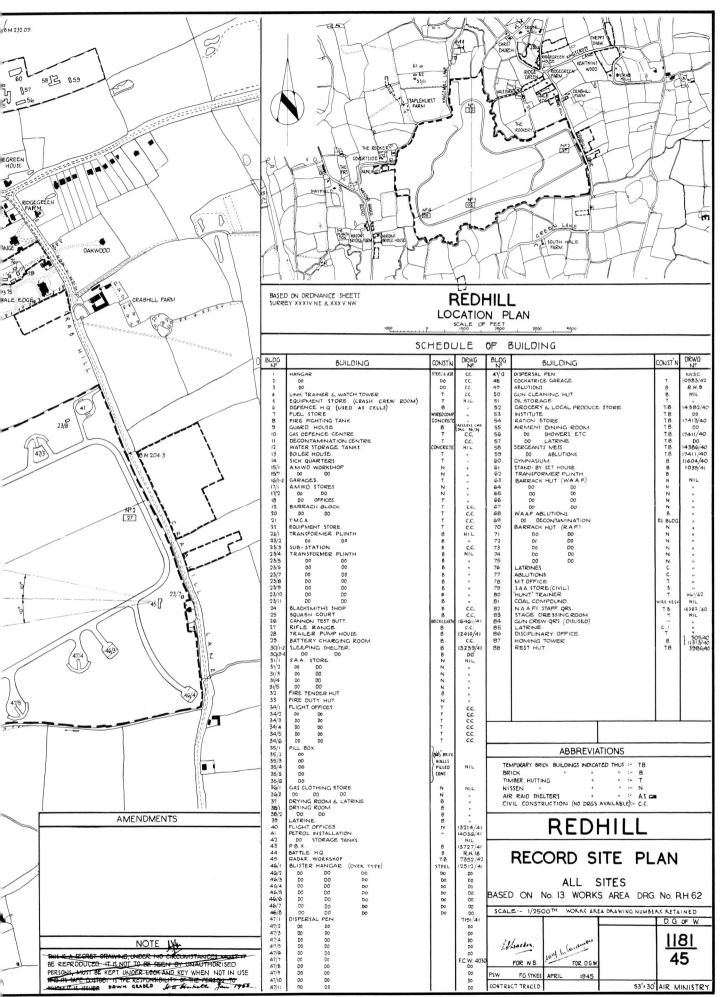

REDHILL
LOCATION PLAN
SCALE OF FEET
1000   0   1000   2000   3000   4000

BASED ON ORDNANCE SHEETS
SURREY XXXIV NE. & XXXV. NW.

SCHEDULE OF BUILDING

BLDG Nº	BUILDING	CONST'N	DRWG Nº	BLDG Nº	BUILDING	CONST'N	DRWG Nº
1	HANGAR	STEEL & ASB	C.C.	47/12	DISPERSAL PEN.		MISC.
2	DO	DO	C.C.	48	COCKATRICE GARAGE.	T.	10983/42
3	DO	DO	C.C.	49	ABLUTIONS.	B.	R.H.9
4	LINK TRAINER & WATCH TOWER	T	C.C.	50	GUN CLEANING HUT.	B.	NIL
5	EQUIPMENT STORE (CRASH CREW ROOM)	T	NIL	51	OIL STORAGE.	T.	"
6	DEFENCE H.Q. (USED AS CELLS)	B	"	52	GROCERY & LOCAL PRODUCE. STORE.	T.B.	14382/40
7	FUEL STORE	WIRED COMP.	"	53	INSTITUTE.	T.B.	DO
8	FIRE FIGHTING TANK	CONCRETE	RESERVE CMD DRG. 96/39	54	RATION STORE.	T.B.	17413/40
9	GUARD HOUSE	B		55	AIRMEN'S DINING ROOM.	T.B.	DO
10	GAS DEFENCE CENTRE	T	C.C.	56	DO SHOWERS, ETC.	T.B.	17411/40
11	DECONTAMINATION CENTRE		C.C.	57	DO LATRINE.	T.B.	DO
12	WATER STORAGE TANKS.	CONCRETE	NIL	58	SERGEANTS' MESS.	T.B.	14386/40
13	BOILER HOUSE.	T	"	59	DO ABLUTIONS.	T.B.	17411/40
14	SICK QUARTERS.	T	"	60	GYMNASIUM.	B	11604/40
15/1	A.M.W.D. WORKSHOP.	N	"	61	STAND-BY SET HOUSE.	B	1039/41
15/2	DO DO	N	"	62	TRANSFORMER PLINTH.	B	"
16/1-2	GARAGES.	T	"	63	BARRACK HUT (W.A.A.F.)	N	NIL
17/1	A.M.W.D. STORES	N	"	64	DO DO	N	"
17/2	DO DO	N	"	65	DO DO	N	"
18	DO OFFICES	T	"	66	DO DO	N	"
19	BARRACK BLOCK.	T	C.C.	67	DO DO	N	"
20	DO DO	T	C.C.	68	W.A.A.F. ABLUTIONS	B.	"
21	Y.M.C.A.	T	C.C.	69	DO DECONTAMINATION.	EX. BLDG	"
22	EQUIPMENT STORE.	T	C.C.	70	BARRACK HUT (R.A.F.)	N	"
23/1	TRANSFORMER PLINTH.	B	NIL	71	DO DO	N	"
23/2	DO DO	B	"	72	DO	N	"
23/3	SUB-STATION	B	C.C.	73	DO DO	N	"
23/4	TRANSFORMER PLINTH.	B	NIL	74	DO DO	N	"
23/5	DO DO	B	"	75	DO DO	N	"
23/6	DO DO	B	"	76	LATRINES.	C.	"
23/7	DO DO	B	"	77	ABLUTIONS.	C.	"
23/8	DO DO	B	"	78	M.T. OFFICE.	T.	"
23/9	DO DO	B	"	79	S.A.A. STORE (CIVIL)	B.	661/42
23/10	DO DO	B	"	80	'HUNT' TRAINER	T.	"
23/11	DO DO	B	"	81	COAL COMPOUND.	WIRE MESH	NIL
24	BLACKSMITHS SHOP.	B	C.C.	82	N.A.A.F.I. STAFF QRS.	T.B.	14382/40
25	SQUASH COURT.	B	"	83	STAGE DRESSING ROOM.	T	NIL
26	CANNON TEST BUTT.	BRICKEARTH	16461/41	84	GUN CREW QRS. (DISUSED)		
27	RIFLE RANGE.	B	C.C.	85	LATRINE.	C.I.	"
28	TRAILER PUMP HOUSE.	B	12410/41	86	DISCIPLINARY OFFICE	T.	505/40
29	BATTERY CHARGING ROOM.	B	C.C.	87	HOMING TOWER		11313/40
30/1-2	SLEEPING SHELTER.	B	13259/41	88	REST HUT	T.B.	3986/40
30/3-4	DO DO	B	DO				
31/1	S.A.A. STORE.	N	NIL				
31/2	DO DO	N	"				
31/3	DO DO	N	"				
31/4	DO DO	N	"				
31/5	DO DO	B	"				
32	FIRE TENDER HUT.	N	"				
33	FIRE DUTY HUT.	N	"				
34/1	FLIGHT OFFICES.	T	C.C.				
34/2	DO DO	T	C.C.				
34/3	DO DO	T	C.C.				
34/4	DO DO	T	C.C.				
34/5	DO DO	T	C.C.				
34/6	DO DO	T	C.C.				
35/1	PILL BOX.						
35/2	DO	9½" BRICK WALLS FILLED CONC.	NIL				
35/3	DO						
35/4	DO						
35/5	DO						
35/6	DO						
36/1	GAS CLOTHING STORE.	N	NIL				
36/2	DO DO DO	N	"				
37	DRYING ROOM & LATRINE.	B	"				
38/1	DRYING ROOM.	B	"				
38/2	DO DO	B	"				
39	LATRINE.	B	"				
40	FLIGHT OFFICES.	N	13214/41				
41	PETROL INSTALLATION.	–	14036/41				
42	DO STORAGE TANKS.		NIL				
43	P.B.X.	B	13727/41				
44	BATTLE H.Q.	B	R.H.18				
45	RADAR WORKSHOP	T.B.	7352/42				
46/1	BLISTER HANGAR. (OVER TYPE)	STEEL	12512/41				
46/2	DO DO DO.	DO	DO				
46/3	DO DO DO	DO	DO				
46/4	DO DO DO	DO	DO				
46/5	DO DO DO	DO	DO				
46/6	DO DO DO	DO	DO				
46/7	DO DO DO	DO	DO				
46/8	DO DO DO	DO	DO				
47/1	DISPERSAL PEN.		7151/41				
47/2	DO DO		DO				
47/3	DO DO		DO				
47/4	DO DO		DO				
47/5	DO DO		DO				
47/6	DO DO		DO				
47/7	DO DO		DO				
47/8	DO DO		DO				
47/9	DO DO		DO				
47/10	DO DO		DO				
47/11	DO DO		DO				

ABBREVIATIONS
TEMPORARY BRICK BUILDINGS INDICATED THUS :- T.B.
BRICK " " " :- B
TIMBER HUTTING " " " :- T
NISSEN " " " :- N
AIR RAID SHELTERS " " :- A.S ▭
CIVIL CONSTRUCTION (NO DRGS AVAILABLE):- C.C.

AMENDMENTS

NOTE
THIS IS A SECRET DRAWING, UNDER NO CIRCUMSTANCES MUST IT
BE REPRODUCED. IT IS NOT TO BE SEEN BY UNAUTHORISED
PERSONS, MUST BE KEPT UNDER LOCK AND KEY WHEN NOT IN USE
AND ITS SAFE CUSTODY IS THE RESPONSIBILITY OF THE PERSON TO
WHOM IT IS ISSUED DOWN GRADED H.S.Herbett Jan 1958

REDHILL
RECORD SITE PLAN
ALL SITES
BASED ON No. 13 WORKS AREA DRG. No. RH 62

SCALE :- 1/2500TH WORKS AREA DRAWING NUMBERS RETAINED

D.G. OF W.

1181
45

FOR W.B. FOR D.G.W.
PSW F.G. SYKES APRIL 1945
CONTRACT TRACED 53" x 30" AIR MINISTRY
FCW 4030

52a

52. REDHILL
No 611 Squadron was amongst the first to receive the new Spitfire IX which represented a vast improvement in performance over its predecessor, the Mk V. No 611 Squadron was based at Redhill at various times during the summer of 1942 from where it flew fighter sweeps and bomber escorts with the Mk IX. *via Chaz Bowyer*

52b

RHOOSE, Glamorgan

Opened: 04/42
Closed: Currently in use as Cardiff Airport
Elevation: 280ft
Pundit code: RH
Formation: 81 (OTU) Gp
Main contractor: Various
Runways: 2 tarmac
Hangars: Blister (4)
User sqns/units:

53 OTU
07/04/42-09/05/43
Spitfire I, II, V; Master III

Opened as a satellite to Llandow 04/42
To Flying Training Command 02/44
To 57 Wing Maintenance Command
11/44

RINGWAY, Cheshire

Opened: 06/38
Closed: Currently in use as Manchester
International Airport
Elevation: 235ft
Pundit code: Not known
Formation: 9 Gp
Main contractor: Various
Runways: 3 concrete/tarmac
Hangars: Bellman (4), A1 (1)
User sqns/units:

Used for brief periods in 1940 by
detachments of 64, 253 and 264 Sqns
for air defence of Manchester

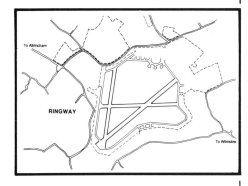

RINGWAY

RIVENHALL, Essex

Opened: 12/44
Closed: 01/46
Elevation: 168ft
Pundit code: RL
Formation: 38 Gp
Main contractor: W. C. French Ltd
Runways: 3 concrete/tarmac
Hangars: Blister (1), T2 (2)
User sqns/units:

295 Sqn
11/10/44-21/01/46
Albemarle I, II, V; Stirling IV

570 Sqn
08/10/44-28/12/45
Albemarle I, II, V; Stirling IV

Opened under control of USAAF 12/43
To 38 Gp RAF Fighter Command 10/44

ROBOROUGH, Devon

Opened: 07/31
Closed: Currently in use as Plymouth
Airport
Elevation: 488ft
Pundit code: Not known
Formation: 10 Gp
Main contractor: Various
Runways: 3 grass
Hangars: Blister (1)
User sqns/units:

247 Sqn
01/08/40-10/02/41
17/02-10/05/41
Gladiator II; Hurricane I

Nominally under RN control but used by
10 Gp Fighter Command for air defence of
Devonport Dockyard 08/40-05/41

ROCHFORD (Southend), Essex

Opened: 1914
Closed: Currently in use as Southend
Airport
Elevation: 25ft
Pundit code: RO
Formation: 11 Gp
Main contractor: Various
Runways: 2 grass
Hangars: Bellman (2), Blister (4)
User sqns/units:

19 Sqn
16-20/08/42
12-20/05/44
Spitfire Vb; Mustang III

54 Sqn
28/10-03/11/39
17/11-02/12/39
16-29/12/39
16/01-14/02/40
23/03-20/04/40
25/06-24/07/40
31/03-20/05/41
Spitfire I, IIa

64 Sqn
27/01-31/03/41
31/03-01/05/42
Spitfire I, IIa, Vb

74 Sqn
22-29/10/39
03-14/11/39
02-16/12/39
29/12/39-14/02/40
20/04-27/05/40
06-26/06/40
26/07-06/08/44
Spitfire I, LFIXe

121 Sqn
03/06-23/09/42
Spitfire Vb

---

127 Sqn
12-23/07/44
Spitfire IX

137 Sqn
12/06-08/08/43
Hurricane IV

222 Sqn
20-27/12/43
04-09/04/44
Spitfire LFIXb

234 Sqn
16/09-15/10/43
Spitfire Vb

264 Sqn
29/10-27/11/40
Defiant I

317 Sqn
02-18/12/43
Spitfire IX

350 Sqn
23/09-07/12/42
12-31/10/43
Spitfire Vb, Vc

402 Sqn
19/08-06/11/41
Hurricane IIb

403 Sqn
02/05-03/06/42
Spitfire Vb

411 Sqn
07-30/03/42
Spitfire Vb

453 Sqn
02/10-24/11/42
07/12/42-01/03/43
14-27/03/43
Spitfire Vb

603 Sqn
03-13/12/40
16/06-09/07/41
Spitfire IIa, Va

611 Sqn
13/12/40-27/01/41
20/05-14/06/41
06-13/09/43
Spitfire I, Va, LFVb

616 Sqn
27/05-06/06/40
Spitfire I

To 11 Gp as forward satellite to
Hornchurch 10/39
Renamed Southend and upgraded to full
satellite status 10/40
Downgraded to forward satellite to
Hornchurch 09/44

ST MARY'S, Scilly Isles

Opened: 1939
Closed: Currently in use as civil airport
Elevation: 100ft
Pundit code: Not known
Formation: 10 Gp
Main contractor: Various
Runways: 3 grass
Hangars: None
User sqns/units:

No squadrons based but used by 87 Sqn (det) 19/05/41-04/42 (Hurricane I, IIc) and 1449 Flt 04/42-17/09/44 (Hurricane IIc)

SCORTON, Yorks

Opened: 10/39
Closed: 1945
Elevation: 200ft
Pundit code: SO
Formation: 13 Gp
Main contractor: Various
Runways: 3 tarmac
Hangars: Blister (12)
User sqns/units:

56 Sqn
15-23/02/44
07-30/03/44
07-28/04/44
Typhoon Ib

122 Sqn
06/10/41-01/04/42
Spitfire IIb, Vc

130 Sqn
10-16/11/43
04/01-13/02/44
Spitfire Vb, Vc

167 Sqn
06/04-01/06/42
Spitfire Vb

219 Sqn
04/10/39-12/10/40
21/10/42-25/04/43
Blenheim If; Beaufighter If

406 Sqn
16/06-04/09/42
Beaufighter IIf, VIf

410 Sqn
01/09-20/10/42
Beaufighter IIf

604 Sqn
24/04/43-25/04/44
Beaufighter VIf; Mosquito XIII, XII

Opened in 13 Gp as satellite to Catterick 10/39

SELSEY, Sussex

Opened: 05/43
Closed: 05/45
Elevation: 20ft
Pundit code: ZS
Formation: 83 Gp/84 Gp, 2 TAF
Main contractor: RAFACS
Runways: 2 steel matting
Hangars: Blister (4)
User sqns/units:

33 Sqn
06-10/08/44
18-19/08/44
Spitfire LFIXe

65 Sqn
31/05-01/07/43
Spitfire Vb

222 Sqn
09/04-30/06/44
06-19/08/44
Spitfire LFIXb

245 Sqn
02/06-01/07/43
Typhoon Ib

329 Sqn
01/07-06/08/44
Spitfire IX

340 Sqn
01/07-14/08/44
Spitfire IXb

341 Sqn
01/07-06/08/44
Spitfire IXb

349 Sqn
11/04-30/06/44
06-19/08/44
Spitfire LFIXe

485 Sqn
07/04-30/06/44
07-19/08/44
Spitfire IXb, IXe

ALG

SHEPHERDS GROVE, Essex

Opened: 04/44
Closed: 07/63
Elevation: 200ft
Pundit code: HP
Formation: 38 Gp
Main contractor: Various
Runways: 3 concrete
Hangars: T2 (2)
User sqns/units:

196 Sqn
26/01/45-16/03/46
Stirling IV, V

299 Sqn
25/01/45-15/02/46
Stirling IV, V

Opened in 3 Gp Bomber Command as a satellite of Stradishall 04/44
To 38 Gp Fighter Command with full station status 01/45

SHERBURN-IN-ELMET, Yorks

Opened: 1917
Closed: 1945
Elevation: 26ft
Pundit code: SH
Formation: 12 Gp
Main contractor: Various
Runways: 1 concrete
Hangars: Blister (5), Various (6)
User sqns/units:

46 Sqn
01/03-20/05/41
Hurricane I

Brief use by 12 Gp Fighter Command 09/39-05/41

SHOREHAM, Sussex

Opened: 02/11
Closed: Currently in use as Shoreham Airport
Elevation: 0ft
Pundit code: SQ
Formation: 11 Gp
Main contractor: Various
Runways: 2 grass
Hangars: Blister (4)
User sqns/units:

253 Sqn
24-30/05/42
Hurricane I, IIa, IIb, IIc

345 Sqn
26/04-16/08/44
Spitfire Vb

FIU
20/08/40-01/41
Beaufighter I; Blenheim I

422 Flt
14/10-18/12/40
Hurricane I

To 11 Gp Fighter Command as a satellite to Tangmere 06/40
Satellite to Ford 11/42

SKEABRAE, Orkney

Opened: 08/40
Closed: 1945
Elevation: 60ft
Pundit code: KJ
Formation: 13 Gp/14 Gp/13 Gp
Main contractor: Various
Runways: 4 tarmac

Hangars: Callender-Hamilton (1), Teesside (12)
User sqns/units:

3 Sqn
07/01-10/02/41
Hurricane I

66 Sqn
09/02-28/06/43
Spitfire Vb, Vc, VI

118 Sqn
10/03-12/07/44
Spitfire Vb, VII

129 Sqn
19/01-13/02/43

132 Sqn
16/02-11/06/42
Spitfire IIb, Vb

164 Sqn
05/05-10/09/42
Spitfire Va

234 Sqn
24/04-26/06/43
Spitfire Vb, VI

253 Sqn
10/02-21/09/41
Hurricane I, IIb

312 Sqn
24/06-21/09/43
Spitfire Vb

313 Sqn
11/07-04/10/44
Spitfire Vb, VII

329 Sqn
03/04-25/05/45
Spitfire IX

331 Sqn
21/09/41-04/05/42
Hurricane IIb; Spitfire IIa, Vb

441 Sqn
30/12/44-03/04/45
Spitfire IX, IXb

453 Sqn
15/10/43-19/01/44
Spitfire Vb

602 Sqn
10/09/42-20/01/43
17/01-12/03/44
Spitfire Va, VI, Vc, Vb, LFVb

611 Sqn
03/10-31/12/44
Spitfire IX

Opened in 13 Gp as a satellite to Kirkwall 08/40

SKITTEN, Caithness

Opened: 12/40
Closed: 05/45
Elevation: 65ft
Pundit code: NS
Formation: 14 Gp
Main contractor: Various
Runways: 3 tarmac
Hangars: Bellman (1), Blister (9)
User sqns/units:

232 Sqn
13-24/10/40
11/11-04/12/40
Hurricane I

260 Sqn
05/12/40-07/01/41
10/02-16/04/41
Hurricane I

607 Sqn
16/04-27/07/41
Hurricane I, IIa, IIb

Opened in 14 Gp Fighter Command as satellite to Castletown 12/40
To Coastal Command 07/41

SNAILWELL, Suffolk

Opened: 03/41
Closed: 1946
Elevation: 70ft
Pundit code: SW
Formation: 12 Gp
Main contractor: Various
Runways: 3 grass
Hangars: Bellman (1), Blister (10)
User sqns/units:

56 Sqn
30/03-29/05/42
01/06-24/08/42
Hurricane IIb; Typhoon Ia, Ib

137 Sqn
24/08-17/09/42
Whirlwind I

152 Sqn
25-31/08/41
Spitfire IIa

181 Sqn
10/12/42-01/03/43
08-24/03/43
Hurricane I; Typhoon Ia, Ib

183 Sqn
08-12/03/43
Typhoon Ib

184 Sqn
15-17/09/43
Hurricane IV

247 Sqn
31/10-05/11/43
Typhoon Ib

Opened in Army Co-operation Command but as a satellite to Duxford 03/41
Achieved full station status 07/41
To 12 Gp Fighter Command 06/43
To 28 Gp Technical Training Command 10/44

SPEKE, Lancs

Opened: 07/30
Closed: Currently in use as Liverpool Airport
Elevation: 65ft
Pundit code: PZ
Formation: 9 Gp
Main contractor: Various
Runways: 3 tarmac
Hangars: Bellman (2), Blister (4)
User sqns/units:

229 Sqn
22/12/40-20/05/41
Hurricane I

303 Sqn
15/07-07/10/41
Spitfire I, IIb; Hurricane I

306 Sqn
07/10-12/12/41
Spitfire IIa

308 Sqn
12-25/09/40
No aircraft

312 Sqn
26/09/40-03/03/41
Hurricane I

315 Sqn
13/03-14/07/41
Hurricane I

Sector Station in 9 Gp Fighter Command 09/40
To Directorate General of Civil Aviation 07/44

STAPLEFORD TAWNEY, Essex

Opened: 06/34
Closed: 05/45
Elevation: 103ft
Pundit code: KZ
Formation: 11 Gp/12 Gp
Main contractor: Various
Runways: 2 grass
Hangars: Blister (4)
User sqns/units:

3 Sqn
23/06-09/08/41
Hurricane IIb, IIc

46 Sqn
01/09-08/11/40
Hurricane I

53. SPEKE
Hurricanes of No 312 (Czech) Squadron overfly one of their number on the ground, late in 1940. DU-W is V6935. *via Chaz Bowyer*

54. STAPLEFORD TAWNEY
Debriefing for pilots of No 46 Squadron, October 1940. Left to right, are: Flg Off Ambrose, 'Vinc' ('Spy'), the Intelligence Officer, Flg Off C.Young, Plt Off P.Leggett, Plt Off P.McGregor, Sgt R.Earp, Plt Off P.Le Fevre. *via Chaz Bowyer*

151 Sqn
29/08-01/09/40
Hurricane I

242 Sqn
09/04-22/05/41
Hurricane IIb

To 11 Gp Fighter Command as a satellite to North Weald 01/40
To 34 Wing Army Cooperation Command 03/43
To 12 Gp Fighter Command 06/43

STAPLEHURST, Kent

Opened: 08/43
Closed: 01/45
Elevation: 100ft
Pundit code: XS
Formation: 83 Gp, 2 TAF; 11 Gp
Main contractor: Various
Runways: 2 steel matting
Hangars: none
User sqns/units:

401 Sqn
07/08-13/10/43
Spitfire Vb

411 Sqn
07/08-13/10/43
Spitfire Vb

412 Sqn
08/08-14/10/43
Spitfire Vb

ALG
To USAAF 04/44
To 11 Gp ADGB 07/44

STONEY CROSS, Hants

Opened: 11/43
Closed: 01/48
Elevation: 373ft
Pundit code: SS
Formation: 10 Gp
Main contractor: George Wimpey & Co Ltd

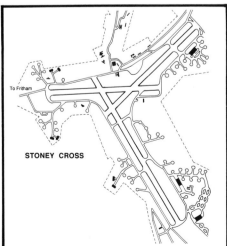

Runways: 3 concrete
Hangars: Blister (6), T2 (4)
User sqns/units:

175 Sqn
19/03-08/04/43
Hurricane IIb

297 Sqn
25/08/43-14/03/44
Albemarle I, II

299 Sqn
04/11/43-15/03/44
Ventura I, II; Stirling IV

Opened in 38 Wing, Army Co-operation Command 11/42
To 10 Gp Fighter Command 06/43
To USAAF 03/44
To RAF Transport Command 11/44

SUMBURGH, Shetlands

Opened: 1933
Closed: Currently in use as civil airport
Elevation: 2ft
Pundit code: UM
Formation: 13 Gp/14 Gp
Main contractor: Various
Runways: 3 tarmac
Hangars: Bellman (3)
User sqns/units:

232 Sqn
17/07-18/09/40
Hurricane I

254 Sqn
16/05-02/08/40
07/01-29/05/41
Blenheim IVf

Sumburgh Fighter Flt
16/05-01/08/40
Gladiator II

To 13 Gp Fighter Command 05/40
To 14 Gp 07/40
To Coastal Command 06/41

SUTTON BRIDGE, Lincs

Opened: 1926
Closed: 1958
Elevation: 9ft
Pundit code: SB
Formation: 11 Gp/81 (OTU) Gp
Main contractor: Various
Runways: 1 grass, 2 steel matting
Hangars: ARS (1), Bellman (2), Blister (12)
User sqns/units:

6 OTU ➡ 56 OTU
09/03-(01/11/40)-27/03/42
Hurricane I

264 Sqn
30/10-07/12/39
No aircraft

266 Sqn
30/10/39-01/03/40
Battle; Spitfire I

Opened as temporary armament practice camp 1926
To Flying Training Command 1936
To 11 Gp Fighter Command 09/39
To Flying Training Command 04/42

SWINGFIELD, Kent

Opened: 08/44
Closed: 04/45
Elevation: 460ft
Pundit code: IF
Formation: 11 Gp
Main contractor: Royal Engineers Airfield Construction Group
Runways: 2 steel matting
Hangars: Blister (4)
User sqns/units: No RAF fighter units based

Unused ALG in 11 Gp ADGB/Fighter Command

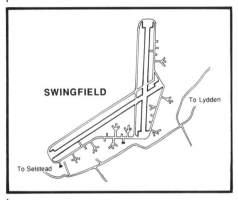

TAIN, Ross-shire

Opened: 09/41
Closed: 11/46
Elevation: 0ft
Pundit code: TN
Formation: 14 Gp
Main contractor: Various
Runways: 3 concrete
Hangars: Bellman (3), Blister (8), T2 (2)
User sqns/units:

17 Sqn
17/09-31/10/41
Hurricane IIa, I, IIb

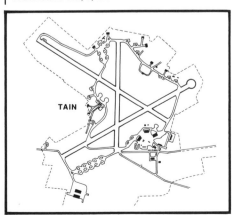

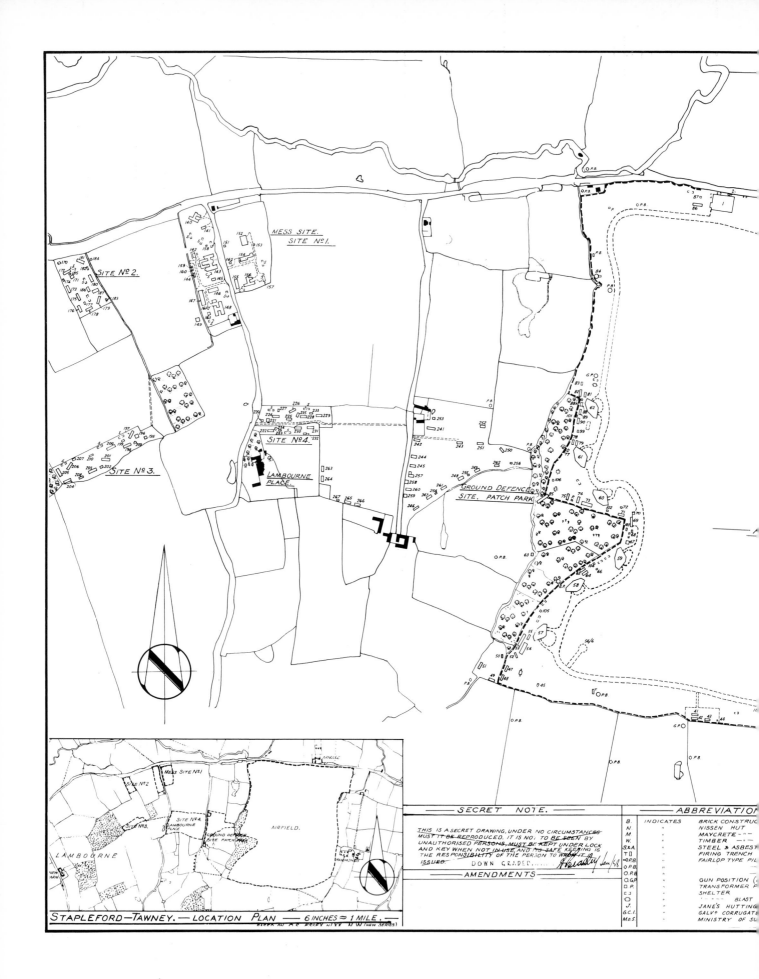

MESS SITE.
SITE Nº1.

SITE Nº 2.

SITE Nº 4.

LAMBOURNE
PLACE.

SITE Nº 3.

GROUND DEFENCE.
SITE. PATCH PARK

ABBREVIATION

	INDICATES	
B.	"	BRICK CONSTRUC
N	"	NISSEN HUT
M.W.	"	MAYCRETE - " -
T	"	TIMBER - " -
S.x.A	"	STEEL & ASBEST
T	"	FIRING TRENCH
O.P.B	"	FAIRLOP TYPE PIL
O.P.B	"	
O.P.B.	"	
Q.G.P.	"	GUN POSITION (
P.	"	TRANSFORMER P
	"	SHELTER
	"	BLAST
J.	"	JANE'S HUTTING
G.C.I.	"	GALVᴰ CORRUGATE
M.O.S.	"	MINISTRY OF SU

LAMBOURNE

AIRFIELD.

MESS SITE Nº 1

SITE Nº 2

SITE Nº 3

SITE Nº 4.

LAMBOURNE
PLACE.

GROUND DEFENCE
SITE PATCH PARK

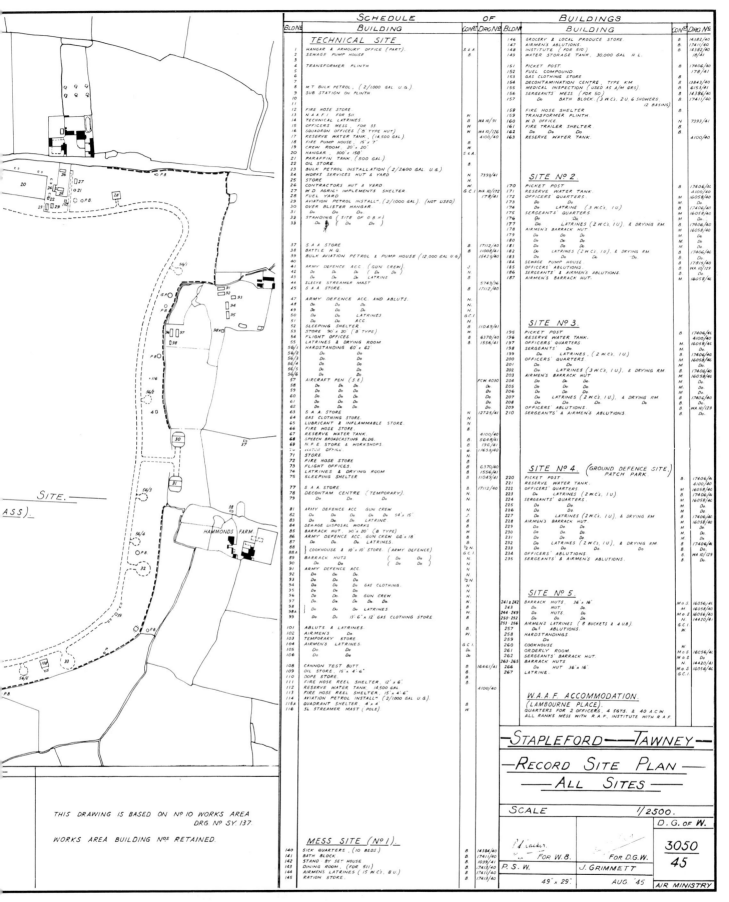

SCHEDULE OF BUILDINGS

BLDNo	BUILDING	CONST	DRG No	BLDNo	BUILDING	CONST	DRG No
	TECHNICAL SITE			146	GROCERY & LOCAL PRODUCE STORE	B	14382/40
				147	AIRMENS ABLUTIONS	B	17411/40
1	HANGAR & ARMOURY OFFICE (PART).	S&A		148	INSTITUTE (FOR 510)	B	14382/40
2	SEWAGE PUMP HOUSE	B		149	WATER STORAGE TANK, 30,000 GAL H.L.		18/41
3							
4	TRANSFORMER PLINTH			151	PICKET POST	B	1746/40
5				152	FUEL COMPOUND		178/41
6				153	GAS CLOTHING STORE	B	
7				154	DECONTAMINATION CENTRE, TYPE KM	B	13843/40
8	MT BULK PETROL, (2/1000 GAL. U.G.)			155	MEDICAL INSPECTION (USED AS A/M. QRS.)	B	6153/41
9	SUB STATION ON PLINTH			156	SERGEANTS' MESS (FOR 50)	B	14386/40
10				157	BATH BLOCK. (3 W.Cs, 2 U, 6 SHOWERS	B	17411/40
11					12 BASINS)		
12	FIRE HOSE STORE.	W		158	FIRE HOSE SHELTER		
13	N.A.A.F.I. FOR 511	W		159	TRANSFORMER PLINTH		
14	TECHNICAL LATRINES	B	WA10/91	160	W.D. OFFICE	N	7393/41
15	OFFICERS MESS, FOR 33	W		161	FIRE TRAILER SHELTER		
16	SQUADRON OFFICES ('B' TYPE HUT)	W	WA10/126	162	Do Do Do		
17	RESERVE WATER TANK, (14,500 GAL.)		4100/40	163	RESERVE WATER TANK		4100/40
18	FIRE PUMP HOUSE, 15' x 7'	W					
19	CREW ROOM, 20' x 20'	W					
20	HANGAR, 300' x 150'	S&A			**SITE No 2.**		
21	PARAFFIN TANK, (500 GAL.)	B		170	PICKET POST	B	1746/40
22	OIL STORE	B		171	RESERVE WATER TANK		4100/40
23	BULK PETROL INSTALLATION (2/2600 GAL. U.G.)			172	OFFICERS QUARTERS	M	16058/40
24	WORKS SERVICES HUT & YARD	N	7393/41	173	Do Do	M	Do
25	STORE	N		174	Do LATRINE (3 W.Cs, I U.)	M	Do
26	CONTRACTORS HUT & YARD	N		175	SERGEANTS QUARTERS	M	16058/40
27	W.D. AGRIC' IMPLEMENTS SHELTER	G.C.I.	WA10/172	176	Do Do	M	Do
28	FUEL YARD		178/41	177	Do LATRINES (2 W.Cs, I U.), & DRYING RM.	B	17406/40
29	AVIATION PETROL INSTALL. (2/1000 GAL.) (NOT USED)			178	AIRMEN'S BARRACK HUT	M	16058/40
30	OVER BLISTER HANGAR			179	Do Do	M	Do
31	Do Do Do			180	Do Do	M	Do
32	STANDING (SITE OF O.B.H.)			181	Do Do	M	Do
33	Do (Do Do)			182	Do LATRINES (2 W.Cs, I U.), & DRYING RM.	B	17406/40
				183	Do Do Do Do	M	Do
37	S.A.A. STORE	B	17112/40	184	SEWAGE PUMP HOUSE	B	17813/40
38	BATTLE H.Q.	B	11008/41	185	OFFICERS ABLUTIONS	B	WA10/129
39	BULK AVIATION PETROL & PUMP HOUSE (12,000 GAL U.G.)		15425/40	186	SERGEANTS' & AIRMENS ABLUTIONS	B	Do
40				187	AIRMENS BARRACK HUT	M	16058/40
41	ARMY DEFENCE ACC. (GUN CREW).	J.					
42	Do Do Do	B.					
43	Do Do Do LATRINE	B.			**SITE No 3.**		
44	SLEEVE STREAMER MAST		5743/36	195	PICKET POST	B	1746/40
45	S.A.A. STORE.	B.	17112/40	196	RESERVE WATER TANK.		4100/40
				197	OFFICERS' QUARTERS	M.	16058/40
47	ARMY DEFENCE ACC. AND ABLUTS.	N.		198	SERGEANTS	M.	Do
49	Do Do	N.		199	Do LATRINES, (2 W.C's, I U.)	B.	17406/40
50	Do Do LATRINES	G.C.I.		200	OFFICERS' QUARTERS	M.	16058/40
51	Do Do ACC.	N.		201	Do Do	M.	Do
52	SLEEPING SHELTER	B.	11049/41	202	Do LATRINES (3 W.Cs, I U.), & DRYING RM.	B.	17406/40
53	STORE 90' x 20' ('B' TYPE)	W		203	AIRMEN'S BARRACK HUT	M.	16058/40
54	FLIGHT OFFICES	B	6370/41	204	Do Do	M.	Do
55	LATRINES & DRYING ROOM	B	1556/41	205	Do Do	M.	Do
56/1	HARDSTANDING 60' x 62'			206	Do Do	M.	Do
56/2	Do			207	Do LATRINES (2 W.Cs, I U.), & DRYING RM	B.	17406/40
56/3	Do			208	Do Do	B.	Do
56/4	Do			209	OFFICERS' ABLUTIONS	B.	WA10/129
56/5	Do			210	SERGEANTS' & AIRMENS ABLUTIONS	B.	Do
56/6	Do						
57	AIRCRAFT PEN (S.E.)		FCW.4030				
58	Do Do		Do				
59	Do Do		Do				
60	Do Do		Do				
61	Do Do		Do				
62	Do Do		Do				
63	S.A.A. STORE	N	12725/41		**SITE No 4.** (GROUND DEFENCE SITE.)		
64	GAS CLOTHING STORE.	N			PATCH PARK.		
65	LUBRICANT & INFLAMMABLE STORE.	B.		220	PICKET POST	B.	1746/40
66	FIRE HOSE STORE.	B.		221	RESERVE WATER TANK.		4100/40
67	RESERVE WATER TANK.	B.	4100/40	222	OFFICERS' QUARTERS	M.	16058/40
68	SPEECH BROADCASTING BLDG.	B.	5649/41	223	Do LATRINES (2 W.C's, I U.)	B.	17406/40
69	N.F.E. STORE & WORKSHOPS	B.	1761/41	224	SERGEANTS' QUARTERS	M.	16058/40
70	WATCH OFFICE	N.	1765/41	225	Do Do	M.	Do
71	STORE	N.		226	Do Do	M.	Do
72	FIRE HOSE STORE	N.		227	Do LATRINES (2 W.Cs, I U.), & DRYING RM	B.	17406/40
73	FLIGHT OFFICES	B.	6370/41	228	AIRMEN'S BARRACK HUT	M.	16058/40
74	LATRINES & DRYING ROOM	B.	1556/41	229	Do Do	M.	Do
75	SLEEPING SHELTER	B.	11049/41	230	Do Do	M.	Do
				231	Do Do	M.	Do
77	S.A.A. STORE	B.	17112/40	232	Do LATRINES (2 W.Cs, I U.), & DRYING RM	B.	17406/40
78	DECONTAM CENTRE (TEMPORARY).	N.		233	Do Do	B.	Do
79	Do Do Do	N.		234	OFFICERS' ABLUTIONS	B.	WA10/129
				236	SERGEANTS' & AIRMENS ABLUTIONS.	B.	Do
81	ARMY DEFENCE ACC. GUN CREW.	N.					
82	Do Do Do Do 54' x 15'	J.					
83	Do Do Do LATRINE.	B.			**SITE No 5.**		
84	SEWAGE DISPOSAL WORKS	B.		241 & 242	BARRACK HUTS, 36' x 16'	MoS.	16056/40
85	BARRACK HUT, 90' x 20' ('B' TYPE)	W.		243	Do HUTS	MoS	16058/40
86	ARMY DEFENCE ACC. GUN CREW 66' x 18'	B.		244-249	Do HUTS	MoS	16056/40
87	Do Do Do LATRINES.	B.		250-252	Do Do	N.	14420/41
88	COOKHOUSE & 10' x 10' STORE. (ARMY DEFENCE)	½ N.		253-256	AIRMENS LATRINES (8 BUCKETS & 4 U.B.)	G.C.I.	
88A	Do Do	G.C.I.		257	Do ABLUTIONS.	W	
89	BARRACK HUTS	N.		258	HARDSTANDINGS		
90	Do (Do Do)	N.		259	Do		
91	ARMY DEFENCE ACC.	N.		260	COOKHOUSE		
92	Do Do	½ N.		261	ORDERLY ROOM	MoS	16056/40
93	Do Do	N.		262	SERGEANTS' BARRACK HUT.	MoS	Do
94	Do Do GAS CLOTHING	N.		263-265	BARRACK HUTS	N.	14420/41
95	Do Do Do GUN CREW	N.		266	Do HUT 36' x 16'	MoS	16056/40
97	Do Do Do	N.		267	LATRINE.	G.C.I.	
98	Do Do LATRINES	N					
98A	Do Do Do	N					
99	15' 6" x 12' GAS CLOTHING STORE	B.			**W.A.A.F. ACCOMMODATION.**		
					(LAMBOURNE PLACE.)		
101	ABLUTS & LATRINES	B.			QUARTERS FOR 2 OFFICERS, 4 SGTS. & 40 A.C.W.		
102	AIRMENS	W.			ALL RANKS MESS WITH R.A.F. INSTITUTE WITH R.A.F.		
103	TEMPORARY STORE						
104	AIRMENS LATRINES.	G.C.I.					
105	Do Do	Do					
106	Do Do	Do					
108	CANNON TEST BUTT.	B.	16461/41				
109	OIL STORE 15' x 4' 6".	B.					
110	DOPE STORE	B.					
111	FIRE HOSE REEL SHELTER, 12' x 6'	B.					
112	RESERVE WATER TANK, 14,500 GAL.		4100/40				
113	FIRE HOSE REEL SHELTER, 15' x 4' 6"						
114	AVIATION PETROL INSTALL. (2/1000 GAL. U.G.)						
115A	QUADRANT SHELTER 4' x 4'	B.					
116	SL STREAMER MAST (POLE)	W					

MESS SITE (No 1).

BLDNo	BUILDING	CONST	DRG No
140	SICK QUARTERS, (10 BEDS)	B.	14384/40
141	BATH BLOCK	B.	17411/40
142	STAND BY SET HOUSE	B.	1039/41
143	DINING ROOM (FOR 511)	B.	17413/40
144	AIRMENS LATRINES (15 W.Cs, 8 U.)	B.	17411/40
145	RATION STORE	B.	17413/40

SITE.
ASS).

HAMMONDS FARM.

THIS DRAWING IS BASED ON No 10 WORKS AREA DRG. No SY.137.

WORKS AREA BUILDING Nos RETAINED.

—STAPLEFORD—TAWNEY—
—RECORD SITE PLAN—
—ALL SITES—

SCALE	1/2500.			
			D.G. OF W.	
P. Walker. FOR W.B.		FOR D.G.W.	**3050**	
P.S.W.	J. GRIMMETT		**45**	
49" x 29"	AUG '45		AIR MINISTRY	

TAIN continued

186 Sqn
07/01-01/03/44
Typhoon Ib; Spitfire Vb

Opened as 14 Gp Sector Station 09/41
To Coastal Command 02/43

TANGMERE, Sussex

Opened: 1918
Closed: 1970
Elevation: 50ft
Pundit code: RN
Formation: 11 Gp
Main contractor: Various
Runways: 2 concrete
Hangars: Bessoneau (2), Blister (16), T2 (1)
User sqns/units:

1 Sqn
01/02/27-09/09/39
23/07-01/08/40
01/07/41-08/07/42
Siskin; Fury; Hurricane I

17 Sqn
19/08-02/09/40
Hurricane I

33 Sqn
03-17/07/44
20-31/08/44
Spitfire LFIXe

41 Sqn
17-20/08/42
05-11/10/42
04/10/43-06/02/44
20/02-11/03/44
Spitfire Vb, XII

43 Sqn
12/12/26-18/11/39
31/05-08/09/40
16/06-01/09/42
Gamecock I; Siskin IIIa; Fury I; Hurricane I, IIa, IIb, IIc

65 Sqn
29/11/40-26/02/41
Spitfire I

66 Sqn
03-07/07/42
16-20/08/42
22/06-06/08/44
Spitfire Vb, Vc, LFIXb

74 Sqn
03-17/07/44
06-20/08/44
Spitfire LFIXe

91 Sqn
04/10/43-08/02/44
20-29/02/44
Spitfire XII

92 Sqn
10/10-30/12/39
Blenheim If

118 Sqn
03-07/07/42
16-24/08/42
Spitfire Vb

124 Sqn
25/09-29/10/42
Spitfire VI

127 Sqn
23/07-06/08/44
Spitfire LFIXe

129 Sqn
28/02-13/03/43
Spitfire Vb

130 Sqn
03-11/08/44
Spitfire XIV

131 Sqn
22-24/08/42
31/08-24/09/42
Spitfire Vb

141 Sqn
23/06-10/08/42
Beaufighter If

145 Sqn
10/05-23/07/40
09/10/40-28/05/41
Spitfire I, IIa

165 Sqn
02/11/42-09/03/43
Spitfire Vb

Fighter Interception Unit (FIU)
18/04-20/08/40
Blenheim; Beaufighter; Defiant

183 Sqn
04/08-18/09/43
01/02-15/03/44
Typhoon Ib

197 Sqn
28/03/43-15/03/44
01-10/04/44
Typhoon Ib

198 Sqn
16-30/03/44
Typhoon Ib

213 Sqn
07/09-29/11/40
Hurricane I

219 Sqn
10/12/40-23/06/42
Blenheim If; Beaufighter If

222 Sqn
19-26/08/44
Spitfire LFIXb

229 Sqn
22-24/06/44
Spitfire IX

238 Sqn
16/05-20/06/40
Spitfire I

257 Sqn
03/02-10/04/44
Typhoon Ib

266 Sqn
23/03-10/04/44
Typhoon Ib

310 Sqn
22-28/06/44
29/06-01/07/44
Spitfire LFIX

312 Sqn
22-28/06/44
29/06-04/07/44
Spitfire HFIX

313 Sqn
22-28/06/44
Spitfire IX

329 Sqn
06-19/08/44
Spitfire IX

331 Sqn
22/06-06/08/44
Spitfire IXb

332 Sqn
21/06-06/08/44
Spitfire IXb

340 Sqn
14-19/08/40
Spitfire IXb

341 Sqn
06-19/08/44
Spitfire IXb

349 Sqn
19-26/08/44
Spitfire LFIXe

401 Sqn
18/04-18/06/44
Spitfire IXb

403 Sqn
18/04-16/06/44
Spitfire IXb

411 Sqn
16-17/04/44
22/04-19/06/44
Spitfire IXb

412 Sqn
24/08-23/09/42
15/04-18/06/44
Spitfire Vb, IXb

416 Sqn
17/04-16/06/44
Spitfire IXb

55. TANGMERE
No 501 Squadron's Hurricane I L2124:H receives attention from its ground crew in early 1940. This particular aircraft went on to serve in a training role with No 7, 5 and 55 OTUs before crashing at Moreton-in-Marsh, Gloucestershire, on 5 December 1940. *via K. Merrick*

56. TANGMERE
Pilots and ground staff of No 486 (NZ) Squadron with one of their Typhoon Ibs, 1943. *R. Beeforth*

57. WARMWELL
Sqn Ldr R.E.Morrow DFC, OC No 402 (RCAF) Squadron, watches from astride the cockpit sill as his Hurricane IIb, BE417:K, is bombed up early in 1942. *via Chaz Bowyer*

TANGMERE continued

421 Sqn
18/04-16/06/44
Spitfire IXb

485 Sqn
19-31/08/44
Spitfire IXe

486 Sqn
29/10/42-31/01/44
Typhoon Ib

501 Sqn
27/11/39-10/05/40
03-07/07/42
Hurricane I; Spitfire Vb, Vc

1455 Flt ➡ 534 Sqn
07/07/41 (04/09/42)-25/01/43
Havoc I, II (Turbinlite); Boston I; Boston III (Turbinlite)

601 Sqn
30/12/39-01/06/40
17/06-19/08/40
02-07/09/40
Blenheim If; Hurricane I

605 Sqn
27/08/39-11/02/40
Gladiator I; Hurricane I

607 Sqn
01/09-10/10/40
Hurricane I

609 Sqn
16-21/03/44
Typhoon Ib

616 Sqn
26/02-09/05/41
23/09-29/10/42
Spitfire IIa, VI

Central Fighter Establishment (CFE)
01-10/45
Typhoon Ib; Tempest V

11 Gp Sector Station 09/39

TARRANT RUSHTON, Dorset

Opened: 10/43
Closed: 09/80
Elevation: 255ft
Pundit code: TK
Formation: 38 Wing/38 Gp
Main contractor: Various
Runways: 3 concrete
Hangars: T2 (4)
User sqns/units:

298 Sqn
04/11/43-05/07/45
Halifax V, III, VII

644 Sqn
23/02/44-01/12/45
Halifax V, III, VII

Opened in 38 Wing Fighter Command 10/43

TEALING, Angus

Opened: 03/42
Closed: 06/45
Elevation: 400ft
Pundit code: TG
Formation: 81 (OTU) Gp/9 Gp
Main contractor: Various
Runways: 2 concrete
Hangars: Blister (8), T1 (3)
User sqns/units:

56 OTU ➡ 1 Combat Training Wing (CTW) ➡ 1 Tactical Exercise Unit (TEU)
27/03/42 (05/10/43)-31/07/44
Hurricane; Master; Lysander; Typhoon; Spitfire

Opened with full station status 03/42
To Flying Training Command 08/44

TERN HILL, Salop

Opened: 01/36
Closed: Currently in use by RAF
Elevation: 280ft
Pundit code: TR
Formation: 9 Gp
Main contractor: Various
Runways: 2 concrete/tarmac
Hangars: C Type (4), Bellman (1), Blister (9)
User sqns/units:

131 Sqn
06/08-27/09/41
Spitfire Ia

306 Sqn
07/11/40-03/04/41
Hurricane I

403 Sqn
30/05-04/08/41
Spitfire I, IIa

605 Sqn
31/03-30/05/41
Hurricane IIa

9 Gp Sector Station 08/40
To Flying Training Command 10/41

THORNEY ISLAND, Hants

Opened: 02/38
Closed: Currently in use by Army
Elevation: 0ft
Pundit code: TC
Formation: 84 Gp, 2 TAF
Main contractor: Various
Runways: 3 concrete
Hangars: Blister (16), C Type (6)
User sqns/units:

164 Sqn
16/03-12/04/44
21/04-18/06/44
Typhoon Ib

183 Sqn
01-11/04/44
22/04-18/06/44
Typhoon Ib

193 Sqn
16/03-06/04/44
Typhoon Ib

198 Sqn
06-22/04/44
30/04-18/06/44
Typhoon Ib

609 Sqn
01-22/04/44
30/04-18/06/44
Typhoon Ib

Opened in 16 Gp Coastal Command 02/38
To 84 Gp, 2 TAF 03/44
To 2 Gp, 2 TAF 06/44

TURNHOUSE, Midlothian

Opened: 1916
Closed: Currently in use as Edinburgh Airport
Elevation: 100ft
Pundit code: TS
Formation: 13 Gp
Main contractor: Various
Runways: 3 concrete
Hangars: Blister (6), C Type (1)
User sqns/units:

3 Sqn
14/09-13/10/40
Hurricane I

64 Sqn
16-17/05/41
06/08-04/10/41
Spitfire IIa

65 Sqn
27/08-29/11/40
Spitfire I

81 Sqn
06/12/41-06/01/42
14/02-15/03/42
Spitfire Va

122 Sqn
05/05-26/06/41
Spitfire I

123 Sqn
10/05-06/08/41
Spitfire I

141 Sqn
04-19/10/39
28/06-11/07/40
30/08-15/10/40
Gladiator I; Defiant I

232 Sqn
03-14/08/42
01/09-25/11/42
Spitfire Vb

242 Sqn
10/04-15/05/42
Spitfire Vb

243 Sqn
02/09-24/11/42
Spitfire Vb

245 Sqn
05/06-20/07/40
Hurricane I

253 Sqn
21/07-23/08/40
Hurricane I

329 Sqn
09/03-03/04/45
Spitfire XVI

340 Sqn
07/11-20/12/41
21/03-30/04/43
30/01-08/02/45
Spitfire IIa, Vb, IXb

341 Sqn
18/01-21/03/43
01-09/02/45
Spitfire Vb, IXb

603 Sqn
14/10/25-16/12/39
05/05-28/08/40
27/02-16/05/41
28/04-07/05/45
DH9A; Wapiti; Hart; Hind; Gladiator II;
Spitfire I, IIa, LFXVIe

607 Sqn
10/10-08/11/40
Hurricane I

13 Gp Sector Station 09/39

TWINWOOD FARM, Beds

Opened: 04/42
Closed: 06/45
Elevation: 275ft
Pundit code: TF
Formation: 81 (OTU) Gp/9 Gp
Main contractor: Various
Runways: 3 concrete
Hangars: Blister (6)
User sqns/units:

51 OTU
19/04/42-14/06/45
Blenheim; Beaufighter; Beaufort; Havoc;
Hudson; Wellington;
Mosquito; Hurricane

Opened as satellite to Cranfield 04/42

USWORTH, Durham

Opened: 10/16
Closed: Currently in use as Sunderland
Airport
Elevation: 120ft

Pundit code: Not known
Formation: 13 Gp/81 (OTU) Gp
Main contractor: Various and John Laing
& Son Ltd
Runways: 2 concrete/tarmac
Hangars: Blister (3), Callender (1),
Lemella (1)
User sqns/units:

43 Sqn
08/09-12/12/40
Hurricane I

64 Sqn
01-16/05/40
Spitfire I

607 Sqn
04/06-01/09/40
12/12/40-16/01/41
Hurricane I

55 OTU
14/03/41-28/04/42
Hurricane X

62 OTU
23/06/42-30/06/43
Anson

13 Gp with full station status 09/39
To C&M 04/44

VALLEY, Anglesey

Opened: 02/41
Closed: Currently in use by RAF
Elevation: 26ft
Pundit code: VY
Main contractor: Various
Formation: 9 Gp
Runways: 3 tarmac
Hangars: Bellman (3), T2 (3)
User sqns/units:

125 Sqn
14/11/43-25/03/44
Beaufighter VIf; Mosquito XVII

131 Sqn
04/03-16/04/42
Spitfire Vb

157 Sqn
26/03-07/05/44
Mosquito II, VI

242 Sqn
16/09-01/11/41
Hurricane IIb

312 Sqn
03/03-25/04/41
Hurricane I

350 Sqn
13/11/41-19/02/42
Spitfire IIa

406 Sqn
31/03-15/11/43
Beaufighter VIf

456 Sqn
30/06/41-29/03/43
Defiant I; Beaufighter IIf, VIf; Mosquito II

615 Sqn
21/04-11/09/41
Hurricane I, IIb, IIc

Opened in 9 Gp as a Sector Station 02/41
Sector Station transferred to Woodvale
11/43

WARMWELL, Dorset

Opened: 05/37
Closed: 11/45
Elevation: 207ft
Pundit code: XW
Formation: 10 Gp
Main contractor: Various
Runways: 3 grass
Hangars: Bellman (2), Blister (8), T2 (2)
User sqns/units:

19 Sqn
01-14/06/42
Spitfire Vb

41 Sqn
07-18/03/45
Spitfire XIV

118 Sqn
09-18/04/41
Spitfire I, IIa

130 Sqn
30/11-05/12/41
Spitfire IIa, Va, Vb

152 Sqn
12/07/40-09/04/41
Spitfire I, IIa

164 Sqn
20/06-06/08/43
Hurricane IV

174 Sqn
01-21/09/42
Hurricane IIb

175 Sqn
03/03-10/10/42
21/11-04/12/44
Hurricane IIb; Typhoon Ib

181 Sqn
12/01-03/02/45
Typhoon Ib

182 Sqn
03-21/02/45
Typhoon Ib

184 Sqn
04-18/12/44
07-28/05/45
Typhoon Ib

234 Sqn
24/02-05/11/41
23/03-04/04/42
Spitfire I, IIb, Vb

WARMWELL continued

245 Sqn
19/12/44-06/01/45
Typhoon Ib

247 Sqn
21/02-07/03/45
Typhoon Ib

257 Sqn
08/01-12/08/43
17/09/43-20/01/44
Typhoon Ib

263 Sqn
19-23/12/41
13/09/42-20/02/43
15/03-19/06/43
12/07-07/09/43
10/09-05/12/43
06-19/03/44
Whirlwind I; Typhoon Ib

266 Sqn
21/09/42-08/01/43
Typhoon Ib

302 Sqn
05/09-11/10/41
27/04-01/05/42
Hurricane IIb; Spitfire Vb

312 Sqn
20-24/04/42
19-31/05/42
20/02-14/03/43
Spitfire Vb, Vc

350 Sqn
05-15/04/42
18/03-02/04/45
Spitfire IIa, Vb, XIV

401 Sqn
24/10-04/11/44
Spitfire IXb

402 Sqn
06/11/41-04/03/42
14/01-02/02/45
Hurricane IIb; Spitfire XIVe

403 Sqn
04-14/01/45
Spitfire XVI

411 Sqn
15-23/10/44
Spitfire IXe

438 Sqn
19/03-03/04/45
Typhoon Ib

439 Sqn
03-22/04/45
Typhoon Ib

440 Sqn
23/04-08/05/45
Typhoon Ib

443 Sqn
18/12/44-03/01/45
Spitfire IXb

609 Sqn
02/10/40-24/02/41
Spitfire I

610 Sqn
21/02-03/03/45
Spitfire XIV

Opened in Flying Training Command and known as Woodsford 05/37
Renamed Warmwell 07/38
To 10 Gp Fighter Command as satellite to Middle Wallop 07/40
To USAAF 03/44
To RAF 08/44

WELLINGORE, Lincs

Opened: 1935
Closed: 1945
Elevation: 260ft
Pundit code: JW
Main contractor: Various
Formation: 12 Gp
Runways: 2 grass
Hangars: Blister (8)
User sqns/units:

29 Sqn
27/07/40-27/04/41
Blenheim If; Beaufighter If

54 Sqn
02-18/06/42
Spitfire Vb

81 Sqn
01/09-30/10/42
Spitfire Vb

154 Sqn
01/09-01/11/42
Spitfire Vb, Vc

349 Sqn
05-16/08/43
Spitfire Va

402 Sqn
12/02-12/04/44
Spitfire Vb, Vc

412 Sqn
20/10/41-01/05/42
Spitfire IIa, Vb

416 Sqn
29/05-07/06/43
19/09-02/10/43
Spitfire IX, Vb

439 Sqn
01-08/01/44
Hurricane IV

To 12 Gp Fighter Command as RLG to Digby 06/40
To Flying Training Command as RLG to Cranwell 04/44

WEST FREUGH, Wigtownshire

Opened: 01/37
Closed: Currently in use by RAE
Elevation: 55ft
Pundit code: EW
Formation: 13 Gp
Main contractor: Various
Runways: 2 tarmac
Hangars: Bessoneau (1), Bellman (7), Blister (8), F Type (1)
User sqns/units:

130 Sqn
04-12/08/42
Spitfire Vb, Vc

Alternative emergency satellite to Ayr in 13 Gp, but never used for this purpose

---

WEST MALLING, Kent

Opened: 1930
Closed: 1969
Elevation: 308ft
Pundit code: VG
Formation: 11 Gp
Main contractor: Various
Runways: 2 steel matting/concrete
Hangars: Blister (16), J Type (1)
User sqns/units:

3 Sqn
14/05-11/06/43
Typhoon Ib

29 Sqn
27/04/41-13/05/43
01/05-19/06/44
Blenheim If; Beaufighter If, VIf; Mosquito XIII

32 Sqn
05/05-14/06/42
07/07-20/08/42
Hurricane IIb, IIc, I

41 Sqn
19-28/06/44
Spitfire XII

64 Sqn
06-25/09/43
Spitfire Vc

66 Sqn
30/10-07/11/40
Spitfire I

80 Sqn
05/07-29/08/44
Spitfire IX

85 Sqn
13/05/43-01/05/44
21/07-29/08/44
Mosquito II, XV, XII, XIII, XVII

91 Sqn
23/04-21/07/44
Spitfire XIV

58. WELLINGORE
Spitfire Vb AD381 was purchased by Plessey workers for the RAF. Named *The Plessey Spitfire*, it entered service with No 412 (RCAF) Squadron in December 1941. *via Author*

59. WEST MALLING
On 17 April 1943 at 01.10hrs, a Focke-Wulf Fw190A-4 of *II/Schnellkampfgeschwader 10* (*SKG 10*) landed in error at West Malling. Its pilot, Feldwebel Otto Bechtold, had become lost on the first experimental moonlight attack on targets along the Thames Estuary. The aircraft, c/n 7155, was retained by the RAE for trials and evaluation purposes, but crashed and burned out on 13 October 1944 near Collyweston, killing its pilot Flt Lt E.R.Lewendon, OC No 1426 Enemy Aircraft Flight.

The aircraft is pictured here shortly after its arrival and is painted overall in sooty matt black except for the engine cowling. *MAP*

WEST MALLING continued

96 Sqn
08/11/43-20/06/44
Mosquito XIII

124 Sqn
20/09/43-05/01/44
18/01-18/03/44
Spitfire VII

130 Sqn
05/08-18/09/43
Spitfire Vb

141 Sqn
11-25/07/40
Defiant I

157 Sqn
21/07-29/08/44
Mosquito XIX

234 Sqn
05/08-16/09/43
Spitfire Vb

264 Sqn
14/04/41-01/05/42
Defiant I, II

274 Sqn
05/07-17/08/44
Spitfire IX

316 Sqn
04-11/07/44
Mustang III

322 Sqn
20/06-21/07/44
Spitfire XIV

350 Sqn
07-19/09/43
Spitfire Vb

409 Sqn
14/05-19/06/44
Mosquito XIII

410 Sqn
20/10-08/11/43
Mosquito II

485 Sqn
16-22/08/42
Spitfire Vb

486 Sqn
10-29/10/42
Typhoon Ib

1452 Flt ➡ 531 Sqn
07/07/41 (08/09/42)-02/10/42
09/10/42-25/01/43
Havoc I; Havoc I (Turbinlite); Boston III (Turbinlite)

610 Sqn
16-21/08/42
19-27/06/44
Spitfire Vb, XIV

616 Sqn
03-07/07/42
18/03-24/04/44
Spitfire VI, VII

421 Flt
10/40
Hurricane I

To 11 Gp Fighter Command as a satellite to Kenley 06/40

WESTHAMPNETT, Sussex

Opened: 07/40
Closed: Currently in use as civil airport
Elevation: 110ft
Pundit code: WQ
Main contractor: Various
Formation: 11 Gp/83 Gp, 2 TAF
Runways: 3 grass
Hangars: Blister (8), T1 (1)
User sqns/units:

41 Sqn
16/12/41-01/04/42
21/06-04/10/43
28/06-03/07/44
Spitfire I, Vb, XII

65 Sqn
07/10-22/12/41
Spitfire IIb, Vb

91 Sqn
28/06-04/10/43
Spitfire XII

118 Sqn
15-24/08/43
29/08-25/09/44
Spitfire Vb, IXc

124 Sqn
29/10-07/11/42
09/08-25/09/44
Spitfire VI, HFIXe

129 Sqn
29/08-01/11/41
22/12/41-06/07/42
Spitfire IIa, Vb

130 Sqn
19-27/06/44
Spitfire Vb

131 Sqn
07/11/42-22/01/43
Spitfire Vb

145 Sqn
23/07-14/08/40
Hurricane I

167 Sqn
21/05-12/06/43
Spitfire Vb, Vc

174 Sqn
10/10/43-21/01/44
Typhoon Ib

175 Sqn
09/10/43-24/02/44
08/03-01/04/44
Typhoon Ib

184 Sqn
23/04-14/05/44
20/05-17/06/44
Typhoon Ib

245 Sqn
10/10/43-01/04/44
Typhoon Ib

302 Sqn
23/11/40-07/04/41
Hurricane I, IIa

303 Sqn
19-27/06/44
09/08-25/09/44
Spitfire LFVB, IXc

Westhampnett

The clipped-wing Spitfire XII was the first Rolls-Royce Griffon-engined version to enter service and was used primarily for home defence duties in the UK against tip-and-run Focke-Wulf Fw190s, although it was also used in the medium/low-level strike role in the Normandy area of France. Armed with two cannon and four 0.303in machine guns the Mk XII entered service early in 1943, but only two RAF fighter squadrons, Nos 41 and 91, were equipped with the version.

In the early evening of 18 July 1943, the Tangmere Wing (Nos 41 and 91 Squadrons) swept the Poix-Abbeville area as top cover for Typhoons of No 83 Group which were attacking the Luftwaffe fighter airfield at Abbeville. Some of the aircraft of No 41 Squadron were jumped by about 25 Messerschmitt Bf109s.

When Blue Section of No 41 Squadron were bounced, Flg Off Bob Hogarth in EN235 turned left into the enemy aircraft and in the ensuing combat he was shot down. His No 2 (Sgt J.Fisher) dived after him and got in two short bursts at a Bf109 but with little effect. Flying as Yellow 3, Flg Off Slack in EN233 was seen going down on the tail of a Bf109 but, unfortunately, he, too, was not seen again either.

The squadron diarist recorded:'The squadron are very upset at the loss of Flg Off T.A.Slack and Flg Off R.H.W.Hogarth as they had been with the squadron a very long time and were two of our most experienced pilots – Slack with his lively wit and friendly nature was a great favourite with the pilots and ground crews, and Hogarth, with his shy but efficient manner, will be greatly missed.'

60b

60a. WESTHAMPNETT
Spitfire XIIs of No 41 Squadron in
starboard echelon, early in 1944. EB-H
MB794 failed to return from a
beachhead patrol on 9 June 1944. *Rolls-Royce Plc*

60b. The wreckage of No 41 Squadron's
Spitfire XII EN235:C is examined by
Luftwaffe personnel after it was shot
down by Messerschmitt Bf109s on 18
July 1943 near Poix in northern France.
Its pilot, Flg Off Bob Hogarth, was
killed. *via Author*

61. WICK

No 111 Squadron's Hurricane Is are refuelled early in 1940. The nearest aircraft, L2001:B, was lost on 19 June 1940 when it crashed on take-off at Hatfield, killing its pilot Sgt Pascoe. *via Chaz Bowyer*

61

WEST HAMPNETT continued

340 Sqn
07/04-20/07/42
26-28/07/42
Spitfire Vb

350 Sqn
03/07-08/08/44
Spitfire IX

402 Sqn
19-27/06/44
Spitfire Vb, Vc

416 Sqn
25/06-07/07/42
Spitfire Vb

441 Sqn
01-12/04/44
Spitfire IXb

442 Sqn
01-23/04/44
Spitfire IXb

443 Sqn
08-22/04/44
Spitfire IXb

485 Sqn
02/01-21/05/43
Spitfire Vb

501 Sqn
30/04-17/05/43
12-21/06/43
02/07-02/08/44
Spitfire Vb; Tempest V

602 Sqn
13/08-17/12/40
Spitfire I

610 Sqn
15/12/40-29/08/41
20/01-30/04/43
27/06-02/07/44
Spitfire I, IIa, Vb, XIV

616 Sqn
09/05-06/10/41
29/10/42-02/01/43
Spitfire IIa, Vb, VI

83 Gp Support Unit
04/11/44-22/02/45
Mustang; Spitfire

ELG in 11 Gp for Tangmere 12/38
Upgraded to satellite to Tangmere 07/40
To USAAF 07/42
To 11 Gp RAF Fighter Command 10/42
To Air Staff, SHAEF 03/45

WETHERSFIELD, Essex

Opened: 12/41
Closed: Currently in use by RAF and USAF
Elevation: 317ft
Pundit code: UW
Formation: 38 Gp
Main contractor: Various
Runways: 3 concrete
Hangars: T2 (2)
User sqns/units:

196 Sqn
09/10/44-26/01/45
Stirling IV

299 Sqn
09/10/44-25/01/45
Stirling IV

To 38 Gp RAF Fighter Command 11/44

WICK, Caithness

Opened: 09/39
Closed: 1978
Elevation: 114ft
Pundit code: WC
Main contractor: Various
Formation: 13 Gp
Runways: 3 tarmac
Hangars: Bellman (2), C Type (4)
User sqns/units:

3 Sqn
30/05-03/09/40
Hurricane I

41 Sqn
19-25/10/39
Spitfire I

43 Sqn
26/02-31/05/40
Hurricane I

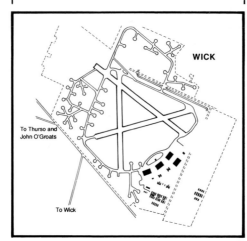

WICK

To Thurso and John O'Groats

To Wick

111 Sqn
27/02-13/05/40
Hurricane I

504 Sqn
22/05-21/06/40
Hurricane I

605 Sqn
28/02-21/05/40
Hurricane I

Opened in 13 Gp with full station status 09/39
Became Sector Station 12/39
To Coastal Command 10/40

WINFIELD, Berwickshire

Opened: 05/42
Closed: 05/45
Elevation: 170ft
Pundit code: IW
Formation: 81 (OTU) Gp/9 Gp/13 Gp
Main contractor: James Miller & Partners Ltd
Runways: 2 tarmac
Hangars: Blister (4)
User sqns/units:

222 Sqn
04-10/08/42
Spitfire Vb

54 OTU
01/05/42-31/10/45
Blenheim I, IV, V; Beaufort I; Beaufighter
I, II, VI; Mosquito II, III, VI, XII, XIII, XVII,
XIX, XXX; Wellington XVIII; Hurricane II

Opened as satellite to Charter Hall 05/42

WINKLEIGH, Devon

Opened: 01/43
Closed: 12/58
Elevation: 540ft
Pundit code: WK
Formation: 10 Gp
Main contractor: Various
Runways: 2 concrete/tarmac
Hangars: Blister (8), T2 (1)
User sqns/units:

406 Sqn
14/04-17/09/44
Beaufighter VIf; Mosquito XII, XXX

Opened in 10 Gp Fighter Command as
a satellite to Exeter 01/43
To USAAF 10/43
To 10 Gp RAF Fighter Command 04/44
To 23 Gp Flying Training Command
11/44

WINKTON, Hants

Opened: 03/44
Closed: 01/45
Elevation: 40ft
Pundit code: XT
Main contractor: Not known
Formation: 11 Gp
Runways: 2 steel matting
Hangars: Blister (4)
User sqns/units:

ALG
Used by USAAF but nominally under
control of 11 Gp RAF Fighter Command

WITTERING, Northants

Opened: 1916
Closed: Currently in use by RAF
Elevation: 250ft
Pundit code: WI
Formation: 12 Gp
Main contractor: Various
Runways: 3 concrete
Hangars: B1 (1), T2 (2)
User sqns/units:

1 Sqn
09/09-15/12/40
Hurricane I

23 Sqn
16/05/38-31/05/40

16/08-12/09/40
Demon; Blenheim If

25 Sqn
27/12/40-16/01/42
Blenheim If; Beaufighter If; Havoc I

32 Sqn
26/05-04/06/40
Hurricane I

68 Sqn
08-27/02/45
Mosquito XXX

74 Sqn
14-21/08/40
Spitfire I

91 Sqn
09-21/05/43
Spitfire XII

118 Sqn
03-17/01/43
Spitfire Vb

141 Sqn
30/04-04/12/43
Beaufighter If, VIf; Mosquito II

151 Sqn
22/12/40-30/04/43
Defiant I, II; Hurricane IIc; Mosquito II

WITTERING continued

152 Sqn
30/09-10/11/42
Spitfire Vb

213 Sqn
18/05/38-09/06/40
Gauntlet II; Hurricane I

229 Sqn
26/06-09/09/40
15-22/12/40
Hurricane I

266 Sqn
14/05-12/08/40
21/08/40-28/09/41
Spitfire I, IIa

349 Sqn
05-08/06/43
Spitfire Va

438 Sqn
19/12/43-10/01/44
Hurricane IV

486 Sqn
09/04-27/09/42
Hurricane IIb; Typhoon Ib

1453 Flt ➡ 532 Sqn
10/07/41 (02/09/42)-09/11/42
Havoc I (Turbinlite); Boston III; Boston III (Turbinlite)

610 Sqn
10/10/39-04/04/40
Spitfire I

FIU
03/04-23/08/44
Beaufighter; Mosquito
To 12 Gp Fighter Command as Sector Station 11/38
To 21 Gp Flying Training Command 03/45

WOODCHURCH, Kent

Opened: 07/43
Closed: 09/44
Elevation: 150ft
Pundit code: XO
Main contractor: RAFACS
Formation: 83 Gp, 2 TAF
Runways: 2 steel matting
Hangars: None
User sqns/units: Used only by RCAF Army co-operation sqns

ALG

WOODVALE, Lancs

Opened: 12/41
Closed: Currently in use by RAF
Elevation: 35ft
Pundit code: OD
Main contractor: Various
Formation: 9 Gp/12 Gp
Runways: 3 asphalt

Hangars: Bellman (3), Blister (9)
User sqns/units:

167 Sqn
12/06/43
(Disbanded, renumbered No 322 Sqn)

195 Sqn
12/02-13/05/43
Typhoon Ib

198 Sqn
15/05-05/06/43
Typhoon Ia, Ib

219 Sqn
27/02-15/03/44
Mosquito XVII

222 Sqn
30/12/43-14/02/44
Spitfire LFIXb

256 Sqn
01/06/42-24/04/43
25/08-25/09/43
Defiant II; Beaufighter If, VIf; Mosquito XII

308 Sqn
12/12/41-01/04/42
Spitfire Vb, IIa

315 Sqn
01/04-05/09/42
Spitfire Vb

316 Sqn
15/02-28/04/44
Spitfire LFVb

317 Sqn
05/09/42-13/02/43
Spitfire Vb

322 Sqn
12/06-15/11/43
30/11-31/12/43
Spitfire Vb

501 Sqn
05-12/06/43
Spitfire Vb

Opened in 9 Gp Fighter Command with full station status 12/41
To RN 05/45

WREXHAM, Denbighshire

Opened: 06/41
Closed: 1945
Elevation: 220ft
Pundit code: RW
Formation: 9 Gp
Main contractor: Sir Alfred McAlpine Ltd
Runways: 3 concrete
Hangars: Bellman (1), Blister (11)
User sqns/units:

96 Sqn
21/10/41-20/10/42
Defiant I, Ia, II: Beaufighter IIf, VIf

Opened in 9 Gp Fighter Command 06/41
To 21 Gp Flying Training Command 02/43

ZEALS, Wilts

Opened: 05/42
Closed: 01/46
Elevation: 550ft
Pundit code: ZL
Formation: 10 Gp
Main contractor: Various
Runways: 3 grass
Hangars: Blister (8), T1 (1)
User sqns/units:

66 Sqn
24/08-26/09/42
29/09-08/10/42
09/10-01/11/42
14/11-23/12/42
Spitfire Vb, Vc

118 Sqn
24/08-23/12/42
Spitfire Vb

132 Sqn
28/02-05/04/43
Spitfire Vb

174 Sqn
12/03-05/04/43
Hurricane IIb

184 Sqn
12/03-05/04/43
Hurricane IId

263 Sqn
19/06-12/07/43
Whirlwind I

410 Sqn
18/06-28/07/44
Mosquito XIII

421 Sqn
01-14/11/42
Spitfire Vb

488 Sqn
12/05-29/07/44
Mosquito XIII

604 Sqn
25-28/07/44
Mosquito XIII

Opened in 10 Gp Fighter Command as Forward Operating Airfield 05/42
To USAAF 08/43
To 10 Gp RAF Fighter Command 04/44
To FAA as HMS *Humming Bird* 04/45

Airfield Locations in Great Britain

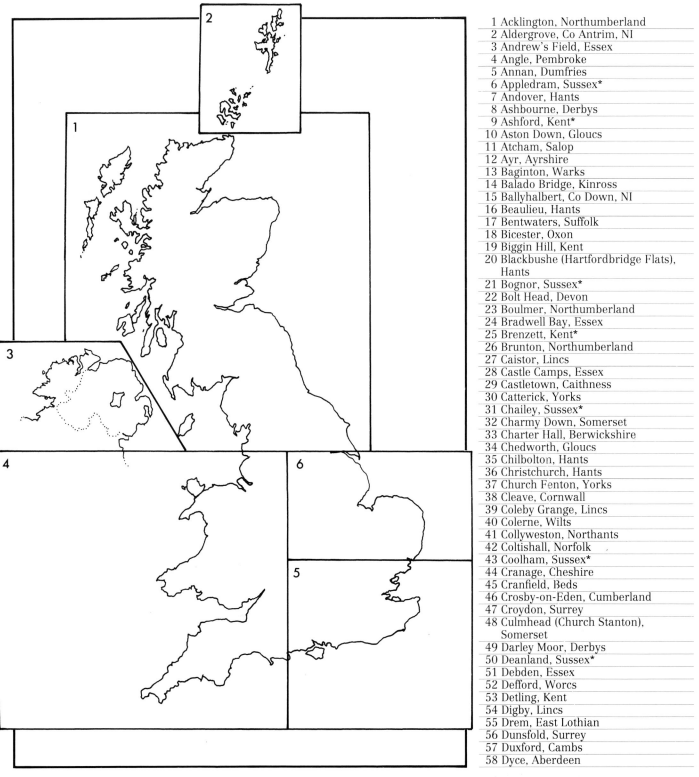

1 Acklington, Northumberland
2 Aldergrove, Co Antrim, NI
3 Andrew's Field, Essex
4 Angle, Pembroke
5 Annan, Dumfries
6 Appledram, Sussex*
7 Andover, Hants
8 Ashbourne, Derbys
9 Ashford, Kent*
10 Aston Down, Gloucs
11 Atcham, Salop
12 Ayr, Ayrshire
13 Baginton, Warks
14 Balado Bridge, Kinross
15 Ballyhalbert, Co Down, NI
16 Beaulieu, Hants
17 Bentwaters, Suffolk
18 Bicester, Oxon
19 Biggin Hill, Kent
20 Blackbushe (Hartfordbridge Flats),
   Hants
21 Bognor, Sussex*
22 Bolt Head, Devon
23 Boulmer, Northumberland
24 Bradwell Bay, Essex
25 Brenzett, Kent*
26 Brunton, Northumberland
27 Caistor, Lincs
28 Castle Camps, Essex
29 Castletown, Caithness
30 Catterick, Yorks
31 Chailey, Sussex*
32 Charmy Down, Somerset
33 Charter Hall, Berwickshire
34 Chedworth, Gloucs
35 Chilbolton, Hants
36 Christchurch, Hants
37 Church Fenton, Yorks
38 Cleave, Cornwall
39 Coleby Grange, Lincs
40 Colerne, Wilts
41 Collyweston, Northants
42 Coltishall, Norfolk
43 Coolham, Sussex*
44 Cranage, Cheshire
45 Cranfield, Beds
46 Crosby-on-Eden, Cumberland
47 Croydon, Surrey
48 Culmhead (Church Stanton),
   Somerset
49 Darley Moor, Derbys
50 Deanland, Sussex*
51 Debden, Essex
52 Defford, Worcs
53 Detling, Kent
54 Digby, Lincs
55 Drem, East Lothian
56 Dunsfold, Surrey
57 Duxford, Cambs
58 Dyce, Aberdeen

59 Earls Colne, Essex
60 East Fortune, East Lothian
61 Eastchurch, Kent
62 Eglinton, Co Londonderry, NI
63 Eshott, Northumberland
64 Exeter, Devon
65 Fairford, Gloucs
66 Fairlop, Essex
67 Fairwood Common, Glamorgan
68 Filton, Bristol
69 Finmere, Bucks
70 Ford, Sussex
71 Fowlmere, Cambs
72 Friston, Sussex
73 Funtington, Sussex*
74 Gatwick, Surrey
75 Goxhill, Lincs
76 Grangemouth, Stirlingshire
77 Gravesend, Kent

78 Great Dunmow, Essex
79 Great Orton, Cumberland
80 Great Sampford, Essex
81 Grimsetter (Kirkwall), Orkney
82 Hampstead Norris, Berks
83 Harrowbeer, Devon
84 Harwell, Berks
85 Hawarden, Flintshire
86 Hawkinge, Kent
87 Headcorn, Kent*
88 Heston, Middx
89 Hibaldstow, Lincs
90 High Ercall, Salop
91 Holmsley South, Hants
92 Honiley, Warks
93 Horne, Surrey*
94 Hornchurch, Essex
95 Hucknall, Notts
96 Hunsdon, Herts

97 Hurn, Hants
98 Hutton Cranswick, Yorks
99 Ibsley, Hants
100 Ipswich, Suffolk
101 Keevil, Wilts
102 Kenley, Surrey
103 King's Cliffe (Wansford),
    Northants
104 Kingsnorth, Kent*
105 Kingston Bagpuize, Berks
106 Kinnell, Angus
107 Kirkistown, Co Down, NI
108 Kirton-in-Lindsey, Lincs
109 Lasham, Hants
110 Lashenden, Kent*
111 Leconfield, Yorks
112 Leicester East, Leics
113 Llanbedr, Merioneth
114 Llandow, Glamorgan
115 Longtown, Cumberland
116 Ludham, Norfolk
117 Lydd, Kent*
118 Lympne, Kent
119 Macmerry, East Lothian
120 Manston, Kent
121 Martlesham Heath, Suffolk
122 Matlaske, Norfolk
123 Maydown, Co Londonderry, NI
124 Mendlesham, Suffolk
125 Merryfield, Somerset
126 Merston, Sussex
127 Middle Wallop, Hants
128 Milfield, Northumberland
129 Montford Bridge, Salop
130 Morpeth, Northumberland
131 Needs Oar Point, Hants*
132 New Romney, Kent*
133 Newchurch, Kent*
134 North Weald, Essex
135 Northolt, Middx
136 Odiham, Hants
137 Ouston, Northumberland
138 Pembrey, Carmarthenshire

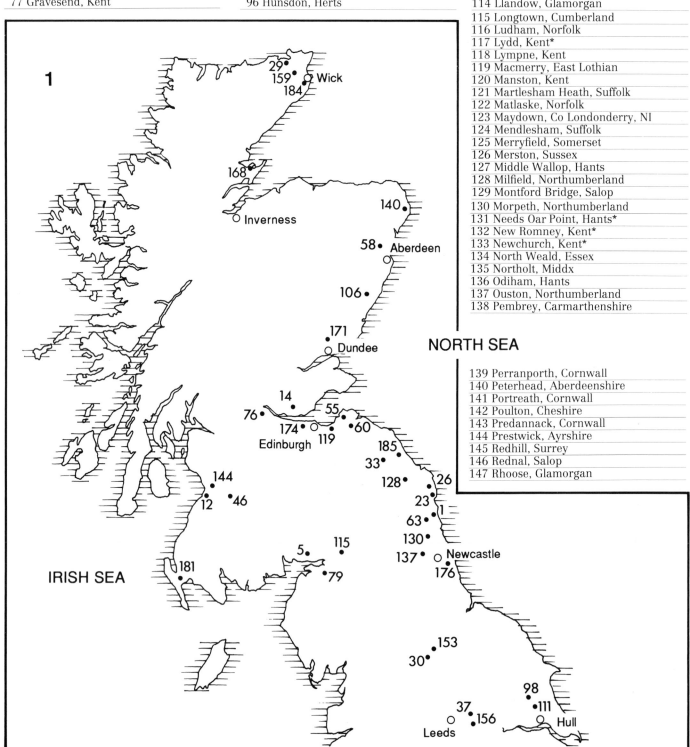

NORTH SEA

139 Perranporth, Cornwall
140 Peterhead, Aberdeenshire
141 Portreath, Cornwall
142 Poulton, Cheshire
143 Predannack, Cornwall
144 Prestwick, Ayrshire
145 Redhill, Surrey
146 Rednal, Salop
147 Rhoose, Glamorgan

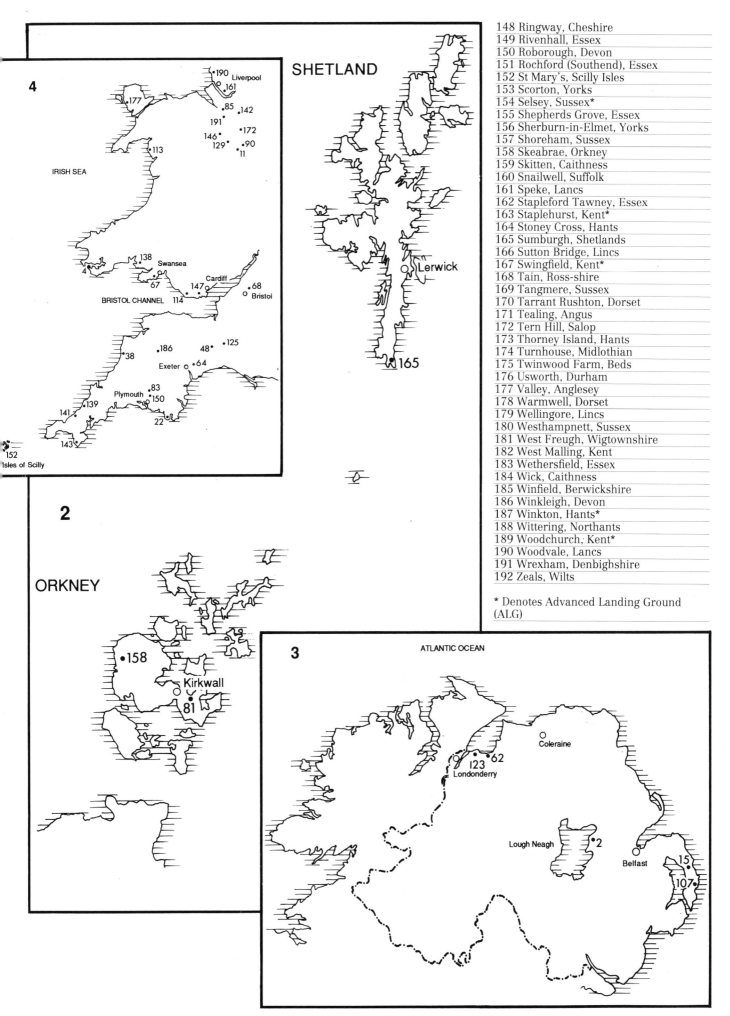

SHETLAND

Lerwick

165

4

190 Liverpool
161
177
85 142
191
172
146
129 90
11
113

IRISH SEA

138
Swansea
67
147
Cardiff
114
68
Bristol

BRISTOL CHANNEL

186
48 125
38
Exeter 64
83
Plymouth
150
141 139
22
143

152
Isles of Scilly

2

ORKNEY

158

Kirkwall

81

3

ATLANTIC OCEAN

Coleraine

123 62

Londonderry

Lough Neagh

2

Belfast

15

107

148 Ringway, Cheshire
149 Rivenhall, Essex
150 Roborough, Devon
151 Rochford (Southend), Essex
152 St Mary's, Scilly Isles
153 Scorton, Yorks
154 Selsey, Sussex*
155 Shepherds Grove, Essex
156 Sherburn-in-Elmet, Yorks
157 Shoreham, Sussex
158 Skeabrae, Orkney
159 Skitten, Caithness
160 Snailwell, Suffolk
161 Speke, Lancs
162 Stapleford Tawney, Essex
163 Staplehurst, Kent*
164 Stoney Cross, Hants
165 Sumburgh, Shetlands
166 Sutton Bridge, Lincs
167 Swingfield, Kent*
168 Tain, Ross-shire
169 Tangmere, Sussex
170 Tarrant Rushton, Dorset
171 Tealing, Angus
172 Tern Hill, Salop
173 Thorney Island, Hants
174 Turnhouse, Midlothian
175 Twinwood Farm, Beds
176 Usworth, Durham
177 Valley, Anglesey
178 Warmwell, Dorset
179 Wellingore, Lincs
180 Westhampnett, Sussex
181 West Freugh, Wigtownshire
182 West Malling, Kent
183 Wethersfield, Essex
184 Wick, Caithness
185 Winfield, Berwickshire
186 Winkleigh, Devon
187 Winkton, Hants*
188 Wittering, Northants
189 Woodchurch, Kent*
190 Woodvale, Lancs
191 Wrexham, Denbighshire
192 Zeals, Wilts

* Denotes Advanced Landing Ground (ALG)

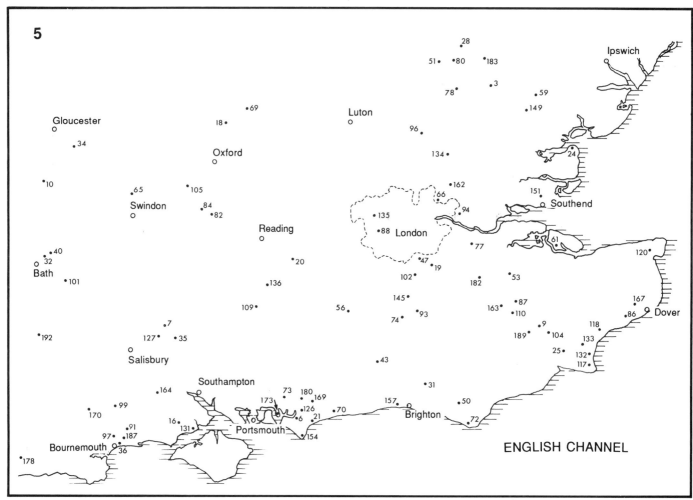

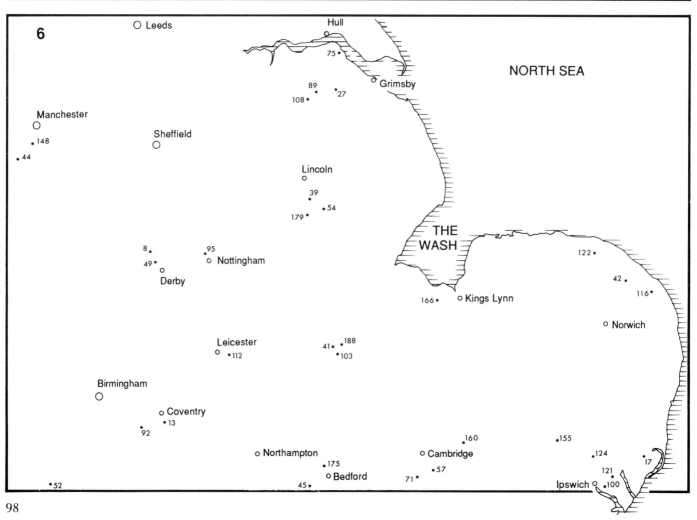

98

War Over the West

By late September 1940 the balance of power in the skies over the British Isles had at last begun to tip in favour of the hard-pressed pilots of RAF Fighter Command. Since early July the mounting fury of Luftwaffe attacks had pushed the endurance of the RAF's men and machines to their uttermost limits. Desperate duels fought high in the often cloudless summer skies of southern England were watched with awe and trepidation by those far below on the ground. West of the main conflict being fought over southeastern England, the counties in the southwest witnessed their fair share of dogfights, too. The aircraft factories of Westland's at Yeovil and the Bristol Aeroplane Co at Filton were significant targets, as were the docks at Avonmouth

and across the Bristol Channel in South Wales. Furthermore, many stray German raiders limping south and homewards to bases in France after bombing targets in the Midlands and northwest England, damaged and with dead and injured on board, often fell to the guns of pursuing RAF fighters before they reached the south coast.

In order to beef up the air defences west of Southampton, the grass airfield of Warmwell near Dorchester in Dorset was transferred to No 10 Group Fighter Command in June 1940 as a Forward Airfield in the Middle Wallop 'Y' Sector. On 12 July No 152 Squadron and its Spitfires were posted in from Acklington, Northumberland, with the prime role of defending the Naval Base at Portland.

They were joined in their task by the Spitfires of No 609 Squadron from nearby Middle Wallop which were detached to Warmwell on a daily basis for operations.

One of No 152 Squadron's Spitfire pilots was a young Australian from Manley, a suburb of Sydney, who had travelled across the world to England in 1938 to enlist in the RAF as a fighter pilot. His name was Kenneth Holland.

Kenneth was reputedly an orphan who had lived at the home of his guardian, Major H.Ripley, in Camelford, Cornwall, since his arrival in England from Australia. On 1 August 1940, at the age of 20, he joined No 152 Squadron at Warmwell and very soon was flying sorties in defence of the West Country. His lamentably short career as a fighter pilot

No 152 Squadron pilots and ground staff at Warmwell in August 1940. To emphasise just how desperate the fight for survival was in the summer of 1940, nine of the 20 pilots in this group were dead within two months of the picture being taken. Back row: groundcrew; Middle row, left to right, are: Sgt H. J. Akroyd (K 08/10/40), Sgt E.Shepperd

(KIFA 18/10/40), Plt Off Richard Hogg (MIA 25/08/40), Intelligence Officer, Plt Off I.Bayles, Plt Off A.Weston, Plt Off W.Beaumont (MIA 23/09/40), Plt Off C.Warren, Plt Off Eric Marrs (MIA 24/07/41), Plt Off F.Holmes, Sgt John Barker (KIA 04/09/40), Sgt L.Reddington (MIA 30/09/40); Front row, left to right, are: Sgt Jack McBean

Christie (KIA 26/09/40), Plt Off T.Wildblood (MIA 25/08/40), Adjutant, Flg Off Peter O'Brien, Flt Lt Derek Boitel-Gill (KIFA 08/41), Sqn Ldr Peter Devitt (OC), Flt Lt F.Thomas, Flg Off E.Hogg, Engineer Officer, Plt Off G.Cox, Sgt Ken Holland (KIA 25/09/40); Front row: The Hon Plt Off Pooch. *A. White*

A Luftwaffe Heinkel He111H-1 crosses the English coast and heads for its target during the Battle of Britain. *via Author*

with the RAF – related below – is, sadly, typical of several hundred other young RAF pilots who died in the service of their country in the high summer of 1940.

The following events which cover 10 days in September 1940 – the height of the Battle of Britain – have been transcribed from Kenneth Holland's combat reports. The action of 25 September in which he met his death has been pieced together from a number of primary and secondary sources, details of which can be found in the bibliography at the end of this book. Comments in square brackets are explanatory notes added by the author.

Sunday 15 September

'Six aircraft of B Flight on patrol sighted 30 He 111s [Heinkel He 111] at 15.40hrs, 7 miles SW of Portland at 15,000ft proceeding to the NW. E/A [enemy aircraft] turned to the SE after attacking Portland. Green Section's three aircraft attacked a straggler from the enemy formation. Green 1 [Plt Off P.O'Brien] made an astern attack, concentrating his fire on the starboard engine. It [E/A] broke away left and down. Green 3 [Sgt K.C.Holland] attacked with a 5 second burst from astern and above and black smoke poured from the starboard engine and E/A began to lose height. Green 2 [Plt Off Weston] attacked E/A...[rest of report missing].'

B Flight claimed one He 111 destroyed and one probable. The aircraft were possibly of *KG55* based at Chartres.

Tuesday 17 September

'I was Blue 2 when Ju 88 [Junkers Ju 88] was sighted. I followed Blue 1 into attack from the starboard beam giving a burst of 2 seconds from 250-200yd. I continued to attack from varying positions and later chased E/A through clouds. E/A was taking evasive action by doing steep turns, diving, sideslipping and throttling back when attacked. I saw engines of E/A had stopped but lost sight of it in thick cloud. After circling round looking for it above cloud, my engine was becoming hot so I landed at Yatesbury [Wiltshire]. My A/C [aircraft] was hit by m/g [machine-gun] fire in 3 places. Rounds fired – 1,650 (very approx).'

Sgt Holland had delivered his attack against a Junkers Ju 88A-1, *Werke Nummer* (*Wk Nr*) 3188 L1+XC of *Stab II/LG1*, at 17,000ft over the town of Shepton Mallet in Somerset. The Ju 88 had been on an operation from its French base at Orleans/Bricy to bomb factories at Speke near Liverpool when it was attacked by Holland at 13.50hrs. Ten minutes later it crash-landed 20 miles to the east at Ladywell Barn near Warminster in the neighbouring county of Wiltshire. From its crew of four, one man was killed in the action and three captured, one of whom

was Major Cramer, the *Gruppe Kommandeur* of *LG1*.

In the engagement Holland's Spitfire suffered damage to its hydraulic, glycol and oil systems, and a punctured starboard tyre. He claimed one-third of the Ju 88 destroyed shared with Plt Offs Eric Marrs and Peter O'Brien of B Flight's Blue Section.

Thursday 19 September

'I was Green 2 ordered to patrol cloud base. R/T [radio telephone] of Green 1 was U/S [unserviceable] so I became Green 1. I was ordered to 15,000ft over Warmwell and was then vectored to Ju 88. As there was cloud at 10,000ft, Green 2 went below the cloud and I went above the cloud at 11,500ft. When cloud broke I went down to given height and sighted Ju 88 ahead on the right two miles away. Green 2 was left behind below cloud. I gave tally-ho, but Green 2 could not find me. I made alternate quarter attacks from left and right from 300 to 200yd, firing one burst of 4 seconds and five each of 2 seconds, aiming first at gunners' positions and then at each engine. E/A took slight evasive action heading for cloud on a southerly course. White return fire after my second attack. I continued to attack and eventually the E/A, now at 8,000ft, dived vertically towards the sea with both engines on fire. As my ammunition was finished, I flew on a northerly course and came to the Isle of Wight. My engine was missing slightly so I made for Portsmouth aerodrome where I landed and after checking engine returned to base. Rounds fired – 2,800.'

This ground-controlled interception and engagement took place at 10,000ft over the English Channel at 16.20hrs and involved a Junkers Ju 88A-1, possibly of *1/KG51* or *3/KG51*. Sgt Holland claimed this Ju 88 as destroyed.

Wednesday 25 September

Shortly after 10.00hrs on the morning of

Wednesday 25 September, 12 Spitfires of No 152 Squadron were patrolling the south coast area near Portland when they were directed by radar controllers at nearby Worth Matravers to intercept a large formation of He 111s apparently making for Yeovil. No 10 Group HQ at Box, Wiltshire, had ordered a total of three fighter squadrons (Nos 152, 238 and 609) to the area but the bombers, which had crossed the coast at Chesil Beach, passed well to the east of Yeovil and headed for the Bristol Aeroplane & Engine Co works at Filton, to the north of Bristol. The force of 57 He 111s of I, II and III *Staffels* of *Kampfgruppe 55* (*KG55*), based at Dreux, Chartres and Villacoublay respectively, to the south and west of Paris, protected by a strong screen of Messerschmitt Bf 110C-4 heavy fighters of *Zerstorergeschwader 26* (*ZG26*) from Arques, five miles southeast of Dieppe, proceeded to drop their deadly cargo of over 100 tons of bombs on the factories, causing 238 casualties among the workers. Having wrought havoc over the defenceless works with little interruption, the German raiders swung to the south and headed for home.

Sgt Kenneth Holland was flying at 20,000ft as Blue 2 with B Flight of No 152 Squadron led by the squadron's CO, Sqn Ldr Peter Devitt (Blue 1). Although Holland was flying almost four miles high, the cramped cockpit of his Spitfire was sweltering and filled with the din from the 12-cylinder Rolls-Royce Merlin engine running at full power just a few feet in front of him. The sound of his breath rasped into the microphone of his oxygen mask. Through the mushy crackle in his headphones came the matter of fact voice of the CO: '100-plus bandits below and to starboard. Let's go and sort them out. Tally-ho!' High over the winding river Avon and flying towards Bath, but some 5,000ft below them, the force of German fighters and bombers droned its way south.

Above:

High over Bath on 25 September, Plt Off Dudley Williams, Green Section leader, started the attack on Hpt Helmut Brandt's Heinkel He111 of KG55 that would cause it to crash minutes later at Woolverton. *A. White*

Above right:

Together, Sgt Kenneth Holland (centre) and Plt Off I.Bayles (right), closed in for the kill on Brandt's badly disabled Heinkel. *via Author/A. White*

One by one the squadron peeled off and dived towards the fleeing bombers. Blue 1 closed in fast on the port stern quarter of a vic of three He 111s. With the safety catch off and the target in his sights he thumbed the fire button: bullets and tracer tore into one of the bombers. Devitt closed to 20yd but he was unable to observe the results of his attack when escaping petrol from his fuel tank, punctured by return fire from the He 111, temporarily blinded him. Uninjured, he managed to force-land his Spitfire at Newton

St Loe on the western outskirts of Bath at 11.55hrs.

Meanwhile, several thousand feet below over Bath, Plt Off Dudley Williams, leader of Green Section, jockeyed for position to attack an He 111P, *Wk Nr* 1525 G1+EP, of *II/KG55* which he had singled out for his attention. This aircraft, based at Chartres, was flown by *Hauptman* Helmut Brandt, *Staffelkapitan* of *6/KG55* (ie: 6th *Staffel*, or squadron, in the IInd *Gruppe*). Before being forced to break off his attack to help deal with the escorting Bf110s of *ZG26*, Williams succeeded in scoring hits in the engines of Brandt's Heinkel. He saw it drop out of formation and sideslip down and away with whisps of smoke trailing from the engines.

The action drifted south towards Frome, leaving the city of Bath beneath a fast-fading swirl of contrails in the sky. Brandt's disabled Heinkel was losing precious height and any chance he may have had of making it safely across the Channel to effect a crash-landing in France was by this stage very slim. Minutes later his hopes were completely dashed as four RAF fighters wheeled in to attack from out

of the sun. The Spitfires of Sgt K.Holland and Plt Off I.Bayles (Black 1), along with two Hurricanes of No 238 Squadron from Middle Wallop, flown by Plt Off J.Urwin-Mann and Sgt R.Little, closed in for the kill.

Holland approached the Heinkel at great speed and overshot, banking into a tight turn before opening fire from about 400yd astern and slightly to port, raking it with the full might of his eight 0.303in Browning machine guns. Bullets smashed into the Heinkel's glazed cockpit, shattering the controls and injuring Brandt in the head, left eye, and all but severing the little finger of his right hand. Struggling along at 2,000ft the bomber rapidly lost height and Brandt, bleeding badly from his head wounds, decided to circle in order to search for a clear space in which to put his stricken aircraft down.

The shattered wreckage of Brandt's Heinkel He111, G1+EP, lies spread over a field near Church Farm at Woolverton. *A. White*

In the meantime, Holland had turned quickly and aligned his Spitfire on the Heinkel's tail for a second attack. However, Brandt's gunner, *Gefreiter* Rudolf Beck, had not been silenced in the first attack and was able to get in a well-aimed burst at close range with his 7.9mm machine gun. The bullets struck home with fatal results: Holland's Spitfire appeared to stop in mid-air before its nose swiftly dropped and the aircraft headed down towards the fields below at Church Farm, Woolverton, four miles north of Frome. *Hauptman* Brandt and two of his crew of four baled out of their

Oberfeldwebel Rudi Kirchoff from Brunswick, Brandt's radio operator died in the crash at Woolverton.
A. White

Below:
He111H, G1+BH of 1/KG55, force-landed at Westfield Farm, Studland, near Swanage, Dorset at 12.10hrs on 25 September. It had been attacked by fighters of Nos 152, 238 and 609 Squadrons in a running fight after bombing Filton. Four of its crew of five survived the ordeal to become PoWs. The white bull on the fuselage side is the insignia of 1/KG55. *A. White*

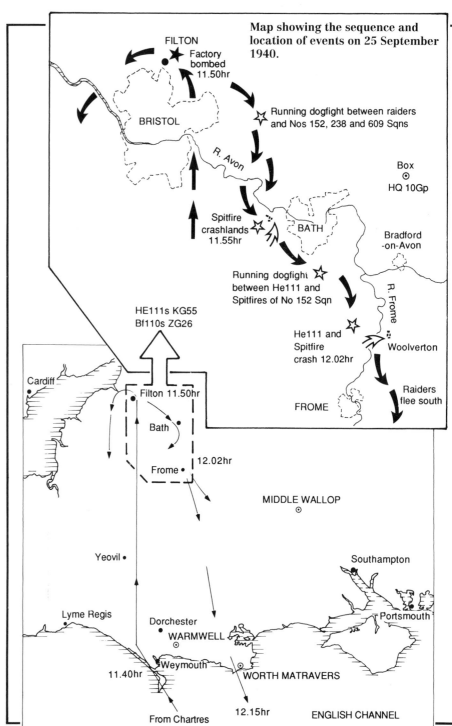

Map showing the sequence and location of events on 25 September 1940.

FILTON
Factory bombed 11.50hr
BRISTOL
R. Avon
Box ⊙ HQ 10Gp
Running dogfight between raiders and Nos 152, 238 and 609 Sqns
Spitfire crashlands 11.55hr
BATH
Bradford -on-Avon
R. Frome
Running dogfight between He111 and Spitfires of No 152 Sqn
He111 and Spitfire crash 12.02hr
Woolverton
Raiders flee south
FROME

HE111s KG55
Bf110s ZG26

Cardiff
Filton 11.50hr
Bath ⊙
Frome ●
12.02hr
MIDDLE WALLOP ⊙

Yeovil ●
Southampton
Portsmouth

Lyme Regis ●
Dorchester ●
WARMWELL ⊙
Weymouth
WORTH MATRAVERS
11.40hr
12.15hr
ENGLISH CHANNEL
From Chartres

wrecked aircraft, leaving it to crash and explode in an adjoining field at 12.02hrs, some 400yd beyond where Holland's Spitfire had come down.

Brandt survived the ordeal but two of his crewmen who jumped too low were killed when their parachutes failed to deploy in time. They were *Oberfeldwebel* Gunter Wittkamp the observer, and *Unteroffizier* Hans Mertz flight engineer. Both radio operator *Oberfeldwebel* Rudi Kirchoff and the gunner *Gefreiter* Rudolf Beck, failed to get out of the aircraft and died in the ensuing inferno. Sgt Holland did not survive either – he was found dead in the cockpit of his Spitfire by villagers.

An eyewitness account by Tom Newman, a local teenager at the time of the event, describes how Holland's Spitfire had crashed in a small field, coming to rest a few yards from the field wall, where

it tipped on its nose with one wheel crumpled beneath it. It is likely Holland was semi-conscious for a short while after being hit because another eyewitness described how the Spitfire's undercarriage had been lowered and it looked as if Holland was going to follow the Heinkel down to the fields and land nearby. A single bullet — coming through a hole in the cockpit canopy, noted by several eyewitnesses after the crash, — must have hit Holland in the head with fatal results; he finally succumbed to his severe head wound and died at the controls of his aircraft as he prepared to land in the field. The Heinkel had disintegrated when it hit the ground and lay in pieces all over a ploughed field.

As if to reinforce the notion that the past is in the present and forever with us, by a strange coincidence the author came

across the dark-green cloth flying helmet belonging to Wittkamp the observer, and the Morse key reputedly from the Heinkel, in a bric-a-brac shop at Glastonbury, Somerset, in September 1992. Inside the helmet, written in ink on one of the ear pieces, was the inscription '*Oberfw* G.Wittkamp. 6.KG55'. On the outside, the thin metal covers to the ear pieces were dented and the paint chipped; the result of Wittkamp's fatal fall, perhaps? The owner of the shop declared that both items had been salvaged in 1940 after the crash by the farmer, Mr Matthews, on whose land the Heinkel had come down. A few months before the author's visit, the farmer's family had passed them on to someone else who, in turn, had sold them to the bric-a-brac shop. Sadly, the inflated price of some £300 asked for the helmet and Morse key together prevented their purchase by the author.

A memorial stone was erected on the spot where Kenneth Holland's Spitfire crashed near to Church Farm, Woolverton. It was later moved to the edge of the field but finally rescued and re-sited next to the village war memorial, where it can be seen to this day. *via Author*

Growing Up in No 10 Group

'Johnny' Johnston was a Geordie and his wartime flying career with Fighter Command was a comparitively long and eventful one. Inevitably known to his friends as 'Johnny', he gained his initial combat experience on Spitfires alongside some of the most famous names that the wartime Command produced. By the time he was grounded late in 1944 he had flown more than 500 hours on Spitfires and Mustangs from airfields in the UK.

His flying career began as a sergeant pilot on Spitfires with No 152 Squadron at Warmwell, Dorset, in the dangerous days of late autumn 1940. From there he was posted with the squadron to Portreath in April 1941 before moving east to join No 92 Squadron at Biggin Hill later that year. There followed a break from operational flying with a spell of instructing at No 61 OTU, Rednal, and at the Central Gunnery School, Sutton Bridge. Then he joined No 234 Squadron prior to D-Day for his second tour, flying in support of the Allied breakout from the Normandy beachhead following the landings on 6 June 1944. He survived a crashlanding in France after being shot down by flak on 14 June, hitching a ride home in Air Chief-Marshal Sir Trafford Leigh-Mallory's personal Dakota. His last sortie was in November 1944 with No 234 Squadron from North Weald on bomber escort duty, flying a Mustang III.

'It was always said that you only remember the good stations because they were mainly the happy ones, and my happy memories were generally quite humorous ones. As far as I was concerned this was indeed true of RAF Warmwell, my first operational airfield, where I grew up very quickly amongst a wonderful crowd of people of all ranks and trades. It was No 152 Squadron that I joined in November 1940 as a sergeant pilot with the huge total of 12½hrs on Spitfires. I'd been trained on Hawker Hart variants followed by a quick trip in a Miles Master where I found the variable pitch airscrew and an undercarriage that could actually be lifted up and down quite a shock to my system.

'Our aircraft were certainly clapped out: they were mainly Spitfire Mk Is and IIs, all with the old pump undercart and the manually-tuned TR9 radios. There were no fancy things for No 10 Group in those days.

'The dispersal atmosphere at Warmwell was marvellous and I was pretty well at home from the beginning. We were not really a very mixed bunch because there were only a few basic types on the squadron: our CO was a time-serving regular as was one flight commander and one other pilot; there were four short service commissioned officers and two officers who had been regular NCO pilots before the war and who had been recalled from the Class A reserve. The other officers were from various University Air Squadrons and who had been given RAFVR commissions. All of the half-dozen or so sergeant pilots were prewar VR. The ground staff were mainly regulars and could only be classed as absolute masters of their trades, especially the NCOs.

'Food in the Officers' Mess was not considered very good at Warmwell, while the Sergeants' Mess was marvellous and fed us like a five-star hotel. On readiness in the afternoons, tea used to be set up at dispersal for the readiness flight and it was strange how many officers just happened to be around at these times doing little odd jobs! We NCOs used to phone down to the Mess and order tea for whatever the number of pilots and we'd be given a very good menu. When the officers' teas arrived they generally comprised of tiny dried up squares of cucumber sandwiches and perhaps a cake of rather indeterminate origin. But when ours arrived there was a tea urn accompanied by a bowl containing plenty of sugar, and lots of sandwiches and salads, sausages and boiled eggs, in sufficient quantity to feed the whole flight. Everyone was there. No wonder there seemed to be more NCOs on our squadron at readiness at any one time than on any other!

'No 609 Squadron were not very lucky in this way. They were in tents over by the old quarry where mud grew better than the grass. Their CO was most upset when the Station Commander refused to allow meals in the Officers' Mess outside normal dining hours. On a fighter squadron this meant that many of his officers missed out on meals.

'But then came the magic day when we got some replacement aircraft which all had that great luxury of luxuries – an automatic undercart. Now, the Station Commander was a bit of a so-and-so who unfortunately used 152's aircraft whenever he wished to fly and we knew that very soon he'd be with us. One sergeant pilot, Jimmy Short, took off to have one or two circuits and try out the new aircraft. So round and round the circuit he went – undercarriage up, undercarriage down, undercarriage up. He was so intent upon this that when he had to come in to let somebody else have a go (we only had about three of them at that time), he came in downwind but he had his undercart down, and crosswind flaps down, then put his undercart up. In all the excitement of this novel feature he'd simply forgotten what was what.

Sgt W. L. H. 'Johnny' Johnston of No 152 (Hyderabad) Squadron, pictured leaning against his Spitfire I at Warmwell in the autumn of 1940.
W.Johnston

No 152 Squadron Faces

Right:
Flt Lt Derek Boitel-Gill – pictured here whilst OC 'A' Flight No 152 Squadron, in autumn 1940 – went on to command the squadron but his flying career was cut brutally short in August 1941 when he was killed in a flying accident. *A. White*

Far right:
Sgts Howard Marsh (left) and Jimmy Short down at the flights, Warmwell, in late 1940. Jimmy Short was shot down on a daylight escort sortie to the French port of Brest on 24 July 1941 where Bomber Command Wellingtons, Hampdens and Fortresses attacked the German cruiser *Prinz Eugen* and battlecruiser *Gneisenau*. The three squadrons of escorting Spitfires found the German fighter opposition was stronger than expected, but Short survived his encounter to become a prisoner-of-war. *W. Johnston*

Above:
Pictured here with Sgt Pilot Edmund Shepperd from the Isle of Wight, the indefatigable Plt Off Pooch, No 152 Squadron's mascot at Warmwell, reputedly sired most of the RAF's bull terriers. Shepperd was a prewar regular who fought with the squadron throughout the Battle of Britain, being credited with four enemy aircraft destroyed. He was killed in a flying accident on 18 October, when his Spitfire inexplicably crashed at Tadnoll Mill near Dorchester. *A. White*

Right:
George White snatches a quick smoke outside No 152 Squadron's dispersal hut at Warmwell in the autumn of 1940. The 'borrowed' sign above him on the hut refers to 'Joe Guppy's Camp' and concerns a local farmer who encouraged prewar campers to use his land near Weymouth. *W. Johnston*

'Fortunately for Jimmy, we were all standing out at dispersal fairly near to the wire, waving and jumping up and down. He spotted us and went round again. But he'd been seen by the Station Commander who was furious and was soon around to our dispersal in his shiny flying boots. He proceeded to give us a blistering lecture about the high cost of new aircraft and made us feel about 6in high. Then off he went just to show us how it should be done. Well, at least that was the intention.

'He came in too low, opened up a little and then carried on as if he was coming in on a deck landing, straight through the barbed wire boundary fence. Then he floated and he floated and obviously his pride just would not allow him to go around again. However, there was one thing he had forgotten: some building contractors were on the aerodrome digging a ditch. Normally there was plenty of room in which to get down, but not if you had floated as he had done. Finally he touched down just a little bit short of the ditch and as his tail came down so did his main wheels – right down into the ditch and there he was lying on his belly.

'The only time I ever recall him setting foot on our dispersal after this episode was during the following spring. We were on a squadron practice formation sortie on a day in early March 1941 when the CO, Sqn Ldr Derek Boitel-Gill – commonly called 'Bottled Gull' – spotted a Hudson down below us escorted by a pair of Hurricanes. It was then that he decided on a piece of real prewar 'bull'. He called us all in tight and then called out for a No 1 attack. We formed up and then on the command down we went in an attack just as if we were at a prewar Hendon air display. We re-formed very tightly and came round to beat up the Hudson and then went merrily on our way.

'When we rejoined the circuit at Warmwell we all noticed a Hudson and some Hurricanes parked on the tarmac. We landed in a tight formation, taxied in and then waited for all the pilots to leave their aircraft before walking in a bunch back to the dispersal hut, discussing the flight. The CO hesitated when he saw an army of brass hats ahead of us waiting outside. One figure stood out from this crowd who we immediately identified as HRH The Duke of Kent. I was standing next to the CO on this occasion when he turned, looked down at me and said: 'Well Johnny, I'll be a flying officer tomorrow. I wonder where that puts you in the line of succession?'

'Naturally, the Station Commander was standing with all the brass hats and it was plain to see he was almost speechless with rage. But quite suddenly he was put firmly in his place and the whole situation was defused when the Duke stepped forward to address the squadron and looked around before he said: "Gentlemen, that was a neat display indeed. Congratulations, I enjoyed it!" And to our relief no more was ever said about it again.'

Sgts Anderson and Howard Marsh after the squadron had moved to Portreath in April 1941. The rudimentary nature of the only building on the airfield at the time of the squadron's arrival is apparent from this photograph. *W. Johnston*

No 152 Squadron converted to the Spitfire IIa in March 1941 and left Warmwell on 19 April 1941 when it was posted in quite a hurry down to the semi-completed airfield of Portreath in Cornwall, situated on the coast some 3½ miles north of Redruth. The airfield had only opened on 7 March and was upgraded in May to become a Sector Station in No 10 Group with satellites at Perranporth and Predannack. Once completed, it was unusual in that it had four tarmac runways.

'At that time we'd never even heard of this place called Portreath and when we got there it was only half-built. On the way down we lost a pilot and didn't even notice he had gone. With no completed runways and no buildings we could move into, we were all accommodated in tents on the clifftop. There was only one solid building and this was used as an office and parachute store. Later on we went into digs in the village which was quite nice.

'During the April blitzes on Plymouth one of our jobs had been to try and catch the morning high-flying Ju88 reconnaissance aircraft which was taking photographs and weather readings for the Luftwaffe's operations on the following night. But he was far too fast for us in our Spitfire IIa's except for one occasion: three of us were scrambled early in the morning from Portreath to try and get up into position to intercept him but one of us had to abort. The other two caught the '88 in and out of cloud near the Eddystone lighthouse and attacked him. Believing we had killed the rear gunner I went in for the second attack and found that we were wrong.

'As I went in for the kill a face appeared at the gun position which had been empty. I'm sure something was thrown out of the Ju88 just as I opened fire so I broke off to port and diving down quite steeply I felt a bit of a jolt. My prop stopped and I kept on diving to gain some speed, in the hope of either restarting my dead engine or even climbing back up to gain a bit of height. When Sgt White, the remaining pilot, came in to make his attack the '88 was heading for home at a speed he couldn't match. But neither could he see me nor raise me on the R/T.

'In the meantime my engine had refused to restart and so I had glided down to make a safe landing just off Roborough's [Plymouth airport] boundary, where in due course I walked in to flying control. The telephones were not working so I was unable to contact my squadron at Portreath to notify them of my safety and whereabouts. In any case, after several nights of heavy bombing there was far too much going on in the city for anyone to bother about just another pilot, so I went out onto the road and hitched a lift which took me to the top end of Plymouth up by Mutley Plain. I walked down to the station with my chute slung over my shoulder. There were no trains; there was hardly any station. But there were some buses running. By bus and lorry I got along to Par where I managed to pick up a train going westwards.

'I didn't get back to base until about 10.30pm and I wandered into our digs to be greeted by George White with "where the hell have you been?".'

Pictured here in the cockpit of his Spitfire I at Warmwell in 1941, Sgt George White was destined to be shot down and killed near Eindhoven, Holland, later that year. Note the squadron's adoption name 'Hyderabad' on the fuselage side. *W. Johnston*

Daylight Bomber Escort

Johnny transferred to No 92 Squadron at Biggin Hill and on 3 October 1941 he was one of eight pilots from the Biggin Hill Wing detailed to provide a bomber escort. Their charges were six Blenheims of No 2 Group Bomber Command who were mounting a daylight raid against a power station near Ostend. All the Blenheims returned safely home but Johnny came close to losing out against a gaggle of Messerschmitt Bf109Fs.

'Coming out from the target there was a very bad mix-up. No 609 Squadron should have executed a normal turn to remain in the same relative position to us when we turned around to come back down the coast, but instead they did a cross-over turn which actually put them in front of us. We were flying in two fours, each in line-astern: in one section was the CO, Sgt Woods-Scawen, Sgt Kingaby and Sgt Cox; I was flying in the other section as No 3 behind 'Chips' Carpenter.

'I checked up and saw a gaggle of fighters above us and to port which I believed to be Spitfires of '609. I had a quick check all around and I was absolutely shattered to see about 30 Bf109Fs and possibly a few FW190s pouring down out of the sun, and '609 were on the wrong side. As far as we were concerned they were out of position.

'Working on the old premise that the worse the language and the louder the voice meant a real emergency, I gave the warning the full works. As I gave it I broke and the others followed smartly. Out of the corner of my eye I saw Don Kingaby on my left breaking violently up and round and back into the gaggle. He was only just in time because his No 2 and No 4 went down at once to the guns of the '109s; had he not broken when he did he would have been sandwiched and would have gone down with them. Sgt Cox lost his tail and was on fire as he disappeared downwards. Woods-Scawen shed pieces of his Spitfire on the way down.

'It transpired later that Don Kingaby's radio had gone U/S quite early on but he had stayed with us to keep up the numbers, seeing there were only eight of us. He decided he would keep his eyes on me because he knew that when I broke he

would break (my sense of self-preservation was rather acute at that time, like his).

'I felt and heard some hits on my aircraft behind me so I didn't fancy hanging around on my own and so I set off at a steady speed, not being sure of what damage my aircraft had suffered. However, the Luftwaffe had decided otherwise and I found myself being overhauled by a gaggle of '109s which formed up behind me in an arc. It looked as if the leader in the middle was being covered by the rest to allow him to take the kill – a practice that was apparently adopted by the Luftwaffe to build up aces.

'They sat behind me so I couldn't turn around or turn away. I was getting gradually lower and lower in the sky; if I tried to turn, a swift burst of gunfire every now and then from my pursuers kept turning me back on track. I'd got to the point where I decided that the next run-in with

my assailants would have to be the last because by now I was right down on the deck.

'Suddenly I was aware of a lone Spitfire coming in from starboard, screaming right along the line of '109s, dropping two of them straight into the water before they even saw him. It climbed away and turned back to come in again and while the '109s were in disarray, the Spitfire came down past me. I saw it was Don Kingaby who was waving madly and pointing to his ears and mouth so I knew his R/T was out. He put his thumb down and waved me home, then turned away again and went back up amongst the '109s.

'Johnny' Johnston in the cockpit of his No 92 Squadron Spitfire Vb at Biggin Hill in July 1941. *W.Johnston*

'I got back to Gravesend alright but found only another three of us had made it back. While we were standing giving our stories in to the old 'Spy' [Sqn Ldr de la Torre, Station Intelligence Officer at Biggin Hill] another aircraft chugged over the hedge sounding very rough. It was 'Chips' Carpenter, fairly well holed. He didn't realise he had been shot through the calf of his leg in the skirmish until an airman asked him where the blood on his flying boots had come from. That made five back safely, two lost, one missing and strayed, from our Wing effort. But then we got a call from Manston saying Don Kingaby was down there, he was OK and would be coming back in 10mins or so. Once he had returned and we had examined his Spitfire, it was evident that the top surface of his wings had actually sprung a few rivets due to the violent manoeuvring with the 109s. His second bar to his DFM came through very quickly after this and I've always felt it was mainly due to his actions in saving me on that day.'

Growing Up Amongst The Aces

Above:
No 92 Squadron's veterans of the Battle of Britain at Biggin Hill, seen here late in 1940. From left to right, are: Flg Off Tony Bartley, Flg Off Alan Wright, Flt Lt Brian Kingcome, with Flg Off Garland at the rear. The first three of these pilots achieved ace status during World War 2 and were each credited with the following kills: Tony Bartley 15, Brian Kingcome 11, Alan Wright nine. All three survived the war.
W. Johnston

Right:
A gun camera sequence showing a Messerschmitt Bf109F being destroyed by an RAF Spitfire pilot. *via Chaz Bowyer*

Below:
The log book page giving details of the disastrous bomber escort sortie of 3 October 1941. *W. Johnston*

Flak Clipped My Wings

Following a spell instructing, Johnny returned to operations on clipped-wing Spitfire Vbs with No 234 Squadron at Deanland, an Advanced Landing Ground in Kent. On D-Day, the squadron provided low cover over the Normandy beaches and escorted the Stirling, Halifax and Albemarle tugs and gliders of No 38 Group to their drop zones. From 6 June onwards, No 234 Squadron flew a pattern of fairly uneventful fighter sweeps from Deanland over the Normandy beachhead with the task of preventing any low-level enemy air attacks on Allied ground forces. In common with the other squadrons similarly tasked, they were not authorised to make any 'freelance' low-level attacks on so-called soft targets, but on occasions the rules were bent to liven things up a little. On D+8, 14 June, things suddenly became much more eventful for Johnny, as he recalls:

'We took off from Deanland at about 1.30pm to go over on beachhead cover and we started our patrol along a line roughly between Bayeux and Caen, just north of the main road, at a height of about 1,500ft. On the second run along the line someone reported on the R/T they had seen something below us that appeared to be different from on our first run. When we turned to come back on the westward leg we opened out a little bit so we could cover more ground.

'According to Operations back at Deanland (which was Army Intelligence), if anything came up we were to chase it because, in their words, we were 'expendable' – which wasn't very nice to think. We thought that we were over our own lines at this time, and according to the map and with the marker of the road, we certainly were. We didn't see anything but quite suddenly, without any warning at all, I got hit.

'I assume it was a very near miss because it was from an 88mm ground battery and you don't got hit by one of those and stay airborne. The shell burst just underneath my starboard wingtip and blew the aircraft some 200ft upwards. I was flying a clipped-wing Mk Vb and the burst took off another 2ft of wingtip, blowing the wing up from the exposed end like a paper bag, leaving the aileron dangling by a piece of wire.

'The aircraft was thrown bodily up into the air by the blast and I half-rolled it to port. While I was on my back I caught a split-second glimpse of the extent of the damage, but then almost immediately another burst caught me directly beneath the port wing close to the wing root, loosening the studs on the port and top engine cowlings and smashing the cockpit hood.

Missing Presumed Killed

Twenty-two year-old Flt Sgt Dennis J.Sims of No 234 Squadron was killed on D-Day, 6 June 1944, returning to Deanland from a beachhead patrol. His aircraft may have disintegrated in mid-air after being hit by flak, or plunged into the sea. Sadly, Sims has no known grave but his name is commemorated on the Commonwealth Air Forces Memorial at Runnymede, Surrey. Sims was brought up in Braintree, Essex and achieved distinction in the Scouting movement as a King's Scout, before joining the RAF to train as a pilot.
W. Johnston

The side door was forced open at the front of the runner, the Perspex was all smashed and the windscreen was starred. Something had grazed the right hand side of my flying helmet above the ear piece, but luckily without injuring me.

'By this time my prop had stopped and I was coming round in the roll. Then yet another burst took the radiator out along with a huge square of skin above it in the top of the port wing. I couldn't get out of the cockpit because the hood had jammed closed and I could only fly the aircraft with both hands and the stick right over to port as far as it would go. At one point I even cocked my leg over the stick to get the aircraft into the turn and keep it there.

'I was now coming down in a flat screaming turn. Funnily enough my pitot head was still working and I had about 200 on the clock. I had made a mental note of a flattish line on the ground from previous trips over the area, which I identified as a rough landing strip and now I aimed to try and put my aircraft down on it.

'All this time the aircraft was trying to tear itself back over to starboard and this proved very heavy on my arms as I tried to keep it pointing roughly in the direction of the flat strip I had seen. I overestimated my position a little but when I was over a hedgerow at the edge of the strip I allowed the controls to centralise a little before I thumped the Spit down on the ground at about 180 IAS and everything went haywire.

'The aircraft broke its back and my right hand shoulder strap snapped under the force of the impact, causing me to thump forward into the gunsight – fortunately, of course, through the hood having been jammed, I still had my goggles down which saved me from a potentially serious facial injury. Amazingly, I didn't even get a black eye, but what I did have was the feeling of a lot of fluid pouring down over my face and for quite some minutes afterwards I thought that I'd lost my right eye.

'I got the shock of my life when, through my blurred vision, a crowd of people dressed in khaki battle dress arrived around my aircraft. They were wrenching away trying to get the hood open and finally tore the damned thing

off, opened the door and hauled me out. It was then I heard a broad Geordie voice saying to me: "By Christ, man, ye haven't half been hit!"

'"God almighty," I thought, "I'm home or I'm dead." I struggled up from the cockpit and they helped me out and over the wing, frightened all the time that the aircraft would blow up.

'Two more pilots from the squadron, one from my flight, had also been hit by the salvo that had clobbered me, but they had been a little more fortunate. One of them, Flt Sgt Joe Fargher, brought his damaged aircraft in with its wheels down, although it did tip up on its nose and he grazed his forehead. The other aircraft flown by Flg Off Bill Painter came in on its wheels without too much trouble.

'The airfield we had landed on was at Coulombs, about 2 miles on the coast side of the Bayeux-Caen road along which we had been patrolling. It was occupied by a crowd from the Airfield Construction Unit to build what was eventually to be B6 Airfield (Coulombs/Cully). The CO of the construction unit fixed a car for us, complete with driver and Bren gun sticking out of the top, and away we drove towards the coast.

'In some of the villages along our route, because of the colour of our uniforms, the locals mistook us for German prisoners under the supervision of the Army driver who was in khaki. One or two even spat at us as we drove past. We also had a few frights along the way because the airstrip we had landed at was at the extreme front of the Allied advance and virtually surrounded by Germans. At one point in our journey there was an awful clanking sound and we weren't sure if there was something wrong with the car until, away to our right, a German halftrack emerged from a wood and drove across a field towards us. We slammed the brakes on and didn't know what to do until all of a

sudden a figure, dressed in the uniform of a British paratrooper, emerged from the hedgerows beside the road and told us not to panic. He explained that he and his lads had just captured the halftrack after a firefight and were driving it away.

'Eventually we arrived at the map reference given to us earlier on by the Army at the airstrip. Here was a huge concentration of tents, vehicles and people milling around all over the place. A wood nearby concealed a battery of 4.5in guns firing away like mad and the noise was terrific. After asking for directions we eventually found a tent from where an Air Cdre Montgomery emerged. He was rather nonplussed to see three RAF pilots in an Army car, complete with parachutes, and he was even more intrigued when I told him our story. He said he couldn't help us or give us any transport (our Army driver was only allowed to take us this far) but with a quizzical look he offered to write out a form to help us on our way. We suggested that our Army driver go and get some food and whilst he was gone we refuelled the car and set off without him

in the direction of the coast, taking it in turns to drive.

'We followed the directions given to us and in due course we arrived at a crossroads where we were waved across by SPs, bypassing huge convoys of trucks. Then we heard the unmistakable sound of aircraft. Quite suddenly, from driving along a country lane bordered by hedges, we emerged onto an airfield. There was a Dakota in front of us and a lot of people standing around it so we drove towards them. I was standing up on the seat of the car at this time, manning the Bren gun, and I noticed an awful lot of brass hats in evidence. There were Army and RAF Regiment personnel everywhere, armed to the teeth. I kicked Fargher to stop and then a burly figure detached himself from the group and walked over to us. He was absolutely furious and started to tear me off an awful strip, then he caught his breath and bawled:

'Do you know who I am and do you know where you are?'

'I'd recognised him by this time and said: "Yes Sir, I know who you are. You're Harry Broadhurst."

'I forgot to give him his rank which he didn't like [Air Vice-Marshal, AOC No 83 Group, 2 TAF], but he was gratified to learn that I actually knew who he was and for this reason he deemed us to be alright.

'It was at this point that another person detached himself from the group of brass hats and walked towards us with a retinue in tow. This, to my great surprise, was Sir Trafford Leigh-Mallory himself

Copy of the actual handwritten pass given to 'Johnny' to ease his journey back to the UK. *W. Johnston*

> To. Flying Control B2
> or. 102 Sub Area HQ. 974849.
>
> Flt. Johnston 234 Sqn. 149 Wing.
> F/O Painter —— "
> A/Sgt Fargher —— "
>
> are returning to UK to rejoin their unit.
> Please help.
>
> 14 June.
> att Montgomery
> A/Cdre.
> AOA. 83 gp.

YEAR 1944		AIRCRAFT		PILOT, OR 1ST PILOT	2ND PILOT, PUPIL OR PASSENGER	DUTY (INCLUDING RESULTS AND REMARKS)
MONTH	DATE	Type	No.			
JUNE	7	SPITFIRE VB	BL415 B	SELF	—	TOTALS BROUGHT FORWARD — Cannon Test etc after inspection
"	8	"	—	"	"	Beach Head cover.
"	10	"	B	"	"	Beach Head cover
"	"	"	B	"	"	Beach Head patrol
"	11	"	B	"	"	Beach Head cover
"	12	"	B	"	"	Beach Head patrol
"	13	"	B	"	"	Beach Head patrol
"	14	"	B	"	"	Beach Head Cover.
"	15	DAKOTA	BJ170	S/Lr Jones	SELF	Life back to England (with the Boss himself)
"	16	DOMINIE	?	W/O Smith	SELF etc.	from Thorny Island to Deanland
"	15	SPITFIRE	BM417 B	SELF		Beach Head Cover.
"	16	"	"	"	"	Beach Head Cover - Freelance
"	17	"	"	"	"	Beach Head Cover - Freelance
"	"	"	"	"	"	Beach Head Cover.
"	"	"	—	"	"	Beach Head Cover.
"	18	"	J	"	"	Beach Head Cover
"	"	"	B	"	"	Beach Head Cover
"	19	"	B	"	"	To Predannock
"	21	"	B	"	"	Shipping Recco
"	23	"	B	"	"	Shipping Recco
"	24	"	I	"	"	Patrol Charlie
"	27	"	B	"	"	Rhubarb
"	30	"	B	"	"	Shipping Recco (Bombs!)

Multi-engine / single-engine totals columns:

SINGLE-ENGINE AIRCRAFT DAY DUAL	PILOT	MULTI-ENGINE DAY DUAL	PILOT	NIGHT 1ST PILOT	2ND PILOT	NIGHT DUAL	1ST PILOT	Remarks	PASS-ENGER	INSTR/CLOUD DUAL	PILOT
87.55	999.10 4.35	20.10	.10		1.20				9.45	15.20	49.30
	.20										
	2.35					Low beach cover / assault area. & inland					
	2.25					& inland sweep					
			1.45			Western beaches & Caen area					
	.40		1.30			Dawn					
	.40		1.30			Dawn					
	1.10					Hit by Flak (aileron - rad + oil) crash landed France (Coulombs)					
						Reached B2 a/f via Adv HQ, 83 Gp HQ. (see line!)			.50		
						Home again.			.35		
	2.15					Not bad going - back home & over again in less than 24 hrs.					
	2.30										
	2.35										
	2.10										
			2.10			Dusk? } Damned silly black Lost P/O Painter by			15		
	.40		1.10			Dawn? } own Flak over Brighton.					
	2.40										
	1.30					Lost Sgt Henderson.					
	1.00					Weather U/s.					
	1.30									10		
	1.20										
	1.45					Vannes etc - Fired at Bridge & two Radar Aerial.					
	1.10					Dropped 1 x 500 lbs on Radar Station in Ushant - MISSED it!!					
87.55	1030.30 4.35	28.15	.10		1.20				11.10	15.20	49.55

GRAND TOTAL [Cols. (1) to (10)] 1152 Hrs. 45 Mins. TOTALS CARRIED FORWARD

Johnny's log book page for the day he was shot down over Normandy.
W. Johnston

[Air Chief-Marshal Sir Trafford Leigh-Mallory, AOC-in-C Allied Expeditionary Air Force] who was extremely intrigued. He could see that Harry Broadhurst was losing his temper so he smoothed things over as we told him what had happened to us, and all that we wanted to do was to get the hell out of it and back to England. The Press corps were also there which meant that this was too good a publicity opportunity to miss and Leigh-Mallory, seeing this, turned things to his advantage. We were taken over to stand outside the Dakota where photographs were taken of us and some beers thrust into our hands. Leigh-Mallory milked the situation for the publicity it generated – downed RAF fighter pilots simply itching to get back home to fly again. By this stage all we wanted to do was to go home.

'We climbed on board the Dakota and it was not long afterwards that we were down at Thorney Island – not bad at all in the time we had been airborne, shot down, and so on. Once Leigh-Mallory and his entourage had left the aircraft they were whisked off back to London, the attitude of all the administration people suddenly changed. They couldn't care less about us now.

'In the Officers' Mess that evening at Thorney Island, with Joe Fargher masquerading as a pilot officer, the three of us listened in to the news on the wireless that "three of our aircraft have been lost today, but the pilots are believed to be safe". Next morning we were ferried back to Deanland in a Dominie, where we told our story once again to the intelligence people and by that afternoon, some 23 hours after I'd been shot down, I was back over France again. I looked down to see the wreckage of my aircraft that by now had been pushed to the edge of the airstrip beside a hedge.'

Sadly, Bill Painter was killed on 17 June by 'friendly' flak over Brighton, returning from a fighter sweep over the beachhead in the Bayeux area. His body was washed up several weeks later. Joe Fargher was shot down again over France the next month and escaped to England with the help of the Maquis, only to be shot down again several months later over the Channel flying a Mustang. He was fortunate to be rescued by an airborne lifeboat which was dropped to him, and he survived the war.

North Weald

At the end of August No 234 Squadron moved north to North Weald in Essex, a Sector Station in No 11 Group ADGB. On 29 September, the squadron relinquished its Spitfire Vbs and in their place received its first few North American Mustang IIIs (P-51C):

'I'd flown the original Mustang Mk I whilst at the Central Gunnery School at Sutton Bridge, and I wasn't very

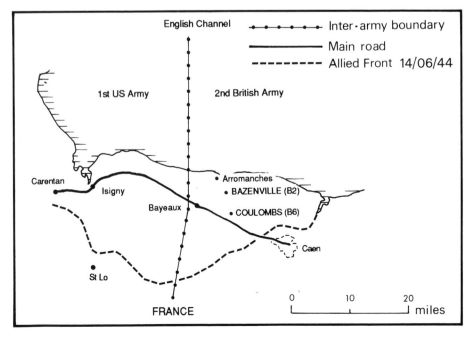

Map to illustrate the location of the events of 14 June 1944, as described by 'Johnny' Johnston.

impressed. But the Mk III was a lovely aircraft to fly, although these ones were hand-me-downs from a Polish squadron and a little bit clapped. We changed the original American R/T harness and throat mics to the standard RAF fit then spent the first couple of weeks in October getting some practice in.

'Operations in the Mustang were completely different to the Spitfire. We were actually going into Germany now, taking Halifaxes and Lancs out to Cologne, Duisberg, Essen, Bonn and Frankfurt in trips lasting up to 3 hours 25 minutes each, which was quite a change from what we'd been used to and a fairly long time when you were strapped in. We flew some of these escorts at 30,000ft and on one occasion we were in open formation at 40,000ft escorting Mosquitoes, coming up to the RV point, when right up through the middle of our wide formation a V2 came up. It looked as thin as a telegraph pole in the split second I saw it before it disappeared from view with a white wobbly trail streaming behind it.

'My last operational trip was to escort Lancasters to Homburg on 2 November 1944. I was then promoted to squadron leader and posted to Manston as Sector Gunnery Officer.'

From then on Johnny moved around a fair bit. He was on the point of being posted to the Far East where he had a squadron of Tempests at Trincomalee nicely lined up for him. Then down went the Atom bomb. Transferring to Transport Command, he was posted to a conversion unit in the Middle East as CFI to convert RAF crews to fly American aircraft that needed returning home under the terms of Lend-Lease. Several months later he was promoted to station commander before resigning his commission as a regular in July 1946, although he remained an officer in the VR until 1959.

Below:
'Johnny' Johnston flew Mustang IIIs on bomber escort sorties with No 234 Squadron from North Weald between August and November 1944. Illustrated are Mustang IIIs of No 19 Squadron. *via Chaz Bowyer*

Pilots, adjutant, intelligence officer and senior ground staff of No 234 Squadron, North Weald, in late 1944. Of the 13 pilots shown here, six were dead or missing within three months of this picture being taken. *W. Johnston*

Above:
On one sortie escorting Mosquitoes, Johnny witnessed from 40,000ft over Holland the launch of a German V2 rocket as it hurtled up through his open formation, bound for London. *via Author*

A Decaying Legacy

During World War 2, Charmy Down and Warmwell were both busy satellite airfields in Fighter Command's No 10 Group, the former to Colerne and the latter to Middle Wallop. Both parent stations have survived into the 1990s, albeit under control of the Army, but their satellites have fared less well. Perched high on a hill north of the city of Bath, the former nightfighter airfield of Charmy Down is now derelict, the runways torn up and the hangars demolished; the former dayfighter airfield of Warmwell east of Dorchester, has been carved from the face of the map by extensive quarrying and housing development, although a handful of hangars and ancillary buildings remain as a mute testimony to the great things it once was part of.

Charmy Down, Somerset

Above:
At more than 680ft above sea level, Charmy Down airfield is virtually invisible from the A46 road below and successfully conceals from prying eyes what little remains of its historic past.
Author

Left:
The derelict brick watchtower stands on the northwest corner of the airfield and is used by the local farmer for storing hay. For a short period after the war it was used as a private dwelling.
Author

Left:
Today, the view through the watchtower's rusting and glassless windows is not one of Hurricanes turning into the wind at the runway threshold, or Turbinlite Havocs thundering along the runway, but of rough pasture and the occasional ponderous tractor. *Author*

Below:
Airfield defences were coordinated from an underground Battle Headquarters with an observation cupola just above the surface. A horizontal slit gave the occupants a 360° view of the airfield. At Charmy Down this cupola is situated adjacent to the watchtower. *Author*

Bottom:
Once the scene of much feverish activity geared to winning a war, the few ancillary buildings still left standing are gradually succumbing to the ravages of time and nature. *Author*

Warmwell, Dorset

Above left:
A new housing estate has been built on the site of the old camp area at Warmwell, the principal reminder of its wartime rôle being a memorial stone in the middle of the estate, erected in 1989. The rest of the airfield has been almost completely erased from the landscape by extensive quarrying. *Author*

Above:
Adjacent to a mobile home park which also occupies part of the old camp area, this is one of just a handful of Warmwell's wartime buildings still left standing, overgrown by nature, derelict and forlorn. *Author*

Centre left:
A handful of wartime T2 hangars and Romney huts are still standing and in good condition, used for agricultural purposes. *Author*

Bottom left:
This is one of two concrete dispersal pans on the northside of the airfield perimeter road, close to the old watchtower. The roar of the Merlin engines has long since faded into the ether, replaced by nothing more than the gentle sounds of the Dorset countryside. *Author*

Warmwell's watchtower has been successfully converted into a private dwelling, although its origins still are plain to see. *Author*

Holy Trinity churchyard, Warmwell, is the last resting place for a number of airmen from Warmwell and other aerodromes further afield. Two victims of the furious struggles in the high summer of 1940 lie side by side at peace in the grassy precincts of the church. Left, Sgt Sidney Wakeling was killed on 25 August when his No 87 Squadron Hurricane, based at Exeter, was shot down in flames during a combat over Portland, his aircraft crashing near Dorchester. Right, Sqn Ldr Terence Lovell-Gregg, OC No 87 Squadron, was shot down and killed in combat over Lyme Bay on 25 August. His Hurricane crashed near Warmwell airfield. *Author*

Appendix I

RAF Fighter Command Headquarters and Air Officer Commanders-in-Chief 1939-45

A Brief Résumé of the Command Structure

Fighter Command's basic organisational structure can be split up as follows into Headquarters RAF Fighter Command set in overall control above Groups, Sectors and Squadrons. The Fighter Command Operations room at Bentley Priory was used mainly for organising reinforcement from one Group to another.

The Groups under the command of an air vice-marshal were arranged in a geographical pattern, each Group covering a particular area of the UK. Each Group was subdivided into Sectors, which comprised a number of fighter stations, satellites and Forward Operating Bases (FOBs), with one station selected as the Sector Station under the command of a group captain. The Group Operations Rooms allocated squadrons to counter a particular raid and generally speaking had a broader picture of events than the Sector Operations Rooms.

Each Fighter Sector was assigned a number of Squadrons which it controlled through its Operations Room. Here the Sector Controller could watch the movements of raids in his area and have radio control of his fighters. During the Battle of Britain period this could number between two and four squadrons, while later in the war the numbers increased and could number six or more.

A Squadron, commanded by a squadron leader or wing commander, could number some 16 aircraft and 20 pilots, plus ground crew of non-commissioned officers and airmen to maintain the aircraft. Each aircraft had its own dedicated airframe rigger and engine fitter whilst the other necessary technical trades like armourers, electricians, instrument technicians and wireless mechanics were allocated to each flight and not to any particular aircraft.

Each Squadron was split into two Flights, 'A' and 'B', each led by a Flight Commander, usually of flight lieutenant rank. Each Flight was further subdivided (when each Flight was operating at the full strength of six aircraft) into three-aircraft Sections identified by a colour-code as follows: 'A' Flight – Red and Yellow sections; 'B' Flight – Blue and Green sections. For example, Green 1 would be leading the second section of 'B' Flight, with Green 2 to his right and Green 3 to his left.

Headquarters

Formed 14/7/36 at Bentley Priory, Stanmore, Middx

Air Officer Commanders-in-Chief (with dates of appointment)

AM H.C.T Dowding – 14/07/36
AM W. Sholto Douglas – 25/11/40
AM T. Leigh-Mallory – 28/11/42
AM R.M Hill – 15/11/43
AM J.M Robb – 14/05/45
(Fighter Command was retitled Air Defence of Great Britain (ADGB) wef 15/11/43; it was retitled Fighter Command again wef 15/10/44)

NO 9 GROUP HEADQUARTERS (NW Midlands)

Formed 09/08/40 at Barton Hall, Preston, Lancashire
(Disbanded summer 1944)

Air Officers Commanding (with dates of appointment)

AVM W.A McClaughry – 16/09/40
AVM J.W. Jones – 10/11/42
AVM L.N. Hollinghurst – 02/07/43
AVM D.F. Stevenson – 07/12/43

NO 10 GROUP (West)

Formed 01/06/40 at Rudloe Manor, Box, Wilts
(Disbanded 04/45)

Air Officers Commanding (with dates of appointment)

AVM C.J.Q. Brand – 15/06/40
AVM A.H. Orlebar – 22/07/41
AVM W.F. Dickson – 04/11/42
AVM C.R. Steele – 05/05/43
Air Cdre A.V. Harvey – 0-3/06/44
AVM J.B. Cole-Hamilton – 10/07/44

NO 11 GROUP (South)

Formed 14/07/36 at Hillingdon House, Uxbridge, Middx

Air Officers Commanding (with dates of appointment)

AVM P.B. Joubert de la Ferte – 14/07/36
AVM E.L.Gossage – 07/09/36
AVM K. Park – 20/04/40
AVM T. Leigh-Mallory – 18/12/40
AVM H.W.L. Saunders – 28/11/42
AVM J.B. Cole-Hamilton – 01/11/44

NO 12 GROUP HEADQUARTERS (Midlands)

Formed 14/07/36 at Watnall, Notts

Air Officers Commanding (with dates of appointment)

AVM T. Leigh-Mallory – 04/12/37
AVM R.E. Saul – 17/12/40
AVM J.O. Andrews – 29/11/42
AVM R.M. Hill – 26/07/43
AVM M. Henderson – 22/11/43
AVM J.W. Baker – 01/01/45

NO 13 GROUP HEADQUARTERS (North)

Formed 24/07/39 at Hucknall, Notts;
Blakelaw Estate, Ponteland Rd, Newcastle-on-Tyne;
Drummossie Hotel, Inverness

Air Officers Commanding (with dates of appointment)

AVM R.E. Saul – 24/07/39
AVM J.O. Andrews – 04/02/41
AVM M. Henderson – 27/11/42
Air Cdre J.A. Boret – 26/01/44-07/05/45

NO 14 GROUP HEADQUARTERS (Scotland, Orkneys, Shetlands)

Formed 20/07/40 at Drummossie Hotel, Inverness
(Later amalgamated with No 13 Group)

Air Officers Commanding (with dates of appointment)

AVM M. Henderson – 20/07/40
AVM J.H. D'Albiac – 10/02/41
AVM R. Collishaw – 21/03/42

NO 22 (ARMY CO-OPERATION) GROUP HEADQUARTERS

Formed 01/07/36 at Farnborough, Hants
(Became Army Co-operation Command on 20/11/40)

Air Officers Commanding (with dates of appointment)

AVM B.E. Sutton – 01/07/36
AM A.S. Barratt – 20/11/40

NO 38 (AIRBORNE FORCES) GROUP HEADQUARTERS

Formed 15/01/42 at Netheravon, Salisbury, Wilts, as No 38 Wing under operational control of Army Co-operation Command;
06/43 – Transferred to Fighter Command control with disbandment of Army Co-operation Command;
10/43 – Reformed as No 38 Group under ADGB control;
10/44 – Marks Hall, Coggeshall, Colchester, Essex

Air Officers Commanding (with dates of appointment)

Air Cdre N. Norman – 15/01/42
Air Cdre W.H. Primrose – 05/43
AVM L.N. Hollinghurst – 06/11/43
AVM J.R. Scarlett-Streatfield – 18/10/44

NO 70 (TRAINING) GROUP HEADQUARTERS

Formed 11/42 at South Farnborough, Hants

Air Officers Commanding (with dates of appointment)

Gp Capt H.R. McL.Reid – 28/11/42 (SASO – acting as AOC)
Air Cdre H.B. Russell – 12/07/43

NO 81 (OTU) GROUP HEADQUARTERS

Formed 12/40 at Autumn Avenue, Worcester

02/42 – Avening, Stroud, Glos
(Disbanded 05/43 and OTU responsibilities assumed by No 9 Gp)

Air Officers Commanding (with dates of appointment)

Air Cdre F.J. Vincent – 16/12/40
Air Cdre W.H. Dunn – 29/07/42

NO 82 GROUP HEADQUARTERS

Formed 21/07/41 at Belfast, NI
(Later amalgamated with No 9 Gp)

Air Officer Commanding (with date of appointment)

Air Cdre G.M. Lawson – 21/07/41

NO 88 (FIGHTER) GROUP HEADQUARTERS

Formed 07/05/45 at Kinellan House, Murrayfield Road, Edinburgh

Air Officer Commanding (with date of appointment)

AVM J.A. Boret – 07/05/45

2nd Tactical Air Force

Headquarters and Air Officer Commanders-in-Chief

Headquarters

Formed 01/06/43 at Bracknell, Berks

Air Officer Commanders-in-Chief (with dates of appointment)

AM J.H. D'Albiac – 01/06/43
AM A. Coningham – 21/01/44

NO 83 (COMPOSITE) GROUP HEADQUARTERS

Formed 05/43 at Gatton Park, Reigate, Surrey
06/44 – Gatwick, Surrey

Air Officers Commanding (with dates of appointment)

AVM W.F. Dickson – 05/43
AVM H. Broadhurst – 25/03/44

NO 84 (COMPOSITE) GROUP HEADQUARTERS

Formed 09/43 at Cowley Barracks, Oxford
06/44 – Chichester

Air Officers Commanding (with dates of appointment)

AVM L.O. Brown – 10/11/43
AVM E.C. Hudleston – 10/11/44

NO 85 (BASE) GROUP HEADQUARTERS

Formed 02/44 at Uxbridge, Middx

Air Officers Commanding (with dates of appointment)

AVM J.B. Cole-Hamilton — 13/02/44
AVM C.R. Steele — 10/07/44
AVM D.A. Boyle – 26/04/45

Appendix II

RAF Fighter Command and Air Defence of Great Britain, Home-based Frontline Unit Strengths 1939-45

The Frontline Groups

At the outbreak of war in September 1939, Fighter Command's frontline force consisted of 31 home-based squadrons, equipped as follows: 14 Hurricane, eight Spitfire, seven Blenheim, one Spitfire/Gladiator, and one Gladiator. They were divided between three Groups and concentrated at 14 airfields in the South, East Midlands, Yorkshire and Scotland.

No 11 Group covered the southeastern counties of Sussex, Kent, Surrey, Middlesex and Essex, and controlled 19 squadrons; No 12 Group covered the Midlands and Yorkshire with nine squadrons; No 13 Group, formed less than two months before the outbreak of war, covered the North of England and Scotland with only three squadrons.

The Orders of Battle that follow show how, from small beginnings, Fighter Command grew not only into a powerful defensive – but also an offensive – force. If we look at the table for March 1943, it is clear to see how the Command had grown: it could then field some 100 frontline squadrons operating from over 50 airfields across the UK.

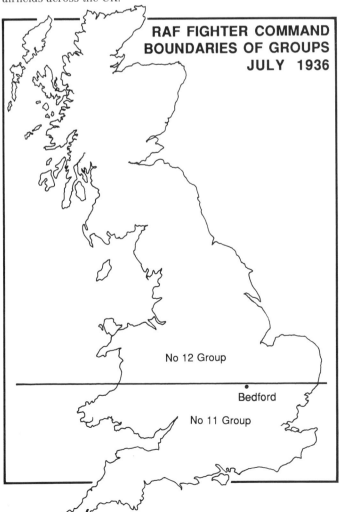

RAF FIGHTER COMMAND
BOUNDARIES OF GROUPS
JULY 1936

No 12 Group

Bedford

No 11 Group

3 September 1939

No 11 Group, HQ: Hillingdon House, Uxbridge, Middx

1 Sqn	Tangmere	Hurricane I
43 Sqn	Tangmere	Hurricane I
501 Sqn	Filton	Hurricane I
3 Sqn	Croydon	Hurricane I
17 Sqn	Croydon	Hurricane I
615 Sqn	Croydon	Gladiator I
601 Sqn	Biggin Hill	Blenheim If
54 Sqn	Hornchurch	Spitfire I
65 Sqn	Hornchurch	Spitfire I
74 Sqn	Hornchurch	Spitfire I
25 Sqn	Northolt	Blenheim If
111 Sqn	Northolt	Hurricane I
600 Sqn	Northolt	Blenheim If
56 Sqn	North Weald	Hurricane I
151 Sqn	North Weald	Hurricane I
604 Sqn	North Weald	Blenheim If
29 Sqn	Debden	Blenheim If
85 Sqn	Debden	Hurricane I
87 Sqn	Debden	Hurricane I

No 12 Group, HQ: Watnall, Notts

66 Sqn	Duxford	Spitfire I
611 Sqn	Duxford	Spitfire I
23 Sqn	Wittering	Blenheim If
213 Sqn	Wittering	Hurricane I
46 Sqn	Digby	Hurricane I
73 Sqn	Digby	Hurricane I
504 Sqn	Digby	Hurricane I
64 Sqn	Church Fenton	Blenheim If
72 Sqn	Church Fenton	Spitfire I

No 13 Group, HQ: Blakelaw Estate, Ponteland, Newcastle-upon-Tyne

41 Sqn	Catterick	Spitfire I
609 Sqn	Catterick	Spitfire I
603 Sqn	Turnhouse	Gladiator II; Spitfire I

15 September 1940

No 9 Group, HQ: Preston, Lancs

308 Sqn	Speke	no a/c

No 10 Group, HQ: Rudloe Manor, Box, Wilts

79 Sqn	Pembrey	Hurricane I
87 Sqn	Exeter	Hurricane I
601 Sqn	Exeter	Hurricane I
247 Sqn	Roborough	Gladiator II
234 Sqn	Middle Wallop	Spitfire I
604 Sqn	Middle Wallop	Blenheim I; Beaufighter If
609 Sqn	Middle Wallop	Spitfire I
152 Sqn	Warmwell	Spitfire I

RAF FIGHTER COMMAND BOUNDARIES OF GROUPS AND SECTORS — JULY 1940

611 Sqn	Digby	Spitfire I; IIa
29 Sqn	Wellingore	Blenheim If; Beaufighter If
264 Sqn	Kirton-in-Lindsey	Defiant I
307 Sqn	Kirton-in-Lindsey	Defiant I
616 Sqn	Kirton-in-Lindsey	Spitfire I
85 Sqn	Church Fenton	Hurricane I
306 Sqn	Church Fenton	Hurricane I

No 13 Group, HQ: Blakelaw Estate, Ponteland, Newcastle-upon-Tyne

54 Sqn	Catterick	Spitfire I
219 Sqn	Catterick	Blenheim If; Beaufighter If
64 Sqn	Leconfield	Spitfire I
302 Sqn	Leconfield	Hurricane I
32 Sqn	Acklington	Hurricane I
610 Sqn	Acklington	Spitfire I
43 Sqn	Usworth	Hurricane I
219 Sqn	Scorton	Blenheim If; Beaufighter If
3 Sqn	Turnhouse	Hurricane I
65 Sqn	Turnhouse	Spitfire I
141 Sqn	Turnhouse	Defiant I
615 Sqn	Prestwick	Hurricane I
111 Sqn	Drem	Hurricane I
263 Sqn	Drem	Hurricane I; Whirlwind I
245 Sqn	Aldergrove	Hurricane I

No 14 Group, HQ: Drummossie, Inverness

145 Sqn	Dyce	Hurricane I

1 January 1941

No 9 Group, HQ: Preston, Lancs

229 Sqn	Speke	Hurricane I
312 Sqn	Speke	Hurricane I
308 Sqn	Baginton	Hurricane I
306 Sqn	Tern Hill	Hurricane I
96 Sqn	Cranage	Hurricane I

No 10 Group, HQ: Rudloe Manor, Box, Wilts

79 Sqn	Pembrey	Hurricane I
263 Sqn	Exeter	Whirlwind I
504 Sqn	Exeter	Hurricane I
247 Sqn	Roborough	Gladiator II/Hurricane I
87 Sqn	Charmy Down	Hurricane I
501 Sqn	Filton	Hurricane I
32 Sqn	Middle Wallop	Hurricane I
93 Sqn	Middle Wallop	Harrow II; Havoc I
604 Sqn	Middle Wallop	Blenheim If; Beaufighter If
152 Sqn	Warmwell	Spitfire I
609 Sqn	Warmwell	Spitfire I
238 Sqn	Chilbolton	Hurricane I

No 11 Group, HQ: Hillingdon House, Uxbridge, Middx

65 Sqn	Tangmere	Spitfire I/IIa
145 Sqn	Tangmere	Hurricane I/Spitfire I
219 Sqn	Tangmere	Blenheim If; Beaufighter If
302 Sqn	Westhampnett	Hurricane I
610 Sqn	Westhampnett	Spitfire I
23 Sqn	Ford	Blenheim If
253 Sqn	Kenley	Hurricane I
615 Sqn	Kenley	Hurricane I
605 Sqn	Croydon	Hurricane IIa
66 Sqn	Biggin Hill	Spitfire IIa
74 Sqn	Biggin Hill	Spitfire IIa
92 Sqn	Biggin Hill	Spitfire I
141 Sqn	Gravesend	Defiant I
264 Sqn	Gravesend	Defiant I
41 Sqn	Hornchurch	Spitfire IIa
64 Sqn	Hornchurch	Spitfire I/IIa
611 Sqn	Southend	Spitfire I, IIa
1 Sqn	Northolt	Hurricane I
601 Sqn	Northolt	Hurricane I
56 Sqn	North Weald	Hurricane I
249 Sqn	North Weald	Hurricane I
85 Sqn	Debden	Hurricane I

No 11 Group, HQ: Hillingdon House, Uxbridge, Middx

213 Sqn	Tangmere	Hurricane I
607 Sqn	Tangmere	Hurricane I
602 Sqn	Westhampnett	Spitfire I
501 Sqn	Kenley	Hurricane I
605 Sqn	Croydon	Hurricane I
72 Sqn	Biggin Hill	Spitfire I
92 Sqn	Biggin Hill	Spitfire I
600 Sqn	Redhill	Blenheim If; Beaufighter If
66 Sqn	Gravesend	Spitfire I
41 Sqn	Hornchurch	Spitfire I
222 Sqn	Hornchurch	Spitfire I
603 Sqn	Hornchurch	Spitfire I
1 (RCAF) Sqn	Northolt	Hurricane I
229 Sqn	Northolt	Hurricane I
303 Sqn	Northolt	Hurricane I
25 Sqn	North Weald	Blenheim If; Beaufighter If
249 Sqn	North Weald	Hurricane I
46 Sqn	Stapleford Tawney	Hurricane I
17 Sqn	Debden	Hurricane I
257 Sqn	Martlesham Heath	Hurricane I
23 Sqn	Ford	Blenheim If
73 Sqn	Castle Camps	Hurricane I

No 12 Group, HQ: Watnall, Notts

310 Sqn	Duxford	Hurricane I
312 Sqn	Duxford	Hurricane I
19 Sqn	Fowlmere	Spitfire I; IIa
74 Sqn	Coltishall	Spitfire I; IIa
242 Sqn	Coltishall	Hurricane I
1 Sqn	Wittering	Hurricane I
266 Sqn	Wittering	Spitfire IIa

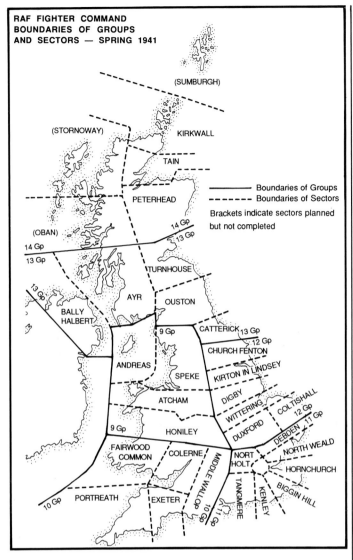

RAF FIGHTER COMMAND BOUNDARIES OF GROUPS AND SECTORS — SPRING 1941

———— Boundaries of Groups
– – – – Boundaries of Sectors

Brackets indicate sectors planned but not completed

17 Sqn	Martlesham Heath	Hurricane I
242 Sqn	Martlesham Heath	Hurricane I

No 12 Group, HQ: Watnall, Notts

19 Sqn	Duxford	Spitfire IIa
310 Sqn	Duxford	Hurricane I
222 Sqn	Coltishall	Spitfire I
257 Sqn	Coltishall	Hurricane I
25 Sqn	Wittering	Blenheim If/Beaufighter If
151 Sqn	Wittering	Defiant I
266 Sqn	Wittering	Spitfire I
2 (RCAF) Sqn	Digby	Hurricane I
46 Sqn	Digby	Hurricane I
29 Sqn	Wellingore	Blenheim If; Beaufighter If
71 Sqn	Kirton-in-Lindsey	Hurricane I
255 Sqn	Kirton-in-Lindsey	Defiant I
616 Sqn	Kirton-in-Lindsey	Spitfire I

No 13 Group, HQ: Blakelaw Estate, Ponteland, Newcastle-upon-Tyne

54 Sqn	Catterick	Spitfire I
256 Sqn	Catterick	Defiant I
600 Sqn	Catterick	Blenheim If; Beaufighter If
213 Sqn	Leconfield	Hurricane I
303 Sqn	Leconfield	Hurricane I
607 Sqn	Usworth	Hurricane I
72 Sqn	Acklington	Spitfire I
258 Sqn	Acklington	Hurricane I
43 Sqn	Drem	Hurricane I
603 Sqn	Drem	Spitfire IIa
602 Sqn	Prestwick	Spitfire I
245 Sqn	Aldergrove	Hurricane I

No 14 Group, HQ: Drummossie, Inverness

111 Sqn	Dyce	Hurricane I
1 (RCAF) Sqn	Castletown	Hurricane I
3 Sqn	Castletown	Hurricane I
260 Sqn	Skitten	Hurricane I

1 May 1942

No 9 Group, HQ: Preston, Lancs

232 Sqn	Atcham	Spitfire Vb
255 Sqn	High Ercall	Beaufighter IIf/VIf
257 Sqn	Honiley	Hurricane I, IIa, IIb, IIc; Spitfire Vb
131 Sqn	Llanbedr	Spitfire Vb
315 Sqn	Woodvale	Spitfire Vb

No 10 Group, HQ: Rudloe Manor, Box, Wilts

312 Sqn	Fairwood Common	Spitfire Vb
402 Sqn	Fairwood Common	Spitfire Vb
263 Sqn	Angle	Whirlwind I
234 Sqn	Portreath	Spitfire Vb
130 Sqn	Perranporth	Spitfire Vb, Vc
310 Sqn	Perranporth	Spitfire Vb
247 Sqn	Predannack	Hurricane I, IIc
600 Sqn	Predannack	Beaufighter VIf
1457 Flt	Predannack	Turbinlite Havoc
307 Sqn	Exeter	Beaufighter IIf/VIf
308 Sqn	Exeter	Spitfire Vb
306 Sqn	Culmhead	Spitfire Vb
125 Sqn	Colerne	Defiant I, II/Beaufighter IIf
1454 Flt	Colerne	Turbinlite Havoc
264 Sqn	Colerne	Defiant II/Mosquito II
87 Sqn	Charmy Down	Hurricane I, IIc
245 Sqn	Middle Wallop	Hurricane IIb, IIc
604 Sqn	Middle Wallop	Beaufighter If
1458 Flt	Middle Wallop	Turbinlite Havoc
175 Sqn	Warmwell	Hurricane IIb
302 Sqn	Warmwell	Spitfire Vb
66 Sqn	Ibsley	Spitfire Vb, Vc
118 Sqn	Ibsley	Spitfire Vb
501 Sqn	Ibsley	Spitfire Vb, Vc

No 11 Group, HQ: Hillingdon House, Uxbridge, Middx

1 Sqn	Tangmere	Hurricane I, IIc
219 Sqn	Tangmere	Beaufighter If
1455 Flt	Tangmere	Turbinlite Havoc
129 Sqn	Westhampnett	Spitfire Vb
340 Sqn	Westhampnett	Spitfire Vb
41 Sqn	Merston	Spitfire Vb
23 Sqn	Ford	Havoc I; Boston III
316 Sqn	Heston	Spitfire Vb
1422 Flt	Heston	??
485 Sqn	Kenley	Spitfire Vb
602 Sqn	Kenley	Spitfire Vb
72 Sqn	Biggin Hill	Spitfire Vb
124 Sqn	Biggin Hill	Spitfire Vb
401 Sqn	Gravesend	Spitfire Vb
29 Sqn	West Malling	Beaufighter If
1452 Flt	West Malling	Turbinlite Havoc
457 Sqn	Redhill	Spitfire Vb
91 Sqn	Hawkinge	Spitfire Vb
64 Sqn	Hornchurch	Spitfire Vb
122 Sqn	Hornchurch	Spitfire Vb
303 Sqn	Northolt	Spitfire Vb
317 Sqn	Northolt	Spitfire Vb
121 Sqn	North Weald	Spitfire Vb
222 Sqn	North Weald	Spitfire Vb
403 Sqn	North Weald	Spitfire Vb
65 Sqn	Great Sampford	Spitfire Vb
313 Sqn	Fairlop	Spitfire Vb
32 Sqn	Manston	Hurricane I, IIb, IIc
174 Sqn	Manston	Hurricane IIb
418 Sqn	Bradwell Bay	Boston III
3 Sqn	Hunsdon	Hurricane IIc
85 Sqn	Hunsdon	Havoc II

1451 Flt	Hunsdon	Turbinlite Havoc
111 Sqn	Debden	Spitfire Vb
350 Sqn	Debden	Spitfire Vb
412 Sqn	Martlesham Heath	Spitfire Vb
157 Sqn	Castle Camps	Mosquito II

No 12 Group, HQ: Watnall, Notts

266 Sqn	Duxford	Spitfire Vb/Typhoon Ia, Ib
609 Sqn	Duxford	Spitfire Vb/Typhoon Ia, Ib
56 Sqn	Snailwell	Typhoon Ia, Ib
68 Sqn	Coltishall	Beaufighter If
137 Sqn	Matlaske	Whirlwind I
151 Sqn	Wittering	Defiant II/Mosquito II
486 Sqn	Wittering	Hurricane IIb
1453 Flt	Wittering	Turbinlite Havoc
411 Sqn	Digby	Spitfire Vb
421 Sqn	Digby	Spitfire Va/Vb
133 Sqn	Kirton-in-Lindsey	Spitfire Vb
253 Sqn	Hibaldstow	Hurricane I, IIa, IIb, IIc
1459 Flt	Hibaldstow	Turbinlite Havoc
19 Sqn	Hutton Cranswick	Spitfire Vb

No 13 Group, HQ: Blakelaw Estate, Ponteland,
Newcastle-upon-Tyne

332 Sqn	Catterick	Spitfire Vb
81 Sqn	Ouston	Spitfire Vb
141 Sqn	Acklington	Beaufighter If
1460 Flt	Acklington	Turbinlite Havoc
242 Sqn	Turnhouse	Spitfire Vb
167 Sqn	Scorton	Spitfire Vb
416 Sqn	Peterhead	Spitfire Vb
410 Sqn	Drem	Defiant I/Beaufighter IIf
611 Sqn	Drem	Spitfire Vb
165 Sqn	Ayr	Spitfire Va/Vb
406 Sqn	Ayr	Beaufighter IIf

No 14 Group, HQ: Drummossie, Inverness

132 Sqn	Skeabrae	Spitfire Vb
331 Sqn	Skeabrae	Spitfire Vb

No 82 Group, HQ: (Northern Ireland)

25 Sqn	Ballyhalbert	Beaufighter If
153 Sqn	Ballyhalbert	Beaufighter If
152 Sqn	Eglinton	Spitfire IIa/Vb
504 Sqn	Kirkistown	Spitfire Vb

1 March 1943

No 9 Group, HQ: Preston, Lancs

96 Sqn	Honiley	Beaufighter VIf
456 Sqn	Valley	Beaufighter IIf/Mosquito II
41 Sqn	High Ercall	Spitfire Vb/XII
195 Sqn	Woodvale	Typhoon Ib
219 Sqn	Scorton	Beaufighter If
256 Sqn	Woodvale	Beaufighter VIf

No 10 Group, HQ: Rudloe Manor, Box, Wilts

125 Sqn	Fairwood Common	Beaufighter VIf
130 Sqn	Perranporth	Spitfire Vc/Vb
602 Sqn	Perranporth	Spitfire Vc/Vb
141 Sqn	Predannack	Beaufighter If
266 Sqn	Exeter	Typhoon Ib
307 Sqn	Exeter	Mosquito II
310 Sqn	Exeter	Spitfire Vb, Vc
313 Sqn	Culmhead	Spitfire Vb, Vc
193 Sqn	Harrowbeer	Typhoon Ib
263 Sqn	Harrowbeer	Whirlwind I
264 Sqn	Colerne	Mosquito II
19 Sqn	Middle Wallop	Spitfire Vc/Vb
164 Sqn	Middle Wallop	Hurricane IId, IV
182 Sqn	Middle Wallop	Typhoon Ib
247 Sqn	Middle Wallop	Hurricane IIb/Typhoon Ib
406 Sqn	Middle Wallop	Beaufighter VIf
257 Sqn	Warmwell	Typhoon Ia, Ib
312 Sqn	Warmwell	Spitfire Vb, Vc
132 Sqn	Zeals	Spitfire Vb
504 Sqn	Ibsley	Spitfire Vb, Vc

616 Sqn	Ibsley	Spitfire VI
174 Sqn	Chilbolton	Hurricane IIb
175 Sqn	Stoney Cross	Hurricane IIb
184 Sqn	Chilbolton	Hurricane IId
412 Sqn	Hurn	Spitfire Vb

No 11 Group, HQ: Hillingdon House, Uxbridge, Middx

129 Sqn	Tangmere	Spitfire Vb
165 Sqn	Tangmere	Spitfire Vb
486 Sqn	Tangmere	Typhoon Ib
610 Sqn	Westhampnett	Spitfire Vb
604 Sqn		Beaufighter If
605 Sqn	Ford	Mosquito II
303 Sqn	Heston	Spitfire Vb
350 Sqn	Heston	Spitfire VC/Vb
515 Sqn	Heston	Defiant II
402 Sqn	Kenley	Spitfire IX/Vb
403 Sqn	Kenley	Spitfire IXb
416 Sqn	Kenley	Spitfire Vb/IX
421 Sqn	Kenley	Spitfire Vb
1 Sqn	Biggin Hill	Typhoon Ib
340 Sqn	Biggin Hill	Spitfire IXb
611 Sqn	Biggin Hill	Spitfire IX
29 Sqn	West Malling	Beaufighter If/VIf
91 Sqn	Hawkinge	Spitfire Vb
122 Sqn	Hornchurch	Spitfire IX
453 Sqn	Southend	Spitfire Vb
306 Sqn	Northolt	Spitfire IX/VB
308 Sqn	Northolt	Spitfire Vb
315 Sqn	Northolt	Spitfire IX, Vb
124 Sqn	North Weald	Spitfire VI, IX
331 Sqn	North Weald	Spitfire IXb
332 Sqn	North Weald	Spitfire IXb
64 Sqn	Fairlop	Spitfire IX/VB
137 Sqn	Manston	Whirlwind I
609 Sqn	Manston	Typhoon Ib
418 Sqn	Bradwell Bay	Boston III
3 Sqn	Hunsdon	Typhoon Ib
85 Sqn	Hunsdon	Mosquito II, XV, XII
157 Sqn	Castle Camps	Mosquito II

No 12 Group, HQ: Watnall, Notts

181 Sqn	Cranfield	Typhoon Ib
183 Sqn	Cranfield	Typhoon Ib
68 Sqn	Coltishall	Beaufighter VIf
118 Sqn	Coltishall	Spitfire Vb
56 Sqn	Matlaske	Typhoon Ib
151 Sqn	Wittering	Mosquito II
411 Sqn	Digby	Spitfire Vb
410 Sqn	Coleby Grange	Mosquito II
302 Sqn	Kirton-in-Lindsey	Spitfire Vb
317 Sqn	Kirton-in-Lindsey	Spitfire Vb
25 Sqn	Church Fenton	Mosquito II
316 Sqn	Hutton Cranswick	Spitfire Vb

No 13 Group, HQ: Blakelaw Estate, Ponteland,
Newcastle-upon-Tyne

401 Sqn	Catterick	Spitfire Vb
198 Sqn	Acklington	Typhoon Ia/Ib
409 Sqn	Acklington	Beaufighter VIf
341 Sqn	Turnhouse	Spitfire Vb
65 Sqn	Drem	Spitfire Vb
197 Sqn	Drem	Typhoon Ib
222 Sqn	Ayr	Spitfire Vb
488 Sqn	Ayr	Beaufighter IIf/VIf

No 14 Group, HQ: Drummossie, Inverness

245 Sqn	Peterhead	Typhoon Ib
234 Sqn	Grimsetter	Spitfire IV, Vb, VI
66 Sqn	Skeabrae	Spitfire Vb, Vc
131 Sqn	Castletown	Spitfire Vb

No 82 Group, HQ: (Northern Ireland)

501 Sqn	Ballyhalbert	Spitfire Vb

Allied Expeditionary Air Force: 2nd Tactical Air Force (2 TAF)

Battle Order – 5 June 1944

Includes tactical/strike (83, 84 Gps) and air defence (85 Gp) elements; excludes No 2 Group squadrons, reconnaissance and AOP units.

No 83 Group

121 Wing	Holmsley South	174, 175, 245 Sqns	Typhoon Ib
122 Wing	Funtington	19, 65 122 Sqns	Mustang III
124 Wing	Hurn	181, 182, 247 Sqns	Typhoon Ib
125 Wing	Ford	132, 453, 602 Sqns	Spitfire IXb
126 Wing	Tangmere	401, 411, 412 Sqns	Spitfire IXb
127 Wing	Tangmere	403, 416, 421 Sqns	Spitfire IXb
129 Wing	Westhampnett	184 Sqn	Typhoon Ib
143 Wing	Hurn	438, 439, 440 Sqns	Typhoon Ib
144 Wing	Ford	441, 442, 443 Sqns	Spitfire IXb

No 84 Group

123 Wing	Thorney Island	198, 609 Sqns	Typhoon Ib
131 Wing	Chailey	302, 308, 317 Sqns	Spitfire IX, IXe
132 Wing	Bognor	66, 331, 332 Sqns	Spitfire IXb, LFIXb
133 Wing	Coolham	129, 306, 315 Sqns	Mustang III
134 Wing	Apuldram	310, 312, 313 Sqns	Spitfire IX, LFIX, LFIXb
135 Wing	Selsey	222, 349, 485 Sqns	Spitfire IXb, LFIXb, LFIXe
136 Wing	Thorney Island	164, 183 Sqns	Typhoon Ib
145 Wing	Merston	329, 340, 341 Sqns	Spitfire IX, IXb
146 Wing	Needs Ore Point	193, 197, 257, 266 Sqns	Typhoon Ib

No 85 Group

141 Wing	Hartfordbridge	264 Sqn	Mosquito XIII
		322 Sqn	Spitfire XIV
147 Wing	Zeals	488 Sqn	Mosquito XIII
148 Wing	West Malling	29, 409 Sqns	Mosquito XIII
		91 Sqn	Spitfire XIV
150 Wing	Newchurch	3, 486 Sqns	Tempest V
		56 Sqn	Spitfire IX
	Bradwell Bay	124 Sqn	Spitfire VII
	Hunsdon	410 Sqn	Mosquito XIII
	Hurn	604 Sqn	Mosquito XIII

Air Defence of Great Britain – Units Attached to 2 TAF

Shoreham	345 Sqn	Spitfire Vb
Friston	350 Sqn	Spitfire Vb, Vc
	501 Sqn	Spitfire Vb

Air Defence of Great Britain

Battle Order – 5 June 1944

No 10 Group, HQ: Rudloe Manor, Box, Wilts

1 Sqn	Predannack	Spitfire IXb
165 Sqn	Predannack	Spitfire IXb
152 Sqn	Predannack	Mosquito XIII
41 Sqn	Bolt Head	Spitfire XII
126 Sqn	Culmhead	Spitfire IXb
131 Sqn	Culmhead	Spitfire VII
616 Sqn	Culmhead	Spitfire VII
610 Sqn	Harrowbeer	Spitfire XIV
263 Sqn	Harrowbeer	Typhoon Ib
68 Sqn	Fairwood Common	Beaufighter VIf
406 Sqn	Winkleigh	Beaufighter VIf, Mosquito XII

No 11 Group, HQ: Hillingdon House, Uxbridge, Middx

33 Sqn	Lympne	Spitfire LF IXe
74 Sqn	Lympne	Spitfire LF IXe
127 Sqn	Lympne	Spitfiree HF IX
64 Sqn	Deanland	Spitfire Vc
234 Sqn	Deanland	Spitfire Vb
611 Sqn	Deanland	Spitfire LF Vb
80 Sqn	Detling	Spitfire IX
229 Sqn	Detling	Spitfire IX
274 Sqn	Detling	Spitfire IX
130 Sqn	Horne	Spitfire Vb
303 Sqn	Horne	Spitfire LF Vb
402 Sqn	Horne	Spitfire Vb, Vc
137 Sqn	Manston	Typhoon Ib
605 Sqn	Manston	Mosquito VI
96 Sqn	West Malling	Mosquito XIII
125 Sqn	Hurn	Mosquito XVII
219 Sqn	Bradwell Bay	Mosquito XVII
456 Sqn	Ford	Mosquito XVII
418 Sqn	Holmsley South	Mosquito XII

No 12 Group, HQ: Watnall, Notts

25 Sqn	Coltishall	Mosquito XVII
316 Sqn	Coltishall	Mustang III
307 Sqn	Church Fenton	Mosquito XII
504 Sqn	Digby (det at Acklington)	Spitfire Vb

Mosquito NFXIII HX428 of No 29 Squadron. *via Author*

No 13 Group, HQ: Blakelaw Estate, Ponteland, Newcastle-upon Tyne

118 Sqn	Skeabrae (det at Sumburgh)	Spitfire Vb, VII
309 Sqn	Drem (det at Peterhead)	Hurricne IIc

1 January 1945

No 10 Group, HQ: Rudloe Manor, Box, Wilts

33 Sqn	Predannack	Tempest V
222 Sqn	Predannack	Tempest V
245 Sqn	Warmwell	Typhoon Ib
443 Sqn	Warmwell	Spitfire IXb

No 11 Group, HQ: Hillingdon House, Uxbridge, Middx

154 Sqn	Biggin Hill	Spitfire VII
322 Sqn	Biggin Hill	Spitfire LFXVIe
611 Sqn	Hawkinge	Spitfire IX
264 Sqn	Odiham	Mosquito XIII
418 Sqn	Blackbushe	Mosquito VI
605 Sqn	Blackbushe	Mosquito VI
1 Sqn	Manston	Spitfire IXb
91 Sqn	Manston	Spitfire IXb/XXI
124 Sqn	Manston	Spitfire HFIXe
406 Sqn	Manston	Mosquito XXX
504 Sqn	Manston	Spitfire IXe
616 Sqn	Manston	Meteor I
29 Sqn	Hunsdon	Mosquito XIII
151 Sqn	Hunsdon	Mosquito XXX
310 Sqn	Bradwell Bay	Spitfire LFIX
312 Sqn	Bradwell Bay	Spitfire HFIX
313 Sqn	Bradwell Bay	Spitfire IX
501 Sqn	Bradwell Bay	Tempest V
19 Sqn	Andrews Field	Mustang III
65 Sqn	Andrews Field	Mustang III
122 Sqn	Andrews Field	Mustang III
306 Sqn	Andrews Field	Mustang III
316 Sqn	Andrews Field	Mustang III
64 Sqn	Bentwaters	Mustang III
118 Sqn	Bentwaters	Spitfire IXc/Mustang III
126 Sqn	Bentwaters	Mustang III
129 Sqn	Bentwaters	Mustang III
165 Sqn	Bentwaters	Mustang III
234 Sqn	Bentwaters	Mustang III
25 Sqn	Castle Camps	Mosquito XXX, VI

No 12 Group, HQ: Watnall, Notts

68 Sqn	Coltishall	Mosquito XVII, XIX
125 Sqn	Coltishall	Mosquito XVII
229 Sqn	Coltishall	Spitfire LFXVIe
303 Sqn	Coltishall	Spitfire LFVb, IXc
307 Sqn	Church Fenton	Mosquito XII/XXX
456 Sqn	Church Fenton	Mosquito XVII, XXX

No 13 Group, HQ: Blakelaw Estate, Ponteland, Newcastle-upon-Tyne

315 Sqn	Peterhead	Mustang III
340 Sqn	Drem	Spitfire IXb
441 Sqn	Skeabrae	Spitfire IX

No 38 Group, HQ: Marks Hall, Earls Colne, Essex

298 Sqn	Tarrant Rushton	Halifax III
644 Sqn	Tarrant Rushton	Halifax III
296 Sqn	Earls Colne	Halifax V
297 Sqn	Earls Colne	Halifax V
196 Sqn	Wethersfield	Stirling IV
299 Sqn	Wethersfield	Stirling IV
295 Sqn	Rivenhall	Stirling IV
570 Sqn	Rivenhall	Stirling IV
190 Sqn	Great Dunmow	Stirling IV
620 Sqn	Great Dunmow	Stirling IV

RAF Fighter Command, Air Defence of Great Britain and 2nd Tactical Air Force

Group Structure (Flying Units) – 1939-45

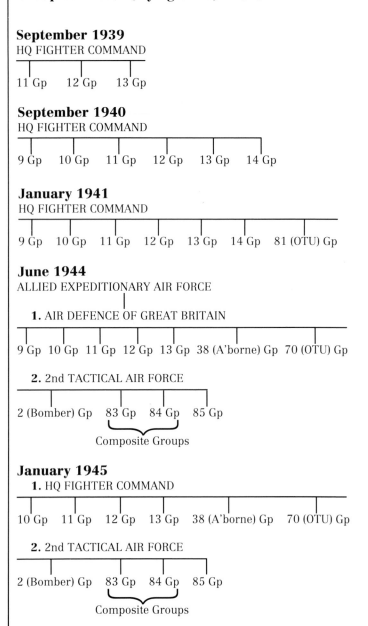

September 1939
HQ FIGHTER COMMAND
11 Gp   12 Gp   13 Gp

September 1940
HQ FIGHTER COMMAND
9 Gp   10 Gp   11 Gp   12 Gp   13 Gp   14 Gp

January 1941
HQ FIGHTER COMMAND
9 Gp   10 Gp   11 Gp   12 Gp   13 Gp   14 Gp   81 (OTU) Gp

June 1944
ALLIED EXPEDITIONARY AIR FORCE

1. AIR DEFENCE OF GREAT BRITAIN
9 Gp   10 Gp   11 Gp   12 Gp   13 Gp   38 (A'borne) Gp   70 (OTU) Gp

2. 2nd TACTICAL AIR FORCE
2 (Bomber) Gp   83 Gp   84 Gp   85 Gp
Composite Groups

January 1945
1. HQ FIGHTER COMMAND
10 Gp   11 Gp   12 Gp   13 Gp   38 (A'borne) Gp   70 (OTU) Gp

2. 2nd TACTICAL AIR FORCE
2 (Bomber) Gp   83 Gp   84 Gp   85 Gp
Composite Groups

Appendix III

RAF Fighter Command Training Unit Strengths 1939-45

The Organisation of Training Groups in Fighter Command

At the oubreak of war in 1939, Fighter Command allocated a number of aircraft and crews to two Group Pools, each under the control of an operational Group, for final operational training prior to joining a squadron. These Group Pools were renamed Operational Training Units (OTU) in the spring of 1940, and at the end of the same year the three OTUs had '50' added to their numbers, becoming Nos 55 OTU, 56 OTU and 57 OTU. In December 1940, No 81 (OTU) Group was formed to incorporate the existing fighter OTUs and in May 1943 it was disbanded, control of OTUs being assumed by No 9 Group which then relinquished its frontline duties. In the summer of 1944 No 9 Group was disbanded and control of individual OTUs devolved onto the existing frontline Groups once more.

3 September 1939

11 Gp Pool	St Athan	Hurricane
12 Gp Pool	Aston Down	Hurricane; Gladiator; Blenheim

Miscellaneous Units

Heston Special Flt	Heston	Blenheim; Spitfire; Hudson

15 September 1940

5 OTU	Aston Down	Spitfire; Hurricane; Blenheim
6 OTU	Sutton Bridge	Hurricane
7 OTU	Hawarden	Spitfire

Miscellaneous Units

Fighter Interception Unit (FIU)	Shoreham	Beaufighter; Blenheim
No 1 Camouflage Unit	Baginton	Reliant; Blenheim; Spitfire
No 2 School of Army Co-operation	Andover	Blenheim; Anson

1 January 1941

No 81 (OTU) Group, HQ: Autumn Avenue, Worcester

54 OTU	Church Fenton	Blenheim; Beaufighter
55 OTU	Aston Down	Spitfire; Hurricane; Blenheim
56 OTU	Sutton Bridge	Hurricane
57 OTU	Hawarden	Spitfire
58 OTU	Grangemouth	Spitfire

Miscellaneous Units

FIU	Shoreham	Blenheim; Beaufighter
Air Fighting Development Unit (AFDU)	Duxford	Spitfire; Hurricane; various
No 1 Camouflage Unit	Baginton	Reliant; Blenheim; Spitfire
No 2 School of Army Co-operation	Andover	Blenheim; Anson

1 May 1942

No 81 (OTU) Group, HQ: Avening, Stroud, Glos

51 OTU	Cranfield; Twinwood Farm	Blenheim; Beaufighter
52 OTU	Aston Down	Spitfire
53 OTU	Llandow; Rhoose	Spitfire
54 OTU	Charter Hall; Winfield	Blenheim; Beaufighter
55 OTU	Annan; Longtown	Hurricane
56 OTU	Tealing; Kinnel	Hurricane
57 OTU	Hawarden	Spitfire
58 OTU	Grangemouth; Balado Bridge	Spitfire
59 OTU	Crosby-on-Eden; Longtown	Hurricane
60 OTU	East Fortune; Macmerry	Blenheim; Beaufighter
61 OTU	Rednal; Montford Bridge	Spitfire

Miscellaneous Units

FIU	Ford	Blenheim; Beaufighter
AFDU	Duxford	Spitfire; Hurricane; various

1 March 1943

No 81 (OTU) Group, HQ: Avening, Stroud, Glos

41 OTU	Hawarden; Poulton	Mustang; Hurricane
51 OTU	Cranfield; Twinwood Farm	Blenheim; Beaufighter
52 OTU	Aston Down	Spitfire
53 OTU	Llandow; Rhoose	Spitfire
54 OTU	Charter Hall; Winfield	Blenheim; Beaufighter
55 OTU	Annan; Longtown	Hurricane
56 OTU	Tealing; Kinnel	Hurricane; Spitfire
57 OTU	Eshott; Boulmer	Spitfire
58 OTU	Grangemouth; Balado Bridge	Spitfire
59 OTU	Milfield; Brunton; Boulmer	Hurricane
61 OTU	Rednal; Montford Bridge	Spitfire
62 OTU	Usworth	Anson

Miscellaneous Units

FIU	Ford	Blenheim; Beaufighter; Mosquito
AFDU	Duxford	Spitfire; Hurricane; various
Fighter Leaders School	Charmy Down	Spitfire

6 June 1944

No 9 Group, HQ: Barton Hall, Preston, Lancs

13 OTU	Bicester; Finmere	Mosquito; Boston
41 OTU	Hawarden; Poulton	Mustang; Hurricane
42 OTU	Ashbourne; Darley Moor	Whitley, Oxford; Anson; Albemarle
51 OTU	Cranfield; Twinwood Farm	Mosquito
53 OTU	Kirton-in-Lindsey; Hibaldstow; Caistor	Spitfire
54 OTU	Charter Hall; Winfield	Beaufighter
57 OTU	Eshott; Boulmer	Spitfire
59 OTU	Boulmer	Hurricane; Typhoon
60 OTU	High Ercall	Mosquito

61 OTU	Rednal; Montford Bridge	Spitfire
62 OTU	Ouston	Anson; Wellington
1 TEU	Kinnelel	Hurricane; Spitfire
2 TEU	Grangemouth; Balado Bridge	Spitfire
3 TEU	Annan	Typhoon; Hurricane

Miscellaneous Units

FIU	Wittering	Mosquito; various
Fighter Leaders School	Milfield; Brunton	Spitfire; Typhoon; Hurricane
ORTU	Hampstead Norris	Albemarle; Tiger Moth; Whitley; Horsa
83 GSU	Redhill	Typhoon
84 GSU	Aston Down	Typhoon; Tempest; Spitfire; Mustang

1 January 1945

Nos 11, 12, 13 and 38 Groups

13 OTU	Harwell; Finmere	Mosquito
41 OTU	Hawarden; Poulton	Mustang; Hurricane
42 OTU	Ashbourne; Darley Moor	Albemarle; Oxford; Anson
51 OTU	Cranfield; Twinwood Farm	Mosquito
53 OTU	Kirton-in-Lindsey; Caistor; Hibaldstow	Spitfire
54 OTU	Charter Hall; Winfield	Mosquito
55 OTU	Aston Down; Chedworth	Typhoon; Hurricane
56 OTU	Milfield; Brunton	Typhoon; Tempest
57 OTU	Eshott; Boulmer	Spitfire
60 OTU	High Ercall	Mosquito
61 OTU	Rednal; Montford Bridge	Spitfire; Mustang
62 OTU	Ouston	Anson; Wellington

Miscellaneous Units

ORTU	Hampstead Norris	Albemarle; Tiger Moth; Whitley; Horsa
FIDS/NFDW	Ford	Mosquito; various
83 GSU	Westhampnett	Mustang; Spitfire
84 GSU	Lasham	Mustang; Spitfire

Hurricane I V6857 of No 401 Squadron went on to serve with Nos 73, 85, 3 Squadrons and No 55 OTU. *via K. Merrick*

Bibliography

Primary Source Material:

PUBLIC RECORD OFFICE, KEW:

AIR 10 3815-3838	Air Ministry Confidential Air Force Lists (Jun 39/Jun 45)
AIR 27 425	No 41 Squadron ORB (Jan 41/Dec 43)
AIR 27 1025	No 152 Squadron ORB
AIR 27 1440	No 234 Squadron ORB (Jan 44/Aug 46)
AIR 50 64	No 152 Squadron Combat Reports

Circumstantial report by Flt Lt Hudson, RAF Old Sarum: *Investigation into No 152 Squadron Spitfire crash following aerial engagement over Woolverton, Somerset, 25 September 1940*

JOHN LAING PLC:
Military contracts listing; miscellaneous papers relating to individual contracts

Secondary Source Material:

Basil Collier, *The Defence of the United Kingdom* (HMSO 1957)

Steve Willis & Barry Hollis, *Military Airfields of the British Isles 1939-1945* (Enthusiast Publications 1990)

Chaz Bowyer, *Fighter Command 1936-1968* (Dent 1980)

Chaz Bowyer, *Mosquito Squadrons of the RAF* (Ian Allan Ltd 1984)

C. Martin Sharp & Michael J. F. Bowyer, *Mosquito* (Faber & Faber Ltd 1967)

Wg Cdr C. G. Jefford, *RAF Squadrons* (Airlife Publishing Ltd 1988)

Robin A. Brown, *A Short History of No 234 Squadron RAF – 1917-1955* (No 234 Squadron)

John Rawlings, *Fighter Squadrons of the RAF and their Aircraft* (Macdonald & Jane's 1969)

Denis Richards & Hilary St G. Saunders, *Royal Air Force 1939-1945* (three volumes) (HMSO 1953, 1954)

Winston G. Ramsey (Ed), The *Battle of Britain Then and Now* (After the Battle 1980)

Sir John Hammerton (Ed), *ABC of the RAF* (The Amalgamated Press Ltd 1941)

Francis K. Mason, *The Hawker Typhoon & Tempest* (Aston Publications Ltd 1988)

Francis K. Mason, *The Hawker Hurricane* (Aston Publications Ltd 1990)

Christopher F. Shores, *2nd Tactical Air Force* (Osprey 1970)

Norman Gelb, Scramble: *A Narrative History of the Battle of Britain* (Michael Joseph, 1986)

Michael J. F. Bowyer, Action Stations 1: *Military Airfields of East Anglia* (Patrick Stephens Ltd [PSL] 1979)

Bruce Barrymore Halpenny, Action Stations 2: *Military Airfields of Lincolnshire and the East Midlands* (PSL 1981)

David J.Smith, Action Stations 3: *Military Airfields of Wales and the Northwest* (PSL 1981)

Bruce Barrymore Halpenny, Action Stations 4: *Military Airfields of Yorkshire* (PSL 1982)

Chris Ashworth, Action Stations 5: *Military Airfields of the South-West* (PSL 1982)

Michael J. F. Bowyer, Action Stations 6: *Military Airfields of the Cotswolds and the Central Midlands* (PSL 1983)

David J. Smith, Action Stations 7: *Military Airfields of Scotland, the North-East and Northern Ireland* (PSL 1983)

Bruce Barrymore Halpenny, Action Stations 8: *Military Airfields of Greater London* (PSL 1984)

Chris Ashworth, Action Stations 9: *Military Airfields of the Central South and South-East* (PSL 1985)

David J. Smith, *Britain's Military Airfields, 1939-45* (PSL 1989)

Wg Cdr T. F. Neil, *From the Cockpit: Spitfire* (Ian Allan Ltd 1990)

Ken Davies, *Ninety Days to Normandy: The Advanced Landing Grounds of 1944* (Niche Publications 1992)

Ken Davies, *New Forest Airfields* (Niche Publications 1992)

Anthony Robinson, *RAF Fighter Squadrons in the Battle of Britain* (Arms & Armour Press, 1987)

Chester Wilmot, *The Struggle for Europe* (Collins 1952)

J. M. Spaight, *Air Power in the Next War* (Geoffrey Bles 1938)